FamilyCircle®
Best-Ever
Cakes
& Cookies

FamilyCircle®
Best-Ever
Cakes
& Cookies

PLUS PIES, TARTS AND OTHER DESSERTS

More than 200 winning recipes with 75 photos

from the editors of Family Circle

Published by Broadway Books
A division of Random House, Inc.
1540 Broadway, New York, New York 10036

BROADWAY BOOKS and its logo, a letter B bisected on the diagonal, are trademarks of
Broadway Books, a division of Random House, Inc.

A Roundtable Press Book
Copyright ©2001 by Roundtable Press, Inc. and G+J USA Publishing
All rights reserved, including the right of reproduction in whole or part in any form.

Printed in China
First Edition September 2001

Library of Congress Cataloging-in-Publication Data

Family Circle best-ever cakes & cookies: plus pies, tarts, and other desserts/from the
editors of Family circle.--1st ed.
    p. cm.
    Includes index.
    ISBN 0-7679-0612-8
    1. Desserts. I. Family circle (New York, N.Y.)

TX773 .F314 2001
641.8'6--dc21   2001025997

FOR ROUNDTABLE PRESS, INC.:

DIRECTORS: Marsha Melnick, Julie Merberg,
Susan E. Meyer

SENIOR EDITOR: Carol Spier

BOOK DESIGN: pink design, inc. nyc

COPY EDITOR: Mary Johnson

EDITORIAL ASSISTANT: Sara Newberry

PRODUCTION: Bill Rose

FOR G+J PUBLISHING:

BOOKS & LICENSING DIRECTOR: Tammy Palazzo

BOOKS & LICENSING COORDINATOR: Sabeena Lalwani

BOOKS & LICENSING ASSISTANT: Carla Clark

FOR FAMILY CIRCLE MAGAZINE:

EDITOR-IN-CHIEF: Susan Kelliher Ungaro

CREATIVE DIRECTOR: Diane Lamphron

EXECUTIVE EDITOR: Barbara Winkler

FOOD DIRECTOR: Peggy Katalinich

SENIOR FOOD EDITOR: Diane Mogelever

SENIOR ASSOCIATE FOOD EDITOR: Julie Miltenberger

EDITORIAL ASSISTANT: Keri Linas

TEST KITCHEN ASSISTANTS: Keisha Davis,
Althea Needham

RECIPE EDITOR: David Ricketts

NUTRITIONIST: Patty Santelli

TEST KITCHEN: JoAnn Brett, Donna Meadow,
Michael Tyrrell, Robert Yamarone

Cover photographs: front, Mark Thomas; spine, Alan Richardson; back, Brian Hagiwara (top and center);
Mark Thomas (middle left, middle right and bottom).

All other photography credits are found on page 240 and constitute an extension of this copyright page.

The recipe shown on the front cover (Celebration Cake) appears on page 22. The recipes shown on pages
2 through 7 appear as follows: Lemon Pie (page 2) on page 102; Pepper-Spice Cookies (page 3, left) on
page 58; Coconut Cream-Filled Cupcakes (page 3, right) on page 46; Carrot Cake (page 6) on page 26;
Cran-Apple Pie (page 7, top) on page 98; Cream Hearts (page 7, middle) on page 189; Strawberry-Chocolate
Shortcake (page 7, bottom) on page 128.

Foreword

Whenever my mother and I go to a restaurant, the first thing we check out is the dessert menu. We come from the Irish "tea and a treat" tradition and get our greatest culinary thrills from scrumptious sweets. We could care less about what's for dinner, we're most passionate about what's for dessert.

Yet, I must confess that when it comes to baking prowess, I did not inherit my mother's second-nature cake-making skills. That's why I absolutely love this newest cookbook of *Family Circle's Best-Ever Cakes & Cookies*. It has inspired me to spend time creating cakes that will make my mom proud as well as baking cookies that will make my kids' day!

So you're in for a real treat. And while you're thumbing through the pages and pictures in this volume, keep this old Russian proverb in mind: "A house is beautiful not because of its walls, but because of its cakes." I couldn't agree more!

SUSAN KELLIHER UNGARO, *Editor-in-Chief*

Contents

Introduction

When I was growing up, my mom had to make my birthday cakes two ways: with frosting for the rest of the family, without just for me. I was completely satisfied with the tender cake and saw no need at all to gild the lily. She also had trouble coaxing me into trying her legendary pie made with fruit from our very own cherry tree out back.

That was then. This is now. Now, I can turn to an irresistible sour-cream chocolate layer cake with light-as-air frosting (page 22), or a sweet-tart lemon pie with a crunchy almond garnish (page 102). Now, I have in my hands *Family Circle's Best-Ever Cakes & Cookies*, with more than 200 of our favorite picks from our fabulous dessert files. And now, for my own children I can bake up Jumbo Chocolate Chip Cookies (page 62) or Halloween Cupcakes (page 204), and build on what will become their memories of mom's homemade desserts.

Having sampled each and every pie, cake, tart and torte in this book, I can testify that they meet our criteria: Beautiful to look at, guaranteed to please. And even the ones that look complicated are completely manageable—they may take a little time, but our how-to photos will help you through any tricky steps.

These days, since it's my turn as baker for my own family, I know *Family Circle's Best-Ever Cakes & Cookies* is where I'll be looking for inspiration for a creamy mousse, a fruity crumble or a birthday cake—with all its frosting!

BAKER'S CREDO

For truly irresistible treats, take these helpful hints to heart.

- Always read the recipe from start to finish before you begin. Make sure you have all the ingredients called for. Be sure to allow sufficient time to complete all the steps.

- If the recipe calls for room-temperature butter, take butter out of refrigerator about one hour in advance. If the recipe calls for beating the eggs, remove them at the same time as the butter. If they are to be separated, leave them in the fridge until needed. Unless a recipe states otherwise, use large eggs.

- Heat oven to desired temperature 10 to 15 minutes before baking.

- Measure accurately. For dry ingredients, use nested cups in ¼-, ⅓-, ½- and 1-cup sizes. Spoon ingredients such as flour and sugar into the appropriate size cup, then level top by sweeping excess away with the straight edge of a knife. For shortening (and brown sugar when indicated), pack cup firmly before leveling off. For liquids, use measures, generally made of glass, with increments on the side and a pouring spout.

- If a recipe calls for sifted flour, sift directly onto a piece of waxed paper, spoon into a measuring cup and level off excess flour.

- Use all that you measure. If measuring shortening or a thick liquid such as corn syrup or vegetable oil, run a rubber scraper around the inside of the measuring cup to make sure you remove the entire contents.

- Because accurate temperature is crucial for success, place an oven thermometer, available at kitchen supply stores, in your unit to serve as a check.

- For expert results, refer to the special features placed throughout this book—they give detailed technical advice on different aspects of dessert making. They're listed on the table of contents under each chapter title. And you can recognize their pages by their pink stripe borders.

PEGGY KATALINICH, *Food Director*

Feather-Light Chocolate Cake, page 20

Italian Ricotta Cheesecake, *page 52*

Cakes

Berry-Capped Cupcakes, *page 48*

Triple-Layer Chocolate Crumb Cake

A light coating of extra cake crumbs adds pizzazz and a hint of the goodness inside.

MAKES *16 servings*
PREP *30 minutes*
BAKE *at 375° for 35 minutes*

Cake

3⅓ cups cake flour (not self-rising)
1½ teaspoons baking powder
1½ teaspoons baking soda
1 teaspoon salt
1½ cups (3 sticks) unsalted butter or margarine, at room temperature
3⅓ cups packed light-brown sugar
4 eggs
4 squares (1 ounce each) unsweetened chocolate, melted and cooled slightly
1 cup buttermilk
1 cup boiling water
1 tablespoon vanilla

Milk Chocolate Cream Frosting

18 ounces (3 cups) milk chocolate chips
½ cup (1 stick) unsalted butter or margarine, at room temperature
1 cup sour cream
1½ teaspoons vanilla
¼ teaspoon salt
1 box (1 pound) confectioners' sugar (about 4 cups)

1. Prepare cake: Place oven racks in second and fourth positions. Heat oven to 375°. Grease three 9 x 1½-inch-round layer-cake pans. Line 4 cups in a standard 12-muffin pan with paper liners.

2. Combine flour, baking powder, baking soda and salt in a small bowl.

3. With a mixer on low speed, beat butter and brown sugar in a large bowl until combined. Increase speed to medium and beat until creamy. Add eggs, one at a time, beating well after each addition. Beat in chocolate.

4. Add flour mixture to egg mixture, alternating with buttermilk and ending with flour mixture, beating after each addition. Beat in boiling water and vanilla until smooth and well blended (batter will be thin).

5. Using dry measures, pour 3⅔ cups batter into each prepared round cake pan. Divide remaining batter equally among lined muffin cups.

6. Bake in heated 375° oven, 20 minutes for cupcakes and 30 to 35 minutes for cake layers, or until a wooden pick inserted in center of each comes out clean. Let cupcakes cool in pans 5 minutes; unmold onto a wire rack to cool completely. Cool cake layers in pans on wire racks 15 minutes. Turn out cakes onto racks and cool completely.

7. Prepare frosting: Melt chocolate chips in a small heavy saucepan over low heat; stir until smooth. Let cool 15 minutes.

8. Beat together butter and melted chocolate in a large bowl until creamy. Beat in sour cream, vanilla and salt. Gradually beat in confectioners' sugar until smooth, creamy and spreadable.

9. Tear cupcakes into pieces. Place in a food processor. Whirl until coarsely ground.

10. Place 1 cake layer on a serving plate. Spread top with 1 cup frosting. Add second cake layer; spread with 1 cup frosting. Top with third cake layer. Spread a thin coating of frosting around sides and top of cake.

11. Set aside 1 cup remaining frosting. Working on a small section at a time, frost sides of cake and sprinkle with cupcake crumbs; press with hand or a spoon to adhere. Gather any crumbs that fall off and use for next section. When sides are covered, frost top of cake with reserved 1 cup frosting.

Double-Chocolate Fudge Cake

Back in 1952, when it was first published, this fudgy cake recipe was a winner. And it still is!

MAKES *12 servings*
PREP *20 minutes*
COOK *about 15 minutes*
BAKE *at 350° for 30 to 33 minutes*
REFRIGERATE *30 minutes*

Cake

4   squares (1 ounce each) unsweetened chocolate, chopped
2   cups all-purpose flour
2   teaspoons baking powder
½   teaspoon baking soda
½   teaspoon salt
¾   cup (1½ sticks) butter or margarine, at room temperature
1½ cups packed light-brown sugar
2   whole eggs
1   teaspoon vanilla
1   cup plus 2 tablespoons milk

Creamy Fudge Frosting

4   egg yolks
2   cups granulated sugar
1   cup milk
2   tablespoons butter or margarine
8   squares (1 ounce each) unsweetened chocolate, chopped
2   teaspoons vanilla

Garnish

¼   cup semisweet chocolate chips
24 whole blanched almonds

1. Heat oven to 350°. Coat two 8-inch round layer-cake pans with nonstick cooking spray.

2. Prepare cake: Melt chocolate in top of a double boiler over barely simmering, not boiling, water, stirring until smooth. Remove from heat and cool to room temperature.

3. Sift flour, baking powder, baking soda and salt into a medium-size bowl.

4. Beat butter in a large bowl until creamy. Beat in brown sugar. Add whole eggs, one at a time, beating after each. Add vanilla and melted chocolate.

5. Sift flour mixture into butter mixture in 3 additions, alternating with milk and ending with flour mixture, beating after each addition. Pour into prepared pans.

6. Bake in heated 350° oven 30 to 33 minutes or until a wooden pick inserted in center of cake layers comes out clean. Cool cake layers in pans on wire racks 10 minutes. Loosen edges with a knife; turn cake layers out onto racks. Cool completely.

7. Prepare frosting: Beat egg yolks in a medium-size bowl with mixer on medium speed until thick and lemon-colored. Gradually beat in 1 cup sugar until very light in color, 5 to 7 minutes. Beat in milk. Transfer mixture to a medium-size saucepan and add butter and remaining 1 cup sugar. Slowly bring to boiling over medium heat, whisking occasionally, 12 to 15 minutes. Boil, whisking, 1 minute. Remove from heat. Using a wooden spoon, stir in chocolate until melted; add vanilla. Transfer to a medium-size bowl. Refrigerate 30 minutes or until a spreading consistency.

8. Beat frosting on medium speed until light and fluffy, 4 minutes. Frost cake, using 1 cup to sandwich layers, 1½ cups for sides and ½ cup for top.

9. Prepare garnish: Melt chocolate in top of a double boiler over barely simmering, not boiling, water, stirring until smooth. Dip one end of each almond into chocolate and then stand it, dipped side down, at edge of cake, forming a ring.

Mint-Berry Chocolate Cake

A hint of mint flavors the layers, while a burst of raspberries and chocolate-covered mint leaves—edible, too—makes for a striking presentation.

Mint-Berry Chocolate Cake

MAKES *16 servings*
PREP *20 minutes*
BAKE *at 350° for 45 minutes*
REFRIGERATE *4 hours*

Cake

2¾ cups all-purpose flour
2¼ cups sugar
1 cup unsweetened cocoa powder
2 teaspoons baking soda
½ teaspoon baking powder
1½ teaspoons salt
3 eggs
1½ cups buttermilk
1 cup water
¾ cup (1½ sticks) unsalted butter or margarine, melted
1 to 2 teaspoons mint extract

Chocolate Ganache Frosting and Glaze

1 cup heavy cream, plus 2 tablespoons for thinning glaze, if needed
8 squares (1 ounce each) semisweet chocolate, chopped
1 teaspoon vanilla

Garnish

1 to 2 bunches mint sprigs with large leaves
½ cup semisweet chocolate chips
2 tablespoons solid vegetable shortening
½ cup white chocolate chips
½ cup raspberries or strawberries

1. Heat oven to 350°. Grease two 8 x 2-inch (6½ cups total volume) heart-shaped layer-cake pans or two 9 x 2-inch round or square cake pans; line bottoms with waxed paper. Grease paper; dust paper and pans with flour.

2. Prepare cake: With a mixer on low speed, mix flour, sugar, cocoa powder, baking soda, baking powder and salt in a large bowl until combined.

3. Add eggs, buttermilk, water, butter and mint extract; beat 30 seconds, until dry ingredients are moistened. Increase speed to medium; beat 2 minutes. Pour batter into prepared pans, dividing equally.

4. Bake cake layers in heated 350° oven 45 minutes for hearts or 9-inch rounds, 40 to 45 minutes for 9-inch squares, or until a wooden pick inserted in center of each comes out clean.

5. Cool cake layers in pans on wire racks 10 minutes. Turn out onto racks to cool completely.

6. Prepare frosting and glaze: Bring cream to boiling in a medium-size saucepan over medium heat; remove from heat. Add chocolate and stir until melted and smooth; stir in vanilla. Pour half of cream mixture into a small bowl; cover with plastic wrap and refrigerate 2 hours or until a good spreading consistency. Cover remaining mixture in pan; let stand at room temperature to use as glaze.

7. Prepare garnish: Separate enough large mint leaves from stems to form a ring around top of cake. Wash, drain and thoroughly pat dry.

8. Meanwhile, melt semisweet chips and 1 tablespoon shortening in a small, heavy saucepan over low heat, stirring until smooth. Repeat with white chips and remaining 1 tablespoon shortening in another pan.

9. Brush tops of half of mint leaves with semisweet chocolate mixture and half with white chocolate mixture. If chocolates harden, return saucepans to low heat, stirring as needed. Place coated leaves over a rolling pin to give them a rounded shape. Set aside on a sheet of waxed paper to harden. Re-coat if desired.

10. If tops of cooled cake layers are rounded, flatten them by using a serrated knife to slice off rounded portion. Invert 1 layer on a serving plate. Spread ⅓ to ½ cup chilled frosting over top. Invert second layer on top. Spread remaining refrigerated frosting on sides of cake, using a long, thin metal spatula to smooth evenly. Refrigerate 1 hour.

11. Pour room-temperature glaze over top of cake. (Glaze should be thick, but pourable. If too thick, gently fold in 1 to 2 tablespoons heavy cream; avoid creating bubbles.) Use a long, thin metal spatula to smooth glaze over top and sides of cake. Refrigerate 1 hour or until glaze is firm.

12. Spoon raspberries onto top center of cake. Arrange chocolate-coated mint leaves around berries.

CHOCOLATE MINT LEAVES

Brush each mint leaf with melted chocolate, then drape over a rolling pin to give a rounded shape.

Brazilian Forest Cake

Cherries, banana slices and Brazil nuts are tucked into the filling and frosting of this towering triumph. Let it serve as centerpiece for your next party.

MAKES *12 servings*

PREP *45 minutes*

BAKE *at 350° for 20 to 22 minutes*

REFRIGERATE *2 hours*

Cake Layers

¼ cup unsweetened cocoa powder
3 tablespoons instant espresso coffee powder
1 teaspoon ground cinnamon
¾ cup boiling water
3 tablespoons butter, cut into small pieces
1¼ cups all-purpose flour
1 teaspoon baking powder
¼ teaspoon baking soda
⅛ teaspoon salt
2 eggs
1 cup sugar
1½ teaspoons vanilla

White Chocolate Cream Frosting

2 teaspoons unflavored gelatin
3 tablespoons cold water
3 cups heavy cream
6 squares (1 ounce each) white chocolate, chopped (1 cup)
1½ teaspoons vanilla

Filling and Garnishes

1 large banana
2 teaspoons lime juice
1½ cups halved maraschino cherries
1 cup chopped Brazil nuts or blanched almonds, toasted (see page 231)
10 whole maraschino cherries with stem
Chocolate shaved into curls

1. Heat oven to 350°. Coat two 8-inch round layer-cake pans with nonstick cooking spray. Line bottoms of pans with waxed paper. Coat paper with spray; dust with flour.

2. Prepare cake: Stir together cocoa powder, espresso powder, cinnamon and boiling water in a cup until smooth. Stir in butter until melted.

3. Mix flour, baking powder, baking soda and salt in a medium-size bowl. With a mixer on medium speed, beat eggs in a large bowl until frothy. On high speed, gradually beat in sugar 4 minutes or until light. On low speed, beat in vanilla, cocoa mixture and flour mixture until blended. Pour batter into prepared pans, dividing equally.

4. Bake in heated 350° oven 20 to 22 minutes or until a wooden pick inserted in center of cake layers comes out clean and tops spring back when lightly pressed with a fingertip. Cool cakes in pans on wire racks 10 minutes. Turn out cakes onto racks to cool completely.

5. Prepare frosting: Sprinkle gelatin over cold water in a cup; let stand to soften. Combine ¾ cup heavy cream and white chocolate in a small saucepan. Stir over medium heat until chocolate is melted, about 2 minutes. Add softened gelatin; stir until smooth. Transfer to a large bowl. Stir in remaining 2¼ cups heavy cream and vanilla. Refrigerate 1 hour, stirring occasionally, until well chilled. Beat on high speed until thick enough to spread, about 5 minutes.

6. Peel banana; cut into ¼-inch-thick slices. Toss slices with lime juice in a small bowl.

7. Using a serrated knife, split each cake layer horizontally in half for a total of 4 layers. Place 1 layer, cut side up, on a platter. Spread with generous ½ cup frosting. Arrange ¾ cup halved cherries on top. Place second cake layer, cut side up, on top. Spread with generous ½ cup frosting; arrange banana slices on top.

Place third cake layer, cut side up, on top. Spread with generous ½ cup frosting; arrange remaining halved cherries over frosting. Place remaining layer, cut side down, on top. Spread layer of frosting over sides and top of cake. Spread any remaining frosting on top.

8. Pat toasted nuts onto sides of cake. Arrange whole cherries and chocolate curls on top. Cover loosely with plastic wrap and refrigerate at least 1 hour before serving.

Bittersweet Chocolate Cakes

Almonds meet chocolate, resulting in a comforting richness in each and every bite.

MAKES *36 cakes*

PREP *30 minutes*

BAKE *at 350° for 15 minutes*

2   cups all-purpose flour
⅔   cup unsweetened cocoa powder
1½ teaspoons ground cinnamon
1   teaspoon baking powder
1   teaspoon baking soda
½   teaspoon salt
¼   teaspoon ground nutmeg
1   cup (2 sticks) butter, at room temperature
1½ cups packed light-brown sugar
3   eggs
2   teaspoons vanilla
1½ cups sour cream
5   squares (1 ounce each) bittersweet chocolate, chopped
1   cup blanched whole almonds, chopped

Ganache Frosting

2¼ cups heavy cream
18 ounces bittersweet chocolate, chopped

Sliced almonds for garnish (optional)

1. Heat oven to 350°. Coat a standard 12-muffin pan with nonstick cooking spray (see note, below).

2. Whisk together flour, cocoa powder, cinnamon, baking powder, baking soda, salt and nutmeg in a large bowl.

3. In a second large bowl, beat butter on medium speed until smooth, 1 minute. Gradually beat in brown sugar, then beat on medium-high 3 minutes or until fluffy. Add eggs, one at a time, beating well after each addition. Beat in vanilla.

4. On low speed, beat flour mixture into butter mixture in 3 additions, alternating with sour cream and ending with flour; beat 2 minutes. Fold in chocolate and almonds. Divide one-third of batter among muffin cups, filling each halfway; set remaining batter aside.

5. Bake in heated 350° oven 15 minutes or until tops spring back when lightly pressed with a fingertip. Cool cakes in pan on a wire rack 10 minutes. Turn out cakes onto rack; cool.

6. Recoat pan with spray and repeat with another third of batter; repeat again with remaining batter.

7. Prepare ganache: Bring cream to boiling in a small saucepan over medium-high heat. Place chocolate in a medium-size bowl. Pour cream over chocolate; stir until chocolate is melted and mixture is smooth.

8. Place wire racks over a jelly-roll pan. Place cakes, top side down, on racks. Pour about 2 tablespoons ganache evenly over each cake, covering completely; smooth with a small spatula.

9. Garnish each cake with 2 or 3 sliced almonds if desired. Refrigerate for 1 hour or until ganache is firm.

NOTE: *For larger cakes, use a jumbo 6-muffin pan. Bake in 2 batches, 25 minutes each. For ganache, use 1½ cups heavy cream and 12 ounces bittersweet chocolate. Makes 12.*

Chocolate Mousse Cake

Raspberry preserves between the layers lend fruity flair, and keep the calories and fat in check. One slice weighs in with fewer than 300 calories and 10 grams of fat. So don't wait; indulge.

MAKES *8 servings*
PREP *25 minutes*
BAKE *at 350° for 10 minutes*
REFRIGERATE *1 hour*

Cake

1   cup all-purpose flour
⅓   cup unsweetened cocoa powder
1   teaspoon baking powder
1   teaspoon baking soda
¼   teaspoon salt
⅓   cup granulated sugar
2   tablespoons butter or margarine, at room temperature
1   egg
1   teaspoon vanilla
1   cup low-fat (1%) milk

Filling

¾   cup low-fat (1%) milk
1   tablespoon strawberry or other fruit-flavored liqueur
1   teaspoon vanilla
½   teaspoon almond extract
1   box (3.9 ounces) chocolate instant pudding-and-pie-filling mix
1   cup frozen nondairy whipped topping, thawed
½   cup seedless raspberry preserves

1   tablespoon confectioners' sugar for dusting
    Fresh flowers for garnish (optional)

1. Heat oven to 350°. Grease two 9-inch round layer-cake pans.

2. Prepare cake: Whisk together flour, cocoa powder, baking powder, baking soda and salt in a small bowl.

3. In a large bowl with mixer on medium speed, beat granulated sugar and butter 30 seconds to blend. Add egg and vanilla; increase speed to high; beat 1 minute.

4. On low speed, beat flour mixture into butter mixture in 3 additions, alternating with milk and ending with flour mixture, until smooth and fluffy. Spread batter in prepared pans, dividing equally.

5. Bake cake layers in heated 350° oven until tops spring back when lightly pressed with a fingertip and sides begin to pull from sides of pan, 10 minutes. Cool cake layers in pans on wire racks 10 minutes. Run a thin knife around edges; invert onto racks and cool completely.

6. Prepare filling: Combine milk, liqueur, vanilla and extract in a medium-size bowl. Add pudding-and-pie-filling mix; beat on medium-low speed 2 minutes. Fold in whipped topping. Refrigerate 3 to 5 minutes.

7. Place 1 cake layer on a serving plate. Spread with ¼ cup raspberry preserves. Spread filling over top. Spread remaining preserves over second cake layer; invert over filling. Cover with plastic wrap and refrigerate until filling is firm, 1 hour. Before serving, dust top with confectioners' sugar and garnish with flowers if desired.

Chocolate Mousse Cake

Feather-Light Chocolate Cake

Three tiers of light and tender cake layered with a chocolate-flavored whipped cream and topped with chocolate curls and candied violets—a combination that can't be beat. Shown on page 10.

MAKES *16 servings*

FREEZE *20 minutes*

PREP *30 minutes*

BAKE *at 350° for 25 minutes*

Cake

- 2 cups granulated sugar
- ¾ cup boiling water
- ¾ cup unsweetened cocoa powder
- 1 cup buttermilk
- 2 teaspoons vanilla
- 2¾ cups cake flour (not self-rising)
- 2¾ teaspoons baking powder
- ¾ teaspoon baking soda
- ½ teaspoon salt
- ¾ cup (1½ sticks) unsalted butter, at room temperature
- 4 eggs

Chocolate-Cream Frosting

- 2 squares (1 ounce each) semisweet chocolate
- 1 tablespoon unsalted butter
- 1¼ cups heavy cream
- 1 tablespoon confectioners' sugar
- 1 teaspoon vanilla

Garnishes (optional)

Semisweet chocolate, shaved into curls
Candied violets

1. Prepare cake: Place granulated sugar in a small heavy-duty plastic food-storage bag; seal; freeze 20 minutes.

2. Meanwhile, adjust oven rack to top of lower third of oven. Heat oven to 350°. Grease three 9 x 2-inch round layer-cake pans. Line bottoms with waxed paper. Grease paper; dust paper and pans with flour.

3. Pour boiling water over cocoa powder in a small bowl; stir to dissolve. Stir in buttermilk and vanilla until smooth; mixture should be cool.

4. Place a large mixing bowl and beaters in freezer 5 minutes.

5. Meanwhile, sift together flour, baking powder, baking soda and salt onto a piece of waxed paper. Repeat twice.

6. With a mixer on medium speed, beat butter in chilled bowl 3 minutes, until light in color. With mixer running, add chilled sugar in a stream. Beat 3 to 4 minutes, until fluffy. Add eggs, one at a time, beating 30 seconds after each addition; beat 1 to 2 minutes, until mixture is airy.

7. Fold in two-thirds of flour mixture; fold in cocoa mixture. Fold in remaining flour mixture. Pour batter into prepared pans, dividing equally.

8. Bake in heated 350° oven 25 minutes or until center of cake layers springs back when lightly pressed with fingertip. Cool cake layers in pans on wire racks 10 minutes. Turn out onto racks to cool completely. Peel off waxed paper.

9. While cake layers bake and cool, prepare frosting: Combine chocolate, butter and ¼ cup cream in a small saucepan over very low heat and heat until chocolate and butter melt; stir until smooth. Remove pan from heat and let mixture cool. With mixer on medium-high speed, beat 1 cup cream, confectioners' sugar and vanilla in a medium-size bowl just until soft peaks form; do not overbeat. Fold one-third of whipped cream into chocolate mixture just until combined. Fold chocolate mixture into remaining whipped cream just until combined.

10. Place 1 cake layer on a serving plate. Spread top with one-third of frosting. Place second cake layer on top; spread with one-third of frosting. Repeat with remaining layer and frosting. Garnish with chocolate curls and candied violets if desired. Cover loosely with plastic wrap and refrigerate until serving.

Chocolate Peanut Butter Squares

For adults who haven't lost their taste for peanut butter: A dense cake and cream cheese frosting both spiked with chopped milk chocolate PB cups. Wow!

MAKES *16 squares*

PREP *15 minutes*

BAKE *at 350° for 35 to 40 minutes*

COOL *1 hour*

Cake

1⅓ cups all-purpose flour
1½ teaspoons baking powder
½ teaspoon salt
1 cup granulated sugar
6 tablespoons (¾ stick) butter, cut into small pieces
3 squares (1 ounce each) bittersweet chocolate, coarsely chopped
¼ cup unsweetened cocoa powder
1 cup milk
2 eggs, lightly beaten
1 teaspoon vanilla
¾ cup coarsely chopped miniature milk-chocolate peanut butter cups (about 15)

Frosting

1 package (3 ounces) cream cheese, at room temperature
¼ cup (½ stick) butter, at room temperature
1 cup confectioners' sugar
1 teaspoon vanilla
¼ cup coarsely chopped miniature milk-chocolate peanut butter cups (about 4)

1. Heat oven to 350°. Butter and flour an 8 x 8 x 2-inch glass baking pan.

2. Prepare cake: Whisk together flour, baking powder and salt in a medium-size bowl.

3. Combine sugar, butter, chocolate and cocoa powder in a large bowl. Bring milk to boiling in a small saucepan over medium heat. Pour milk over chocolate mixture; whisk until chocolate has melted and mixture is smooth. Stir in eggs and vanilla. Whisk in flour mixture. Fold in peanut butter cups. Pour batter into prepared pan.

4. Bake in heated 350° oven 35 to 40 minutes or until a wooden pick inserted in center comes out clean. Cool cake in pan on a wire rack 1 hour.

5. Prepare frosting: With a mixer on medium speed, beat together cream cheese and butter in a medium-size bowl until smooth and creamy. Gradually beat in sugar and vanilla.

6. Spread frosting over top of cake. Sprinkle with peanut butter cups. Cut into squares.

Celebration Cake

Two kinds of chocolate plus cocoa powder meld scrumptiously in each slice. Shown on front cover.

MAKES *24 servings*

PREP *25 minutes*

BAKE *at 350° for 25 to 30 minutes*

REFRIGERATE *3 hours*

Cake

- 6 squares (1 ounce each) semisweet chocolate, chopped
- 2¼ cups all-purpose flour
- 2 tablespoons unsweetened cocoa powder
- 1 teaspoon baking soda
- ½ teaspoon baking powder
- ½ teaspoon salt
- ¾ cup (1½ sticks) unsalted butter, at room temperature
- 1⅓ cups granulated sugar
- 1 teaspoon vanilla
- 3 eggs
- 1 container (8 ounces) sour cream
- ¼ cup water

Fluffy Whipped Cream Frosting

- 3 cups heavy cream
- 2 ounces white baking chocolate, chopped
- 1 teaspoon vanilla
- 6 tablespoons confectioners' sugar
  White chocolate shaved into curls for garnish (optional)

1. Heat oven to 350°. Grease three 9 x 2-inch round layer-cake pans; dust with flour.

2. Prepare cake: Place two-thirds (4 ounces) of chopped chocolate in a glass bowl; microwave at 100% power 2 minutes, stirring once. Add remaining chocolate and stir until melted. Cool slightly.

3. Sift flour, cocoa powder, baking soda, baking powder and salt onto a piece of waxed paper.

4. With a mixer on medium speed, beat butter and granulated sugar in a large bowl 3 minutes or until fluffy. Beat in vanilla. Beat in eggs, one at a time. Beat in melted chocolate.

5. Mix sour cream and water in a small bowl. With mixer on low speed, beat flour mixture into butter mixture in 3 additions, alternating with sour cream and ending with flour mixture; beat on medium-high speed 3 minutes. Spread batter in prepared pans, dividing equally.

6. Bake in heated 350° oven 25 to 30 minutes or until a wooden pick inserted in center of cake layers comes out clean; do not overbake. Cool cake layers in pans on wire racks 15 minutes; turn out onto racks. Cool completely.

7. Prepare frosting: Place 2½ cups cream, a large mixing bowl and clean beaters in refrigerator. In a medium-size saucepan over medium heat, bring remaining ½ cup cream to boiling. Remove from heat. Add chopped white chocolate and stir until melted. Pour into a medium-size bowl; refrigerate until chilled, about 1 hour.

8. Add chilled cream, chocolate mixture, vanilla and sugar to large chilled bowl; beat on medium speed 3 minutes or until stiff enough to spread but not grainy.

9. Place 1 cake layer on a serving plate. Spread with 1 cup frosting. Top with second cake layer and another 1 cup frosting. Place third layer on top; spread remaining frosting over top and sides. Chill cake at least 2 hours for easy cutting. Garnish with white chocolate curls if desired.

Celebration Cake

Pear Cake

This recipe can be assembled ahead and then baked just before you are ready to eat it— great when you want a warm dessert after dinner. Simply peel the pear, mix the batter, combine everything in the pan and store it, covered, in the fridge.

MAKES *8 servings*

PREP *20 minutes*

BAKE *at 350° for 35 minutes*

Batter

- 6 tablespoons (¾ stick) unsalted butter, at room temperature
- ⅔ cup packed light-brown sugar
- 2 eggs
- ¼ cup heavy cream
- 1 cup all-purpose flour
- 1 teaspoon ground ginger
- 1 teaspoon finely chopped fresh ginger
- ¼ teaspoon salt

Pears and Topping

- 2 ripe firm pears
- 1 tablespoon unsalted butter, melted
- 2 tablespoons light-brown sugar
- ¾ cup heavy cream
- ¼ teaspoon ground ginger
- 1 tablespoon confectioners' sugar

1. Heat oven to 350°. Coat a 10-inch pie plate with nonstick cooking spray.

2. Prepare batter: With a mixer on medium speed, beat butter and sugar in a medium-size bowl until well blended. Add eggs, one at a time, beating well after each addition. On low speed, beat in cream, flour, ground ginger, fresh ginger and salt. Batter will be stiff. Scrape into prepared pie plate, smoothing top.

3. Prepare pears and topping: Peel pears; quarter each lengthwise; cut out cores. One at a time, slice each pear quarter crosswise into ¼-inch-thick slices and arrange it on batter, creating a wheel

spoke pattern; gently press slices into batter. Drizzle top with melted butter; sprinkle with brown sugar. (If you wish, cover and refrigerate until ready to bake.)

4. Bake cake in heated 350° oven 35 minutes, until lightly browned. Meanwhile, on medium-high speed, beat cream, ginger and confectioners' sugar in a medium-size bowl until stiff peaks form. Serve cake warm, with whipped cream.

Orange Pecan Bundt Cake

When a buttery cake bursts with pecans and the richness of sour cream, all it needs is a final dusting of confectioners' sugar.

MAKES *16 servings*

PREP *20 minutes*

BAKE *at 350° for 40 to 45 minutes*

- 2 cups all-purpose flour
- 1 teaspoon baking soda
- ¾ teaspoon salt
- 1 package (8 ounces) pecan pieces
- 1½ cups granulated sugar
- ¾ cup plus 2 tablespoons butter (1¾ sticks), at room temperature
- 4 eggs
- 1 container (8 ounces) sour cream
- ½ cup frozen orange juice concentrate, thawed
- 2 tablespoons grated orange rind
- 2 teaspoons vanilla
  Confectioners' sugar for dusting

1. Heat oven to 350°. Butter a 12-cup bundt pan; dust with flour.

2. Sift together flour, baking soda and salt into a medium-size bowl.

3. Place pecan pieces and ½ cup sugar in a food processor; whirl until finely ground.

4. With a mixer on medium speed, beat together butter and remaining 1 cup sugar in a medium-size bowl until light and fluffy, about 3 minutes. Beat in eggs, one at a time, beating well after each addition. Beat in sour cream, orange juice concentrate, orange rind and vanilla. Stir in pecan mixture, then flour mixture. Spoon batter into prepared pan.

5. Bake in heated 350° oven 40 to 45 minutes or until a wooden pick inserted in center of cake comes out clean. Cool cake in pan on a wire rack 5 minutes. Invert cake onto rack and remove pan; cool cake completely. Dust top with confectioners' sugar.

Rich Ginger Sheet Cake

Fresh ginger gives this moist cake an unexpected zing, while honey lends a sweet note to the cream topping.

MAKES *16 servings*

PREP *35 minutes*

BAKE *at 350° for 55 minutes*

Cake

3 whole eggs
2 egg yolks
1½ cups milk
3 tablespoons grated fresh ginger
1 tablespoon vanilla
3 cups cake flour (not self-rising)
2 cups granulated sugar
1 tablespoon baking powder
1 teaspoon salt
¼ cup (½ stick) unsalted butter, at room temperature
¾ cup vegetable oil

Honey-Cream Frosting

1 package (8 ounces) cream cheese, at room temperature
3 tablespoons honey
½ teaspoon salt
5 cups confectioners' sugar
   Fresh flowers for garnish (optional)

1. Adjust oven rack to top of lower third of oven. Heat oven to 350°. Grease a 13 x 9 x 2-inch baking pan; line bottom with waxed paper. Grease paper; dust paper and pan with flour.

2. Prepare cake: With a mixer on medium speed, beat whole eggs, egg yolks, 1¼ cups milk, ginger and vanilla in a medium-size bowl until blended.

3. Whisk together flour, granulated sugar, baking powder and salt in a large bowl. On low speed, beat remaining ¼ cup milk, butter and oil into flour mixture, beating just until dry ingredients are moistened. Increase speed to medium and beat 1½ minutes or until blended.

4. Add one-third of egg mixture to flour mixture; beat on medium speed 20 seconds, until blended. Repeat until all egg mixture is used, scraping down sides after each addition. Pour into prepared pan.

5. Bake in heated 350° oven 55 minutes or until a wooden pick inserted in center of cake comes out clean. Cool cake in pan on a wire rack 15 minutes. Turn out onto rack to cool completely. Peel off waxed paper. Invert cake onto a serving platter.

6. Prepare frosting: On medium speed, beat cream cheese, honey and salt in a medium-size bowl 3 minutes or until creamy. On low speed, gradually beat in sugar, beating until frosting is a spreading consistency.

7. Spread frosting over sides and top of cake. Garnish with flowers if desired.

Carrot Cake

Since heavy add-ins like shredded carrots tend to fall to the bottom of this batter, gently stir them in at the last minute. If you do, you will be rewarded with a virtuoso version of this classic.

Carrot Cake

MAKES *16 servings*

PREP *40 minutes*

BAKE *at 375° for 45 minutes,*
then at 350° for 30 minutes

Cake

3   cups all-purpose flour
1   cup packed dark-brown sugar
¾   cup granulated sugar
1   tablespoon baking powder
1½ teaspoons ground ginger
½   teaspoon baking soda
½   teaspoon ground cloves
½   teaspoon ground nutmeg
½   teaspoon salt
4   eggs
1¼ cups vegetable oil
¼   cup orange juice
1   tablespoon vanilla
1   pound carrots, peeled and shredded
    (4½ cups)
1   cup sweetened flake coconut
1   cup chopped walnuts
½   cup golden raisins

Cream-Cheese Glaze

1   package (3 ounces) cream cheese,
    at room temperature
⅔   cup sifted confectioners' sugar
2   to 2½ tablespoons milk
    Toasted coconut (see page 231) for
    garnish (optional)

1. Adjust oven rack to top of lower third of oven. Heat to 375°. Grease a 10-inch (12-cup) tube pan; dust with flour.

2. Whisk together flour, sugars, baking powder, ginger, baking soda, cloves, nutmeg and salt in a large bowl. Make a well in center.

3. With a mixer on medium speed, beat eggs in a small bowl 1 minute or until frothy. Stir in vegetable oil, orange juice and vanilla.

4. Pour egg mixture into well in flour mixture; stir rapidly with a wooden spoon until well mixed. Beat on medium speed 3 minutes, until blended. Stir in carrots, coconut, walnuts and raisins. Pour batter into prepared pan.

5. Bake in heated 375° oven 45 minutes. Lower oven temperature to 350°. Bake 30 minutes. Cool cake in pan on a wire rack 15 minutes. Turn out cake onto rack to cool completely.

6. Prepare glaze: Beat cream cheese and sugar in a small bowl until smooth. Beat in enough milk to make glaze a good pouring consistency.

7. Place cake on a serving platter. Pour glaze over cake, letting it drip down sides. Scatter coconut on top if desired.

Pumpkin Bundt Cake

Pumpkin puree replaces some of the fat, and reduced-fat cream cheese cuts some more. The result? A mere 204 calories and 5 grams of fat with plenty of rich goodness to spare.

MAKES *16 servings*

PREP *10 minutes*

BAKE *at 350° for 35 minutes*

Cake

- 3 cups cake flour (not self-rising)
- 2½ teaspoons pumpkin pie spice
- 2 teaspoons baking powder
- ¼ cup (½ stick) unsalted butter, at room temperature
- 1 cup granulated sugar
- 1¼ cups canned solid-pack pumpkin puree
- 2 whole eggs
- 2 egg whites
- 1 teaspoon vanilla
- ½ cup evaporated skim milk

Glaze

- 4 ounces less-fat cream cheese
- ½ cup sifted confectioners' sugar
- 2 tablespoons skim milk
- 1 teaspoon grated lemon rind
- ¼ teaspoon lemon juice
- ¼ teaspoon vanilla

1. Heat oven to 350°. Lightly coat a 10-inch (12-cup) bundt pan with nonstick cooking spray.

2. Whisk together flour, pie spice and baking powder in a medium-size bowl.

3. With a mixer on medium speed, beat together butter and sugar in a large bowl 3 minutes or until light and fluffy. Beat in pumpkin puree, whole eggs, egg whites and vanilla.

4. Beat flour mixture into butter mixture in 3 additions, alternating with evaporated milk and ending with flour mixture. Pour into prepared pan.

5. Bake in heated 350° oven 35 minutes or until a wooden pick inserted in center of cake comes out clean. Cool cake in pan on a wire rack 10 minutes. Turn out cake onto rack to cool completely.

6. Meanwhile, prepare glaze: On medium-high speed, beat together cream cheese, confectioners' sugar, skim milk, lemon rind, lemon juice and vanilla in a medium-size bowl until well blended and a good pouring consistency. Pour glaze over cake, letting it drip down sides.

Piña Colada Pound Cake

Crushed pineapple, lime juice and coconut come together for a glittering taste of the tropics. It's even better when the flavors have a chance to meld for a day or two.

MAKES *16 servings*

PREP *15 minutes*

BAKE *at 325° for 60 minutes*

Cake

2½ cups all-purpose flour
½ teaspoon baking soda
½ teaspoon salt
1 cup (2 sticks) butter, softened
2 cups sugar
4 eggs
1 container (8 ounces) vanilla yogurt
¼ cup canned crushed pineapple
1 teaspoon grated lime rind
1 teaspoon coconut extract
½ teaspoon vanilla

Glaze

½ cup confectioners' sugar
2 teaspoons lime juice

Garnishes (optional)

Sugared fruit (see page 231)
Sweetened flake coconut
Lemon rind and lime rind, cut into thin strips

1. Prepare cake: Heat oven to 325°. Grease a 10-inch (12-cup) bundt pan. Dust pan with flour.

2. Whisk together flour, baking soda and salt in a medium-size bowl.

3. In another medium-size bowl, with a mixer on medium speed, beat butter and sugar until light and fluffy, about 3 minutes. Beat in eggs, one at a time, beating well after each addition.

4. Mix together yogurt, pineapple, lime rind, coconut extract and vanilla in a small bowl. Beat flour mixture into butter mixture in 3 additions, alternating with yogurt mixture and ending with flour mixture, beating until smooth. Pour into prepared pan.

5. Bake in heated 325° oven 60 minutes or until a wooden pick inserted in center of cake comes out clean. Cool cake in pan on a wire rack 15 minutes. Turn out cake onto rack to cool completely.

6. Prepare glaze: Whisk together confectioners' sugar and lime juice in a small bowl until a good drizzling consistency. Drizzle over cake. Scatter sugared fruit, flake coconut and strips of rind on top if desired.

White Cake with Triangular Twirls

A lacy chocolate triangle stands up proudly to give each serving of this pure white cake a dramatic accent.

MAKES *16 servings*

PREP *2 hours*

BAKE *at 325° for 35 minutes*

REFRIGERATE *30 minutes*

Cake

4 cups sifted cake flour (not self-rising)
3¼ teaspoons baking powder
¾ teaspoon salt
1¼ cups (2½ sticks) unsalted butter or margarine, at room temperature
1⅔ cups granulated sugar
6 egg whites
2 teaspoons vanilla
1 cup water

Buttercream Frosting

1 cup (2 sticks) unsalted butter or
  margarine, at room temperature
6 to 8 tablespoons milk
2 teaspoons vanilla
1 teaspoon salt
8 cups sifted confectioners' sugar

Triangular Twirls

1 package (6 ounces) semisweet chocolate
  chips (1 cup)
2 tablespoons solid vegetable shortening

1. Heat oven to 325°. Grease two 9 x
   2-inch round layer-cake pans. Line
   bottoms with waxed paper; grease
   paper. Dust paper and pans with flour.

2. Prepare cake: Mix flour, baking powder
   and salt on a piece of waxed paper.

3. With a mixer on medium speed, beat
   butter and sugar in a large bowl until
   light and fluffy. Add egg whites, one at
   a time, beating after each addition.
   Beat in vanilla.

4. On low speed, beat flour mixture into
   butter mixture, alternating with water
   and ending with flour mixture, beating
   after each addition. Pour batter into
   prepared pans, dividing equally.

5. Bake in heated 325° oven 35 minutes, or
   until a wooden pick inserted in center
   of cake layers comes out clean. Cool cake
   layers in pans on wire racks 10 minutes.
   Turn out onto racks to cool completely.

6. Prepare frosting: On medium speed, beat
   together butter, milk, vanilla, salt and
   2 cups sugar in a large bowl until
   smooth and creamy. Gradually beat in
   remaining sugar until a good spreading
   consistency.

7. Meanwhile, melt chocolate and
   shortening in a small saucepan over low
   heat, stirring until smooth.

8. Using a pencil and ruler, draw 8 tall
   triangles on a sheet of waxed paper,
   making the 2 long sides of each 4 inches
   long and the base 2⅛ inches across.
   Place paper, pencil mark side down, on
   a baking sheet.

9. Pour melted chocolate mixture into a
   pastry bag fitted with a medium writing
   tip. Pipe chocolate outline of 1 triangle
   in a smooth steady line, then fill in
   interior with a random lacy pattern.
   Repeat with remaining triangles.
   Refrigerate triangles on baking sheet
   30 minutes or until set.

10. If tops of cooled cake layers are rounded,
    flatten them by using a serrated knife to
    slice off rounded portion. Invert 1 layer
    on a serving plate. Spread ½ to ¾ cup
    frosting over top of cake. Invert second
    cake layer on top. Reserve about ¼ cup
    frosting; spread remainder over sides
    and top of cake, using a long, thin metal
    spatula to smooth as evenly as possible.

11. Spoon reserved frosting into a pastry
    bag fitted with a star tip; pipe a small
    rosette in center of cake top.

12. Using a long, thin metal spatula,
    carefully loosen triangles from waxed
    paper. Spacing at even intervals on top
    of cake, stand each triangle upright on a
    long side; anchor its tip in central rosette
    and gently press triangle into frosting.

TRIANGULAR TWIRLS

First pipe outline of each
triangle on waxed paper.
Then fill each with a
random lacy pattern.

Marbled Angel Food Cake with Strawberries

A showy ribbon of chocolate adds extra flavor as well as artistic appeal without tilting the calorie scales on this naturally trim treat. And this recipe is versatile to the max: Leave out the cocoa powder for a classic snowy version. Or use cherry filling in place of the cocoa to create a lush and flavorful spiral of pink—see the variation, below.

MAKES *10 servings*

PREP *20 minutes*

BAKE *at 350° for 40 minutes*

COOL *1 hour*

Cake

- 1 cup cake flour (not self-rising)
  Pinch ground nutmeg
- 12 egg whites (1¾ cups)
- 1½ teaspoons cream of tartar
- 1⅓ cups superfine sugar
- ¼ cup unsweetened cocoa powder

Topping

- 3 cups fresh strawberries, hulled and sliced
- 3 tablespoons granulated sugar
- ¼ cup orange juice

1. Heat oven to 350°.

2. Prepare cake: Sift together cake flour and nutmeg into a medium-size bowl.

3. With a mixer on medium speed, beat egg whites and cream of tartar in a large bowl until frothy. Beat in superfine sugar, 2 tablespoons at a time, and then beat 5 to 7 minutes, until stiff, glossy peaks form.

4. Fold flour mixture into egg white mixture in 2 additions, until incorporated. Transfer half of batter to a clean medium-size bowl; gently fold in cocoa powder.

5. Spoon white batter alternately with chocolate batter into an ungreased 10-inch tube pan. Swirl a sharp knife through batters to create a marbled pattern.

6. Bake cake in heated 350° oven 40 minutes or until springy when touched and a wooden pick inserted in center of cake comes out clean. If pan has no legs extending above the rim, invert onto a wine or similar weighted bottle, placing center of tube over neck of bottle. Cool 1 hour.

7. Meanwhile, prepare topping: Combine strawberries, sugar and orange juice in a bowl. Let stand to allow flavors to blend.

8. Run a thin metal spatula around side of pan and tube to loosen cake. Turn cake out onto a serving plate. Serve cake slices topped with strawberry mixture.

Cherry Variation

Prepare the Marbled Angel Food Cake with the following changes. In step 2, omit nutmeg. In step 3, add 1 teaspoon cherry extract when beating egg whites. In step 4, force ¼ cup cherry pie filling through a sieve; discard solids and fold puree into half of cake batter. Proceed with step 5, substituting cherry batter for chocolate batter; then bake and cool as directed. Omit topping.

Marbled Angel Food Cake with Strawberries

Lemon Poppy Seed Cake

Create three lemony layers, encase them in a sprightly frosting, then bring the result to a bake sale and watch the profits roll in!

MAKES *16 servings*

PREP *30 minutes*

STAND *1 hour*

BAKE *at 350° for 30 to 35 minutes*

Cake

3 jars (1.25 ounces each) poppy seeds (¾ cup)
2¼ cups milk
4½ cups cake flour (not self-rising)
1½ tablespoons baking powder
1½ teaspoons salt
6 egg whites
2½ cups granulated sugar
1¼ cups (2½ sticks) unsalted butter or margarine, at room temperature
2 tablespoons grated lemon rind

Lemon Buttercream Frosting

1¼ cups (2½ sticks) unsalted butter or margarine, at room temperature
2½ boxes (1 pound each) confectioners' sugar
½ cup fresh lemon juice
¼ cup grated lemon rind
⅛ teaspoon salt
Grated lemon rind for garnish (optional)

1. Prepare cake: Combine poppy seeds and 1 cup milk in a small saucepan. Bring to boiling over medium-low heat. Remove from heat; cover; let stand 1 hour.

2. Heat oven to 350°. Grease three 9 x 2-inch round layer-cake pans; dust paper and pans with flour.

3. Combine cake flour, baking powder and salt and sift into a medium-size bowl.

4. With a mixer on high speed, beat egg whites in a large bowl until foamy. Beat in 1 cup sugar, 1 tablespoon at a time, until soft peaks form.

5. In another large bowl, beat together butter and remaining 1½ cups sugar on medium speed until smooth and creamy, about 3 minutes. Beat in poppy-seed mixture and lemon rind.

6. On low speed, beat flour mixture into butter mixture in 3 additions, alternating with remaining 1¼ cups milk and ending with flour mixture, beating until smooth.

7. Fold egg whites into batter until no streaks of white remain. Pour batter into prepared pans, dividing equally.

8. Bake in heated 350° oven 30 to 35 minutes or until tops of cake layers spring back when lightly pressed and a wooden pick inserted in center of each comes out clean. Using a thin metal spatula, gently loosen sides of cake layers. Cool cake layers in pans on wire racks 10 minutes. Invert onto wire racks to cool completely.

9. Prepare frosting: Beat butter on high speed in a large bowl until fluffy. On low speed, beat in confectioners' sugar in 3 additions, alternating with lemon juice; beat on medium speed until smooth and creamy. Stir in lemon rind and salt.

10. If tops of cooled cakes are rounded, flatten them by using a serrated knife to slice off rounded portion.

11. Invert 1 cake layer on a serving plate. Spread about ¾ cup frosting over top. Place second layer, bottom side down, on top. Spread about ¾ cup frosting over top. Place third layer, bottom side down, on top. Frost top and sides of cake with remaining frosting. Garnish top with lemon rind if desired.

Fluffy Coconut Cake

An old-fashioned cake with a touch of Southern hospitality, this is especially welcome at summertime picnics or wintertime open houses—or anytime, for that matter.

MAKES *12 servings*
PREP *30 minutes*
BAKE *at 350° for 25 minutes*
COOK *frosting 7 minutes*

Cake

1   cup (2 sticks) butter, at room temperature
2   cups sugar
5   whole eggs
3   cups all-purpose flour, sifted
1   tablespoon baking powder
1¼ cups milk
1   teaspoon vanilla

7-Minute Frosting

2   egg whites
1½ cups sugar
⅛ teaspoon salt
½ cup water
1   tablespoon light corn syrup
½ teaspoon vanilla
½ teaspoon lemon extract
1½ cups unsweetened flake coconut

1. Heat oven to 350°. Grease three 9-inch round layer-cake pans. Dust pans with flour.

2. Prepare cake: With a mixer on medium speed, beat butter in a large bowl until creamy. Gradually add sugar, beating thoroughly, until light and fluffy. Add whole eggs, one at a time, beating well after each addition.

3. Combine flour and baking powder in a small bowl. Add flour mixture to butter mixer in 3 additions, alternating with milk and ending with flour, beating thoroughly after each addition. Beat in vanilla. Pour batter into prepared pans, dividing equally.

4. Bake in heated 350° oven 25 minutes or until a wooden pick inserted in center of cake layers comes out clean. Cool cake layers completely in pans on wire racks.

5. Prepare frosting: Combine egg whites, sugar, salt, water and corn syrup in a medium-size heavy saucepan. Heat over very low heat, beating constantly with a hand mixer and scraping down sides of the pan to prevent sugar crystals from forming, until soft peaks form, about 7 minutes total. Remove saucepan from heat. Add vanilla and lemon extract; beat 1 minute.

6. Turn out cake layers from pans. Place 1 layer on a serving plate; slide thin strips of waxed paper under layer to keep plate clean. Spread a small amount of frosting over top of cake and sprinkle with a little shredded coconut. Place second layer on top; frost and sprinkle with coconut. Top with third layer. Frost top and sides of cake. Sprinkle remaining coconut over top and sides, patting lightly to adhere coconut to sides. Remove waxed paper strips.

Macadamia Upside-Down Cake

Take pineapple upside-down cake to new heights with the addition of another of Hawaii's great products: buttery macadamia nuts.

MAKES *8 servings*

PREP *25 minutes*

BAKE *at 350° for 35 minutes*

¾ cup macadamia nuts (3 ounces), chopped
1 can (8½ ounces) crushed pineapple, drained
6 tablespoons (¾ stick) butter or margarine
⅓ cup packed dark-brown sugar
¼ cup dark corn syrup
2 teaspoons water
8 glacé cherries
1 cup all-purpose flour
1 teaspoon baking powder
⅛ teaspoon salt
2 eggs
⅔ cup granulated sugar
½ cup milk
1½ teaspoons vanilla

1. Position oven rack in lower part of oven. Heat oven to 350°. Grease an 8 x 8 x 2-inch square cake pan.

2. Combine nuts and pineapple in a small bowl.

3. Melt butter in a small saucepan. Transfer 2 tablespoons melted butter to a small cup and reserve. Add brown sugar, corn syrup and water to butter remaining in saucepan. Bring to boiling; cook 30 seconds, stirring to dissolve sugar. Pour into prepared baking pan. Scatter glacé cherries over brown-sugar mixture; sprinkle nut-pineapple mixture on top.

4. Stir together flour, baking powder and salt on a sheet of waxed paper.

5. With a mixer on medium speed, beat eggs in a large bowl until foamy, about 30 seconds. Gradually add granulated sugar, beating constantly. Beat in flour mixture just until blended. Add milk, reserved melted butter and vanilla; beat until blended. Pour into prepared pan.

6. Bake in lower part of heated 350° oven 35 minutes or until a wooden pick inserted in center of cake comes out clean. Immediately run a thin metal spatula around edge of pan to loosen cake. Cool cake in pan on a wire rack 15 minutes.

7. Invert cake onto rack and remove pan. Replace any nuts or cherries that have fallen off. Cool cake at least 10 minutes more before serving or cool completely.

EASY CHOPPING

When you need finely chopped nuts, use a chopping bowl and chopper. Or arrange nuts on a chopping board and chop them with a sharp chef's knife, rocking it from tip to end. Chopping nuts in a food processor is not recommended—it is very easy to overprocess them.

Apple Caramel Cake

Butter and brown sugar pair up with apples and pecans for a gooey topping; go over-the-top and serve with a scoop of vanilla or butter pecan ice cream.

MAKES *8 servings*

PREP *15 minutes*

BAKE *at 375° for 30 minutes*

¾ cup (1½ sticks) unsalted butter, melted
1⅓ cups packed light- or dark-brown sugar
1¾ teaspoons pumpkin-pie spice or ground cinnamon
1 cup pecan halves
2 medium-size Granny Smith apples, cored and sliced into thin wedges
2 cups all-purpose flour
¾ teaspoon salt
½ teaspoon baking soda
¾ cup water

1. Heat oven to 375°.

2. Coat sides of a 9-inch round or 9 x 9 x 2-inch-square cake pan with nonstick cooking spray. Place 3 tablespoons butter in bottom of pan; swirl to coat bottom. Sprinkle ⅓ cup brown sugar and ¼ teaspoon pie spice over butter. Arrange 12 pecan halves, flat side up, around edge of bottom of pan. Arrange apple slices in pan. Chop remaining pecans.

3. Whisk together flour, salt, baking soda and remaining 1½ teaspoons pie spice in a medium-size bowl until combined.

4. In a second medium-size bowl, with a mixer on medium speed, beat together remaining melted butter and remaining 1 cup brown sugar until smooth. Stir in water. Stir in flour mixture and chopped nuts just until combined. Spoon batter evenly over apples in pan.

5. Bake in heated 375° oven 30 minutes or until a wooden pick inserted in center of cake comes out clean. Cool cake in pan on a wire rack 10 minutes. Invert cake onto a serving plate and remove pan. Replace any nuts or apples that have fallen off. Serve warm.

Apple Caramel Cake

Strawberry Jelly Roll

In this crowd-pleasing favorite, the sweet-tart flavor of strawberry comes through in three different ways: Flavored cream cheese, jam and the fresh berry itself.

MAKES *10 servings*

PREP *30 minutes*

BAKE *at 375° for about 12 minutes*

REFRIGERATE *at least 1 hour*

Cake

8   egg whites
½   teaspoon cream of tartar
¾   cup granulated sugar
¼   cup vegetable oil
1   teaspoon vanilla
¾   cup sifted self-rising cake flour
3   tablespoons confectioners' sugar

Filling

1   container (8 ounces) strawberry-flavor cream cheese, at room temperature
¼   cup sour cream
¼   cup strawberry jam
1½   cups chopped strawberries (1 pint)

Garnishes *(optional)*

Confectioners' sugar
Whole strawberries

1. Prepare cake: Heat oven to 375°. Coat a 15½ x 10½ x 1-inch jelly-roll pan with nonstick cooking spray. Line bottom of pan with waxed paper; lightly coat waxed paper with cooking spray.

2. Beat egg whites and cream of tartar in a large bowl until foamy. Gradually add ¼ cup granulated sugar and beat until soft peaks form.

3. Beat together oil and remaining ½ cup granulated sugar in a second large bowl until well mixed, about 1 minute. Beat in vanilla.

4. Stir cake flour into oil mixture. Gently fold in one-quarter of egg whites until completely blended, then gently fold in remaining egg whites. Spread batter evenly in prepared pan.

5. Bake in heated 375° oven about 12 minutes or until top is very lightly browned and springs back when lightly touched.

6. Loosen cake around edges with a thin knife. Sprinkle top with confectioners' sugar. Cover with a clean kitchen towel. Top with a slightly larger baking sheet; invert. Remove pan, then waxed paper. Starting from a short side, roll up cake and towel together. Place seam side down on a wire rack to cool.

7. Prepare filling: Stir together cream cheese, sour cream and jam in a medium-size bowl. Gently fold in strawberries.

8. Unroll cake. Spread filling over cake, leaving ½-inch border all around edges of cake. Carefully re-roll cake. Refrigerate at least 1 hour.

9. Place cake, seam side down, on a serving platter. Trim ends of cake. If desired, sprinkle roll evenly with confectioners' sugar and garnish with strawberries.

ROLLED-CAKE HINTS

Starting from a short side, roll up warm cake and towel together.

Spread filling over cooled cake. Then, starting from a short side, re-roll cake.

Strawberry Chiffon Cake

Starring in a 1969 story aptly called "Temptation, Thy Name Is Dessert!" this berry-cream filled creation is still a show-stopper. More berries for garnish? Why not!

MAKES *12 servings*

PREP *60 minutes*

BAKE *at 325° for 1 hour 10 minutes*

2⅓ cups sifted cake flour (not self-rising)
1⅓ cups granulated sugar
1 tablespoon baking powder
¼ teaspoon salt
2 eggs, separated
1 cup milk
⅓ cup vegetable oil
1 teaspoon vanilla
1 cup heavy cream
2 cups strawberries, hulled and sliced
½ cup (1 stick) butter or margarine, at room temperature
1 box (1 pound) confectioners' sugar, sifted (about 4½ cups)
Strawberries for garnish (optional)

1. Heat oven to 325°. Grease and flour a 10-cup ovenproof bowl.

2. Combine flour, 1 cup granulated sugar, baking powder and salt and sift into a large bowl.

3. Beat egg whites in a small bowl until foamy. Beat in remaining ⅓ cup granulated sugar, 1 tablespoon at a time, until soft peaks form.

4. Stir ⅔ cup milk, oil and vanilla into flour mixture; beat on medium speed 1 minute. Add egg yolks and remaining ⅓ cup milk; beat 1 minute. Using a rubber spatula, fold in egg whites until no streaks of white remain. Spoon into prepared 10-cup bowl.

5. Bake in heated 325° oven 1 hour 10 minutes or until top springs back when lightly pressed with a fingertip.

Cool cake in bowl on a wire rack 10 minutes. Loosen around edge with a thin metal spatula; turn out onto rack; cool completely.

6. Turn cake flat side up. With a sharp knife trim off crown to make flat. Carefully cut a cone-shaped piece from center, leaving a cake shell about 1 inch thick. Slice a ½-inch-thick piece from wide end of cone to use as a "lid" for cake filling; reserve remainder of cone for another use.

7. Beat cream in a medium-size bowl until stiff peaks form. Fold 1½ cups strawberries into whipped cream; reserve remaining ½ cup berries.

8. Spoon strawberry cream into hollow in cake; cover with inverted cake slice "lid." Place a serving plate top side down over cake and carefully invert cake and serving plate. Refrigerate.

9. Beat together butter and 1 cup confectioners' sugar in a medium-size bowl on medium speed until smooth and creamy, about 3 minutes. Mash reserved ½ cup strawberries; beat into butter mixture alternately with 3 cups confectioners' sugar until smooth and spreadable. Spread a thin layer, about ¾ cup, over cake; reserve remaining frosting.

10. Attach a star tip to a pastry bag. Beat remaining ½ cup confectioners' sugar into remaining frosting. Spoon frosting into bag; pipe into rosettes on cake top and around outside edge of base. Refrigerate cake until ready to serve.

11. If desired, garnish piped rosettes with additional whole or halved strawberries just before serving.

Orange Cake

It's easy to section oranges: Simply slice off top and bottom so orange sits flat, then run knife blade along curve of orange to remove skin and white pith. Holding the orange, cut along the dividing white membranes to remove each section. Voilà! The secret sweet ingredient is ready.

MAKES *16 servings*

PREP *15 minutes*

BAKE *at 350° for 25 to 30 minutes*

Cake

3 cups cake flour (not self-rising)
2½ teaspoons baking powder
¼ teaspoon salt
1¼ cups (2½ sticks) unsalted butter, at room temperature
1¾ cups granulated sugar
4 eggs
1 tablespoon finely grated orange rind
2 teaspoons vanilla
¾ cup orange juice

Filling

¼ cup water
3 tablespoons granulated sugar
2 tablespoons orange-flavored liqueur
½ cup heavy cream
1 tablespoon confectioners' sugar
¼ teaspoon vanilla
2 to 3 oranges, sectioned

Garnishes

Confectioners' sugar
Fresh mint sprig (optional)

1. Prepare cake: Heat oven to 350°. Generously grease two 9 x 2-inch round layer-cake pans; dust pans with flour.

2. Whisk together flour, baking powder and salt in a medium-size bowl.

3. With a mixer on medium speed, beat butter in a large bowl until smooth. Gradually beat in sugar until smooth and creamy. Add eggs, one at a time, beating well after each addition. Beat in orange rind and vanilla.

4. On low speed, add flour mixture to butter mixture in 3 additions, alternating with orange juice and ending with flour mixture, until well blended. Scrape batter into prepared pans, smoothing tops.

5. Bake in heated 350° oven 25 to 30 minutes or until a wooden pick inserted in center of cake layers comes out clean. Cool cake layers in pans on wire racks 15 minutes. Turn out cakes onto racks to cool completely.

6. Meanwhile, prepare filling: Stir together water and granulated sugar in a small saucepan until sugar is dissolved. Bring to boiling over medium heat without stirring. Cover and boil 2 minutes. Remove from heat; stir liqueur into syrup.

7. On medium-high speed, beat cream, confectioners' sugar and vanilla in a medium-size bowl until stiff peaks form.

8. Place 1 cake layer, bottom side up, on a platter. Brush with syrup. Spread whipped cream over top of layer. Arrange orange sections in a circular pattern on top of whipped cream. Place second cake, bottom side down, on top. Dust top with confectioners' sugar; garnish with mint if desired.

Orange Cake

Cake Chemistry

Great and glorious cakes are not only a matter of artistry but also of science. Depending upon the method and proportions of ingredients, results will vary from light and airy with a tender crumb to moist, rich and dense. Whatever type of cake you are baking, don't peek until the minimum baking time has elapsed. A blast of cold air can cause the cake to fall.

LIGHT AND AIRY

A layer cake that's tall, light and tender requires a little patience. Beating together the butter and sugar—a process called creaming—is key, and shouldn't be rushed. It takes time for creaming to create volume-producing air bubbles in the batter. Baking powder can't create these bubbles; only thorough creaming can. If you use a mixer, beat for at least 5 minutes and as long as 10 before you add other ingredients. If you mix by hand, consider it your day's workout!

- Butter should be brought to room temperature before creaming. However, a lengthy creaming period can melt butter, causing air bubbles to stop forming. To prevent this, rinse bowl and beaters in ice water you begin, and pause halfway through creaming to dip the outside of the bowl in an ice-water bath.

- If the creamed mixture looks curdled, refrigerate it for 5 to 10 minutes, then continue beating.

- Some recipes instruct you to freeze the sugar before creaming it with the butter. This is a good idea when the creaming time is lengthy—freezing keeps the sugar from getting warm too quickly when it is beaten with the butter, and thus prevents the butter from melting.

- Although butter has the best taste, solid shortening contains fine nitrogen bubbles that increase air volume, making cakes even lighter. Use shortening in chocolate or spice cakes where flavor loss won't be noticeable.

- When a recipe says *add the flour mixture to the butter mixture in 3 additions, alternating with the liquid ingredients*, it is instructing you to beat in most of the flour mixture in the first addition, next beat in the liquids, and then beat in the remaining flour mixture. Be careful not to overbeat. When liquid is added to flour, gluten—a protein in the flour—is activated; it helps to hold the air bubbles during baking, but if gluten is overdeveloped, it can make your cake tough.

MOIST AND RICH

For cakes that are moist, rich and dense, you don't cream the butter and sugar. Instead, you first sift the flour, sugar and other dry ingredients into the mixing bowl, and then add the butter and oil to them. What you're doing at this point is coating the flour's proteins with fat so that when you next add other liquids (such as milk or vanilla extract), no cake-toughening gluten is activated and the cake will stay moist during baking.

FULL OF EXTRAS

Cakes with add-ins such as nuts, shredded carrot or candied fruit offer a bonus in every bite. But those crunchy or chewy tidbits are heavy—to keep them from sinking to the bottom of your cake, follow these tips.

- Batter should be thick and heavy so it will support the add-ins. If the batter is thin, dust the extras with flour before adding. (Dusting sticky extras such as candied fruit also keeps the pieces separate.)

- Add the extras at the last minute, just before pouring the batter into the prepared baking pans.

- Incorporate extras with minimal, gentle, by-hand stirring—not with a mixer—so as not to overmix the batter.

- Be sure to cool goody-filled cakes in or out of the baking pans as instructed—some extras stick to the pan and recipes are tested for the easiest pan removal.

SPONGY AND SPRINGY

Made with little or no flour and relying on eggs for volume, sponge cake comes in several forms: jelly roll, angel food and chiffon. In addition to beating the eggs to create maximum foam, follow this advice.

- Superfine sugar dissolves in eggs faster than granulated sugar, and produces a more stable egg white foam. If you don't have superfine sugar, you can make some by whirling granulated sugar in a food processor or blender.

- To get maximum volume when beating egg whites, first warm the mixing bowl by filling it with warm water, then empty it and dry thoroughly. Add egg whites and beat just until soft peaks form. Add sugar and beat again until stiff, but not dry, peaks form.

- Don't use a plastic mixing bowl; any residual traces of fat in it will prevent egg whites from forming a good foam.

- Many recipes instruct you to *make the ribbon* while beating. This means to beat the egg yolks and sugar until they're lemon yellow and a ribbon of batter drizzled on the surface stays there for a few seconds, or a spatula or beater drawn through the batter leaves a trail.

- Because fat destroys egg foam, always line greased pans with parchment paper or waxed paper. Dust with flour if indicated in the recipe.

- Sponge cakes must be baked until thoroughly done to set their fragile structure. They're ready when the edges shrink away from sides of pan and top springs back when lightly pressed with a fingertip.

- To be sure the cake for a jelly roll will be flexible, never cool it in the hot pan. Instead, loosen the cake around the edges with a thin knife or spatula. Sprinkle the top with confectioners' sugar (or ingredient indicated in recipe). Cover with a clean kitchen towel. Top with a slightly larger baking sheet; invert. Lift off pan, then remove waxed paper. Roll up the cake and towel together. Place seam side down on a wire rack to cool.

- Angel food cakes should be inverted for cooling. Some tube pans come with legs that can be extended for support during cooling. If your pan doesn't have this feature, invert it over the neck of a weighted bottle (a wine or soda bottle filled with sand or raw rice will work well).

ON THE RISE

Most cake recipes include a leavening agent—baking powder or baking soda—in addition to eggs. The general proportion is 1 to 1½ teaspoons baking powder or ¼ teaspoon baking soda for every cup of flour. Cakes featuring heavy add-ins such as nuts, raisins or shredded carrot usually require slightly more leavening agent.

- If your cake doesn't rise, don't assume you haven't spooned in enough baking powder or soda—in fact, you probably used too much. Too much leavening ingredient makes big bubbles that crash into each other, combine and float to the top of the batter, where they pop and release air into the oven.

Chocolate Coffee Cream Roll

Coffee and chocolate seem destined for each other. Witness the affinity here when cocoa and espresso powders give the tender cake its color and personality. The warmth of espresso defines the creamy filling, too. Gild the lily by whipping extra cream to use as a garnish.

Chocolate Coffee Cream Roll

MAKES *10 servings*
PREP *45 minutes*
BAKE *350° for 15 minutes*
COOK *10 minutes*
REFRIGERATE *at least 1 hour*

Cake

4   eggs
¼   cup all-purpose flour
¼   cup plus 2 tablespoons unsweetened cocoa powder
2   tablespoons cornstarch
½   teaspoon ground cinnamon
½   teaspoon baking powder
¼   teaspoon baking soda
⅛   teaspoon salt
¾   cup sugar
2   teaspoons instant espresso coffee powder
1   teaspoon boiling water
1   teaspoon vanilla
½   teaspoon almond extract

Coffee Cream Filling

1½   teaspoons unflavored gelatin
2   tablespoons cold water
½   cup sugar
3   tablespoons cornstarch
1   tablespoon instant espresso coffee powder
    Pinch salt
1   cup milk
2   egg yolks
1   tablespoon butter
1   teaspoon vanilla
¾   cup heavy cream

Garnishes *(optional)*

Whipped cream
Chocolate coffee beans

1. Prepare cake: Separate eggs, placing whites in a large bowl and yolks in a medium-size bowl. Let warm to room temperature.

2. Heat oven to 350°. Coat a 15 x 10 x 1-inch jelly-roll pan with nonstick cooking spray; line pan with waxed paper. Coat paper with spray; dust paper and pan with flour.

3. Sift together flour, ¼ cup cocoa powder, cornstarch, cinnamon, baking powder, baking soda and salt into a small bowl.

4. With a mixer on high speed, beat egg whites until soft mounds form. Gradually beat in ½ cup sugar, 2 tablespoons at a time, until stiff, glossy peaks form.

5. Using clean beaters, beat together remaining ¼ cup sugar and egg yolks until thick and a ribbon forms, about 5 minutes. Dissolve espresso powder in boiling water in a cup; add vanilla and almond extract; pour into egg yolk mixture. Beat at high speed 2 minutes or until thickened and light colored.

6. Stir one-fourth of beaten egg whites into egg yolk mixture. Sift one-third of flour mixture into yolk mixture. Fold yolk mixture into remaining egg whites; then fold in remaining flour mixture. Spread batter evenly in prepared pan.

7. Bake in heated 350° oven 15 minutes or until top springs back when lightly pressed with fingertip.

8. Loosen cake around edges with a thin knife. Sift remaining 2 tablespoons cocoa over cake. Cover with a clean kitchen towel. Top with a slightly larger baking sheet; invert. Remove pan, then waxed paper. With a serrated knife, trim ¼ inch from long sides of cake. Starting from a short end, roll up cake with towel. Place seam side down on a wire rack to cool.

9. Prepare filling: Sprinkle gelatin over water in a cup. Let stand to soften, about 5 minutes. Meanwhile, combine sugar, cornstarch, espresso powder and salt in a medium-size saucepan. Whisk in milk and egg yolks. Bring to boiling over medium heat; cook, stirring, until very thick, about 10 minutes. Remove from heat. Add gelatin, butter and vanilla to custard and whisk until gelatin is dissolved and butter is melted.

10. Scrape custard into a small bowl; place in a larger bowl of ice water. Let stand, whisking frequently, until well chilled, about 5 minutes.

11. Meanwhile, in a small bowl, beat cream until almost stiff peaks form. Fold into cooled coffee custard. Unroll cake; remove towel. Spread filling over cake, leaving a ½-inch border all around. Carefully reroll cake; place seam side down on a serving plate. Garnish top with additional whipped cream and chocolate coffee beans if desired. Refrigerate at least 1 hour or until set.

Brandied Apple Bundt Cake

It's all apple, all the time: chopped apples and applesauce in the batter, apple brandy in the syrup and apple juice in the glaze. A special bonus: Expect the cake to stay moist for a week or so—if you can keep it around that long!

MAKES *16 servings*

PREP *25 minutes*

BAKE *at 350° for about 50 minutes*

Cake

3¼ cups sifted cake flour (not self-rising)
1 teaspoon baking powder
¾ teaspoon salt
½ teaspoon baking soda
½ teaspoon ground cinnamon
½ teaspoon ground nutmeg
⅛ teaspoon ground cloves
½ cup (1 stick) butter, at room temperature
1 cup granulated sugar
3 eggs
1 cup unsweetened applesauce
½ cup sour cream
2 Golden Delicious apples (about 1 pound), peeled, cored and diced

Syrup

½ cup granulated sugar
⅓ cup brandy or Calvados (apple brandy)
¼ cup apple juice

Glaze

1 cup plus 2 tablespoons confectioners' sugar
2 tablespoons apple juice
   Pinch ground nutmeg

1. Heat oven to 350°. Coat a 10-inch bundt pan with nonstick cooking spray.

2. Prepare cake: Sift flour, baking powder, salt, baking soda, cinnamon, nutmeg and cloves into a small bowl.

3. With a mixer on medium-high speed, beat together butter and sugar in a large bowl until smooth and creamy, about 2 minutes. Add eggs, one at a time, beating well after each addition. Beat in applesauce and sour cream. (Mixture may look curdled.) On low speed, slowly add flour mixture, beating until well blended. Gently fold in apples. Scrape batter into prepared pan, smoothing top.

4. Bake in heated 350° oven about 50 minutes or until a wooden pick inserted in center of cake comes out clean.

5. Meanwhile, prepare syrup: Mix sugar, brandy and apple juice in a small saucepan. Cook over medium-low heat until sugar dissolves, stirring occasionally; do not boil. Remove from heat.

6. Transfer cake in pan to a wire rack. Brush top of cake with half of brandy syrup. Let stand 10 minutes. Invert cake onto wire rack and remove pan; place rack over a sheet of waxed paper. Brush cake with remaining syrup; let cool completely.

7. Prepare glaze: Stir together confectioners' sugar, apple juice and nutmeg in a small bowl until smooth. Drizzle over cake. Let harden slightly.

Candy Apple Cupcakes

A meltdown of caramel candies makes the frosting all sticky-delicious—just take care to stir candies frequently to prevent burning.

MAKES *2½ dozen cupcakes*

PREP *30 minutes*

BAKE *at 350° for 25 to 30 minutes*

Apple Butter Cupcakes

3   **cups all-purpose flour**
2   **teaspoons baking soda**
1   **teaspoon salt**
1½ **cups apple butter**
¾   **cup packed light-brown sugar**
¾   **cup granulated sugar**
⅔   **cup butter, melted**
½   **cup sour cream**
2   **eggs**

Caramel Frosting

40 **caramel candies**
6   **tablespoons heavy cream**
15 **candy sticks, halved, for garnish (optional)**

1. Prepare cupcakes: Heat oven to 350°. Line 30 cups in 3 standard 12-muffin pans with paper liners.

2. Whisk together flour, baking soda and salt in a medium-size bowl.

3. With a mixer on low speed, beat apple butter, brown sugar, granulated sugar, butter, sour cream and eggs in a large bowl just until combined. Gradually beat in flour mixture until well blended and smooth.

4. Divide batter equally among prepared muffin cups, filling liners about half full.

5. Bake in heated 350° oven 25 to 30 minutes, until a wooden pick inserted in center of cupcakes comes out clean. Cool cupcakes in pans on wire racks 5 minutes. Remove cupcakes to racks to cool completely.

6. Prepare frosting: Heat caramels and cream in a medium-size heavy saucepan over low heat, stirring frequently, until melted. Cool about 5 minutes.

7. Working carefully and quickly, while mixture is still warm and fluid, spread top of each cupcake with 2 level teaspoons of frosting. (Frosting will be sticky, but if it is too warm, it will not stick to cupcake.) If frosting gets too stiff, reheat just until fluid enough to spread. If desired, insert a candy stick upright in center of each cupcake.

CANDY APPLE CUPCAKE CUES

Working quickly so caramel doesn't set, spread on cupcakes with small metal spatula.

After all the cupcakes have been frosted, insert a candy stick in the center of each.

Coconut Cream-Filled Cupcakes

Remember those packaged goodies from yesteryear with their creamy filling and a candy-like chocolate frosting with a white squiggle on top? Meet the grown-up version, with a coconut-accented center and a coffee-tinged topping. Yum.

Coconut Cream-Filled Cupcakes

MAKES *12 cupcakes*
PREP *30 minutes*
BAKE *375° for 20 minutes*
REFRIGERATE *30 minutes*

Cupcakes

- 3 tablespoons unsweetened cocoa powder
- 1 tablespoon instant espresso coffee powder
- ½ cup boiling water
- 3 tablespoons butter, cut into small pieces
- 1 cup all-purpose flour
- 1 teaspoon baking soda
- ¾ cup granulated sugar
- 1 egg
- 1½ teaspoons vanilla
- ½ cup sour cream
- ⅓ cup sweetened flake coconut

Coconut Cream Filling

- 3 tablespoons butter, at room temperature
- 1 tablespoon solid vegetable shortening
- 1¼ cups confectioners' sugar
- 2 tablespoons milk
- 1 teaspoon coconut extract

Chocolate Frosting

- ¼ cup milk
- 1 teaspoon instant espresso coffee powder
- 3 squares (1 ounce each) semisweet chocolate, chopped
- 1 tablespoon butter
- ¼ cup confectioners' sugar
- ½ teaspoon vanilla

Garnishes *(optional)*

- Curls of fresh coconut or sweetened flake coconut
- Chocolate sprinkles

1. Prepare cupcakes: Heat oven to 375°. Line cups in a standard 12-muffin pan with paper liners.

2. Stir together cocoa powder, espresso powder and boiling water in a small bowl. Add butter; stir until melted; let cool to room temperature.

3. Whisk together flour and baking soda in a small bowl.

4. With a mixer on medium-high speed, beat sugar, egg and vanilla in a large bowl 2 minutes. Beat in cocoa mixture and sour cream. On low speed, beat in flour mixture. Stir in coconut. Divide batter equally among prepared muffin cups, filling liners about three-fourths full.

5. Bake in heated 375° oven 20 minutes or until a wooden pick inserted in center of cupcakes comes out clean. Cool cupcakes in pans on wire racks 5 minutes. Remove cupcakes to racks to cool completely.

6. Prepare filling: Beat together butter and shortening in a medium-size bowl until smooth and creamy. Add confectioners' sugar, milk and coconut extract; beat until fluffy. Spoon filling into a pastry bag fitted with a ¼-inch plain round tip. Insert pastry bag in top of each cupcake; squeeze as much filling into center of each as possible (top of cupcake will start to expand.)

7. Prepare frosting: Heat milk and espresso powder in a small saucepan over medium heat, stirring to dissolve powder. Add chocolate and butter; stir until melted. Remove from heat. Stir in confectioners' sugar and vanilla until smooth. Transfer to a medium-size bowl; refrigerate, stirring occasionally, until well chilled and thickened, about 30 minutes.

8. Frost cupcakes, starting near outer edge and working toward center. If desired, edges can be decorated with curls of fresh coconut, flake coconut or chocolate sprinkles.

Blueberry-Cheesecake Cupcakes

Enjoy all the good taste of a cheesecake with the convenience of a cupcake.

MAKES *12 cupcakes*

PREP *15 minutes*

BAKE *at 325° for 35 to 40 minutes*

12 sugar cookies
1 package (8 ounces) cream cheese, at room temperature
1 cup sugar
2 eggs
½ cup sour cream
½ teaspoon vanilla
½ teaspoon grated lemon rind
3 tablespoons all-purpose flour
1 cup blueberries

1. Heat oven to 325°.

2. Line cups in a standard 12-muffin pan with foil liners. Place a cookie in bottom of each liner; trim cookies to fit if necessary.

3. With a mixer on medium speed, beat together cream cheese and sugar in a large bowl until smooth. Add eggs, beating just until blended. Beat in sour cream, vanilla and lemon rind. On low speed, beat in flour. Stir in blueberries. Spoon batter into prepared muffin cups, dividing equally.

4. Bake in heated 325° oven 35 to 40 minutes, until cupcakes are set. Cool cupcakes in pan on a wire rack 20 minutes. Remove cupcakes from pan to rack to cool completely.

Berry-Capped Cupcakes

Chopped berries in the batter, slices on top—there's something for kids and grown-ups alike to love. Shown on page 11.

MAKES *18 cupcakes*

PREP *15 minutes*

COOK *8 to 10 minutes*

STAND *1 hour*

BAKE *at 350° for 18 to 20 minutes*

Cupcakes

1½ cups chopped strawberries (about 1 pint whole strawberries)
1¼ cups granulated sugar
1 teaspoon grated lemon rind
2 cups cake flour (not self-rising)
1 teaspoon baking powder
½ teaspoon baking soda
¼ teaspoon salt
½ cup (1 stick) butter, at room temperature
3 eggs
1 teaspoon vanilla
¾ cup buttermilk

Frosting

¼ cup (½ stick) butter, at room temperature
1¾ cups confectioners' sugar
2 tablespoons milk
¼ teaspoon vanilla
9 strawberries, halved or quartered, for garnish (optional)
¼ cup strawberry jelly, melted, for garnish (optional)

1. Prepare cupcakes: Heat oven to 350°. Line 18 cups in 2 standard 12-muffin pans with paper liners.

2. Mix chopped strawberries, ¼ cup granulated sugar and lemon rind in a medium-size saucepan. Cook over medium heat, stirring occasionally, 8 to 10 minutes or until sugar is dissolved and mixture is thickened. Spoon into a small bowl; let cool completely, about 1 hour.

3. Mix flour, baking powder, baking soda and salt in a large bowl.

4. With a mixer on low speed, beat together butter and remaining 1 cup granulated sugar in a medium-size bowl until fluffy, about 2 minutes. Add eggs, one at a time, beating after each. Beat in vanilla.

5. On low speed, beat flour mixture into butter mixture in 3 additions, alternating with buttermilk and ending with flour mixture. Swirl in cooled strawberry mixture to create a marble pattern. Divide batter equally among prepared muffin cups.

6. Bake in heated 350° oven 18 to 20 minutes or until cupcakes spring back when gently pressed with a fingertip. Let cool in pans on a wire rack 5 to 10 minutes. Turn out cupcakes onto rack to cool completely.

7. Prepare frosting: Beat together butter, confectioners' sugar, milk and vanilla in a medium-size bowl on low speed until smooth, about 3 minutes. Cover bowl with plastic wrap.

8. If desired, place cut strawberries on a large plate. Liberally brush melted jelly over each piece.

9. Frost tops of cupcakes. Top each with glazed strawberries if using.

Gingham Mini Pound Cakes

Create a frosting napkin of checks and polka dots to drape over orange-flavored mini loaves—great for gifts or snacking.

MAKES *4 loaves (4 slices each)*

PREP *15 minutes plus decorating time*

BAKE *at 350° for 40 minutes*

Cakes

1¼ cups (2½ sticks) unsalted butter, at room temperature
1 cup granulated sugar
3 eggs
2 teaspoons vanilla
3 cups cake flour (not self-rising)
1½ tablespoons poppy seeds
1 tablespoon baking powder
½ teaspoon salt
1 cup orange juice
1 tablespoon grated orange rind

Frosting

½ cup (1 stick) unsalted butter, at room temperature
¼ cup milk
1 box (1 pound) confectioners' sugar
Pinch salt
Pink, yellow and green food coloring

1. Heat oven to 350°. Grease four 5¾ x 3 x 2⅛-inch mini-loaf pans.

2. Prepare cakes: Beat butter in a large bowl with a mixer on medium speed until smooth. Gradually beat in sugar; continue beating until light and fluffy. Add eggs, one at a time, beating well after each addition. Beat in vanilla.

3. Whisk together flour, poppy seeds, baking powder and salt in a medium-size bowl. With mixer on low speed, beat flour mixture into butter mixture in 3 additions, alternating with orange juice and ending with flour mixture. Fold in orange rind. Divide batter equally among prepared pans.

4. Bake in heated 350° oven 40 minutes or until a wooden pick inserted in center of cakes comes out clean. Cool cakes in pans on wire racks 10 minutes. Remove cakes from pans to racks to cool completely.

5. Prepare frosting: Beat together butter, milk, sugar and salt in a medium-size bowl on medium speed until smooth and creamy.

6. To create "gingham napkins," measure out ¾ cup frosting; spread over tops of cakes, dividing equally and making scalloped edges on all sides. Transfer ¼ cup remaining frosting to a small bowl; tint pink. Transfer ¾ cup frosting to a second small bowl; tint yellow. Tint remaining ¾ cup frosting green. Place each color icing in a separate pastry bag fitted with a small writing tip. With green icing, on top of white frosting on 2 loaves, draw lines lengthwise and then crosswise between the scallop peaks, forming a grid. Fill in every other square by piping back and forth with green frosting. Pipe a yellow dot in center of each white square. Repeat with remaining 2 loaves, making yellow squares and pink dots.

NOTE: *If not serving shortly, refrigerate cakes, tightly covered with plastic wrap, or freeze, covered with plastic wrap and then wrapped with foil.*

New York–Style Cheesecake

Graham cracker crust, lemon-flavored filling and sour cream topping—it must be New York.

New York–Style Cheesecake

MAKES *16 servings*
PREP *20 minutes*
BAKE *at 325° for 1 hour 45 minutes*
REFRIGERATE *6 hours or overnight*

Crust

- 1⅔ cups graham cracker crumbs (about 12 whole crackers)
- 2 tablespoons granulated sugar
- 2 tablespoons light-brown sugar
- ¼ teaspoon ground cinnamon
- 3 tablespoons butter, melted

Filling

- 2 packages (8 ounces each) cream cheese, at room temperature
- 1 cup granulated sugar
- ¼ cup all-purpose flour
- ¼ cup heavy cream
- 4 eggs, at room temperature
- 1 teaspoon vanilla
- ½ teaspoon grated orange rind
- ½ teaspoon grated lemon rind
- ¼ teaspoon salt

Topping

- 1 container (8 ounces) sour cream
- 2 tablespoons granulated sugar
- ½ teaspoon vanilla

1. Heat oven to 325°. Wrap outside of a 9-inch springform pan with aluminum foil.

2. Prepare crust: Combine graham cracker crumbs, sugars, cinnamon and butter in a small bowl until well blended. Press crumb mixture over bottom and halfway up sides of prepared pan.

3. Prepare filling: Beat together cream cheese, sugar and flour in a large bowl with mixer on medium speed until smooth and creamy, about 2 minutes. Add cream; beat 30 seconds. Add eggs, one at a time, beating well after each addition. Beat in vanilla, orange rind, lemon rind and salt until well combined. Scrape filling into crust in pan (it will come above crust sides); smooth top.

4. Place springform pan in a large baking pan on oven rack. Pour hot water into large pan to come halfway up sides of springform. Bake in heated 325° oven 1 hour 30 minutes or until center is set.

5. Remove springform pan from water; leave baking pan in oven and leave oven on.

6. Prepare topping: Stir together sour cream, sugar and vanilla in a small bowl. Pour over cake top; spread evenly. Return springform pan to baking pan with water in oven. Bake another 15 minutes or until topping is set.

7. Remove springform pan from water; remove foil. Run a thin knife around inside of pan. Let cake cool in pan on a wire rack. Refrigerate, covered, 6 hours or overnight. Remove sides of pan to serve cake.

We all know they're creamy and delicious; but cheesecakes are easy as well if you practice these helpful tricks.

- When preparing filling, occasionally stop mixer and scrape down sides of bowl to ensure ingredients are evenly blended.

- You can prepare the filling in a food processor. Place the cheese and sugar in the container and whirl to combine, then add the eggs and whirl, incorporate the remaining dry ingredients last.

- Many recipes instruct you to bake a cheesecake in a water bath. The warm water surrounds the cake with a constant gentle heat, which minimizes chances of the custardy filling breaking apart. Be sure to wrap the springform pan with aluminum foil to prevent the filling from leaking out or the water from seeping in.

- To judge doneness, shake the pan—the cake center should be just set, not firm. Overbaking will cause a cheesecake to crack.

- As soon as you remove the cake from the oven, run a thin knife around the inside of the pan, releasing the top ½ inch of cake sides. This helps prevent cracking.

- Always allow the cake to cool completely before removing the sides of the springform pan.

BAKING BATH

Place foil-wrapped springform pan in a larger baking pan on oven rack. Add hot water to baking pan, filling halfway up sides of springform pan.

Italian Ricotta Cheesecake

Toasted pine nuts and an edging of apricot jam provide the perfect finishing note. Shown on page 11.

MAKES *16 servings*
PREP *20 minutes*
BAKE *at 325° for 1 hour 15 minutes*
REFRIGERATE *6 hours or overnight*

Crust

2 tablespoons butter, at room temperature
1 egg
2 tablespoons sugar
¼ teaspoon vanilla
⅛ teaspoon lemon extract
1 cup all-purpose flour
¾ teaspoon baking powder
¼ teaspoon salt
3 tablespoons pine nuts (pignolis), toasted (see page 231)
1 egg white, lightly beaten

Filling

1¼ pounds ricotta cheese
1 cup sugar
5 eggs
4 teaspoons all-purpose flour
1 teaspoon vanilla
½ teaspoon grated lemon rind

Topping

2 tablespoons apricot jam
9 tablespoons pine nuts (pignolis), toasted

1. Prepare crust: Wrap outside of a 9-inch springform pan with aluminum foil.

2. Beat butter, egg and sugar in a medium-size bowl until combined, 2 minutes. Beat in vanilla and lemon extract. Sift flour, baking powder and salt onto a piece of waxed paper. Beat flour mixture into egg mixture until a dough forms.

3. Shape dough into a disc and place between 2 sheets of waxed paper. Roll out into a 10-inch round crust. Peel off top sheet of paper; invert crust into a 9-inch springform pan. Without stretching, press crust onto bottom and sides of pan; peel off remaining paper. If there are holes in crust, press closed with fingers.

4. Scatter nuts over crust; lightly press nuts into crust. Brush pastry with a small amount of egg white; discard remainder of white. Wrap bottom and sides of pan with aluminum foil.

5. Heat oven to 325°.

6. Prepare filling: Beat together ricotta, sugar, eggs, flour, vanilla and lemon rind in a medium-size bowl until well combined, about 2 minutes. Pour into crust in pan.

7. Place springform pan in a large baking pan on oven rack. Pour hot water into large pan to come halfway up sides of springform. Bake in heated 325° oven 1 hour 15 minutes or until center is set. If top of filling begins to brown too much, cover loosely with aluminum foil.

8. Remove springform pan from water; remove foil. Run a thin knife around inside of pan. Let cake cool in springform pan on a wire rack. Refrigerate, covered, 6 hours or overnight, until thoroughly chilled.

9. Prepare topping: Remove sides of pan. Melt jam in a small saucepan. Brush around top edge of cake, making a 1-inch border. Sprinkle border with nuts.

Chocolate Cheesecake

Scatter almonds on the sides and top, then brace yourself for a triple hit of chocolate—in the crust, cheese mixture and whipped cream.

MAKES *16 servings*

PREP *20 minutes*

BAKE *at 325° for 1 hour 10 minutes*

REFRIGERATE *6 hours or overnight*

Chocolate Crust

1¼ cups chocolate-wafer cookie crumbs (about 28 cookies)
¼ cup slivered blanched almonds, ground
¼ cup (½ stick) butter, melted
2 tablespoons sugar
¼ teaspoon salt

Filling

1 package (12 ounces) semisweet chocolate chips (2 cups)
3 packages (8 ounces each) cream cheese, at room temperature
¾ cup sugar
1 tablespoon cornstarch
4 eggs, at room temperature
1 container (8 ounces) sour cream
1 teaspoon vanilla

Garnish

½ cup sliced almonds
½ cup heavy cream
1 tablespoon packaged pre-melted unsweetened chocolate
½ teaspoon vanilla

1. Heat oven to 325°. Wrap outside of a 9-inch springform pan with aluminum foil.

2. Prepare chocolate crust: Mix crumbs, almonds, butter, sugar and salt in a medium-size bowl. Pat evenly over bottom of prepared pan.

3. Prepare filling: Melt chocolate chips in top of a double boiler over barely simmering, not boiling, water. Beat cream cheese, sugar and cornstarch in a large bowl until creamy, 2 minutes. Add eggs, one at a time, beating well after each addition. Beat in melted chocolate, sour cream and vanilla. Pour filling over crust in pan.

4. Place springform pan in a large baking pan on oven rack. Pour hot water into large pan to come halfway up sides of springform. Bake in heated 325° oven 1 hour 10 minutes or until center is set.

5. Remove springform pan from water; remove foil. Run a thin knife around inside of pan. Let cake cool in springform pan on a wire rack. Refrigerate, uncovered, 6 hours or overnight.

6. Prepare garnish: Remove sides of pan. Sprinkle a few sliced almonds onto center of cake top. Cover cake sides with remaining almonds, pressing lightly to adhere. Beat cream, unsweetened chocolate and vanilla in a medium-size bowl until stiff peaks form; spoon into a pastry bag fitted with a medium-size tip. Pipe rosettes around top edge of cake, spacing them about 1 inch apart.

Two-Tone Brownies, *page 68*

Cookies

No-Bake Marshmallow-Chip Clusters, *page 59*

Sugar Cookies Plus!

Everyone needs a basic sugar cookie and this is one of our best. Even better, we offer 7 additional ways to shape and flavor the basic recipe. Shown on page 54.

Shown on page 54.

MAKES *5 dozen cookies*
PREP *20 minutes*
REFRIGERATE *2 hours*
BAKE *at 350° for 10 to 12 minutes*

Basic Sugar Cookies

1½ cups all-purpose flour
1½ teaspoons baking powder
¼ teaspoon salt
1 cup sugar
½ cup (1 stick) butter, at room temperature
1 egg
1 teaspoon vanilla

1. Combine flour, baking powder and salt in a small bowl.

2. With a mixer on medium speed, beat sugar, butter, egg and vanilla in a large bowl 2 minutes, until smooth and creamy. Using a wooden spoon, stir in flour mixture. Shape into a 15-inch-long log; wrap in plastic wrap and refrigerate at least 2 hours or up to 3 days.

3. Heat oven to 350°.

4. Cut dough into ¼-inch-thick slices. Place on ungreased baking sheets, reshaping into rounds if necessary.

5. Bake in heated 350° oven 10 to 12 minutes or until cookies are lightly golden around edges. Remove baking sheets to wire racks and cool 1 minute. Remove cookies to racks and let cool completely.

Thumbprint Cookies

Prepare Sugar Cookie dough steps 1 and 2. Heat oven to 350°. Cut log into ½-inch-thick slices. Roll each slice into a ball. (If sliced dough is too stiff to work with, let soften at room temperature about 10 minutes.) Place on ungreased baking sheets, spacing about 2 inches apart. Indent center of each ball by pressing with your thumb. Spoon about ½ teaspoon any flavor jam into each indentation. Bake 12 to 14 minutes or until lightly golden around edges.

MAKES about 30 cookies.

Lemon Sugar Cookies

Prepare Sugar Cookie dough steps 1 and 2, beating 4 teaspoons grated lemon rind into butter mixture. Heat oven to 350°. Cut log into ¼-inch-thick slices. Place on ungreased baking sheets. Sprinkle about 3 tablespoons decorating sugar over slices, dividing equally. Bake 8 to 10 minutes or until cookies are golden around edges.

MAKES about 60 cookies.

Almond Sugar Cookies

Toast ¾ cup slivered almonds (see page 231); cool. Grind nuts (you should have ¾ cup). Prepare Sugar Cookie dough steps 1 and 2, adding ½ cup ground nuts to dry ingredients (reserve remaining nuts) and beating ½ teaspoon almond extract into butter mixture. Heat oven to 350°. Cut log into ¼-inch-thick slices. Place on ungreased baking sheets. Sprinkle ⅛ to ¼ teaspoon reserved ground nuts over each slice. Bake 8 to 10 minutes or until cookies are golden around edges.

MAKES about 60 cookies.

Ginger Sugar Cookies

Prepare Sugar Cookie dough steps 1 and
2, adding another ¼ cup flour and
1 teaspoon ground ginger to dry ingredients
and beating 1 tablespoon mild molasses
into butter mixture. Heat oven to 350°.
Cut log into ¼-inch-thick slices. Place on
ungreased baking sheets. Lightly dip tines
of a fork into some flour; firmly press a
crisscross design onto each slice. Bake at
350° for 8 to 10 minutes or until cookies
are slightly darkened around edges.

MAKES about 40 cookies.

Chocolate Chip Sugar Cookies

Prepare Sugar Cookie dough steps 1 and
2, stirring 1 cup chocolate chips into mixed
dough and shaping dough into a 10-inch-
long log. Heat oven to 350°. Cut log into
½-inch-thick slices. Place on an ungreased
baking sheet. Bake 12 to 15 minutes or until
cookies are lightly golden around edges.

MAKES about 20 cookies or crusts for
2 Golden Baked Alaskas, page 164.

Mocha Sugar Cookies

Prepare Sugar Cookie dough steps 1 and
2, adding ¼ cup unsweetened cocoa powder
and an additional ¼ teaspoon salt to dry
ingredients. Stir 1 teaspoon instant espresso
powder into egg before beating it into butter
mixture. Heat oven to 350°. Cut log into
¼-inch-thick slices. Place on ungreased
baking sheets. Bake 8 to 10 minutes or until
slightly darkened around edges.

When cookies are cool, melt 3 ounces
semisweet chocolate; spoon into a small
plastic bag. Snip off a corner of bag and
drizzle chocolate over 30 cookies. In the
same way, melt and drizzle 3 ounces white
baking chocolate over remaining 30 cookies.

MAKES 60 cookies.

Nutty Chocolate Chip Cookies

Prepare Sugar Cookie dough steps 1 and
2, adding ¼ cup unsweetened cocoa powder
to dry ingredients and stirring ½ cup mini
chocolate chips and ½ cup finely chopped
dry-roasted unsalted peanuts into mixed
dough. Heat oven to 350°. Cut log into
½-inch-thick slices. Place on ungreased
baking sheets. Measure 2 tablespoons
granulated sugar onto a piece of waxed
paper. For each cookie, dampen bottom of a
small glass with water and dip into sugar;
press down on cookie to flatten to about
2 inches in diameter. Bake 12 to 15 minutes
or until cookies are slightly darkened around
edges.

When cookies are cool, mix 1¼ cups creamy
peanut butter with ½ cup confectioners'
sugar. Spread half of cookies with 2 teaspoons
mixture. Sandwich with remaining cookies.

MAKES 15 sandwich cookies.

COOKIES AT THE READY

This recipe offers yet another plus: You can make
up a batch of dough and refrigerate it for up to 3 days
or freeze for up to 3 months, then enjoy the homemade
taste whenever the spirit moves you. When ready to use,
thaw frozen dough in the refrigerator.

Pepper-Spice Cookies

Ground black pepper is the unexpected ingredient that gives a special kick to the more usual mix of cardamom, cinnamon and cloves.

Pepper-Spice Cookies

MAKES *2 to 3 dozen cookies*
PREP *30 minutes*
REFRIGERATE *2½ hours*
BAKE *at 375° for 8 to 10 minutes*

½   cup (1 stick) unsalted butter, at room temperature
½   cup packed light-brown sugar
2   tablespoons granulated sugar
1   egg
1   teaspoon vanilla
1⅓ cups all-purpose flour
½   teaspoon baking powder
½   teaspoon ground cardamom
½   teaspoon ground cinnamon
¼   teaspoon ground black pepper
⅛   teaspoon ground cloves
    Pinch salt
2   teaspoons grated orange rind

1. Beat together butter and sugars in a medium-size bowl until light and fluffy. Beat in egg and vanilla.

2. Sift flour, baking powder, cardamom, cinnamon, black pepper, cloves and salt onto a piece of waxed paper. Stir into butter mixture. Stir in orange rind. Cover bowl; refrigerate until dough is firm enough to roll, 2 hours.

3. Lightly butter 2 large baking sheets. Roll out dough on a well-floured surface to ⅛-inch thickness. Cut into rounds or other shapes using cookie cutters. Using a spatula, carefully transfer to baking sheets. Refrigerate until cutouts are firm, 30 minutes.

4. Meanwhile, heat oven to 375°.

5. Bake cookies in heated 375° oven until edges are golden, 8 to 10 minutes. Transfer cookies from baking sheets to wire racks to cool.

Island Cookies

Banana, dried pineapple, coconut and macadamia nuts complement the chocolate chips in these aptly named treats.

MAKES *about 4 dozen cookies*

PREP *15 minutes*

BAKE *at 375° for 10 to 12 minutes*

1⅔ cups all-purpose flour
¾ teaspoon baking powder
½ teaspoon baking soda
½ teaspoon salt
¼ teaspoon ground nutmeg
6 tablespoons (¾ stick) unsalted butter, at room temperature
¾ cup packed light-brown sugar
⅓ cup granulated sugar
1 cup mashed ripe banana
1 egg
1 teaspoon vanilla
1 package (12 ounces) semisweet chocolate chips (2 cups)
1 cup sweetened flake coconut
6 rings dried pineapple, chopped
½ cup chopped macadamia nuts

1. Heat oven to 375°.

2. Sift flour, baking powder, baking soda, salt and nutmeg into a medium-size bowl.

3. With a mixer on medium-high speed, beat butter in a large bowl until creamy. Add sugars and mashed banana; beat until light and fluffy. Beat in egg. Beat in vanilla.

4. On low speed, beat in flour mixture. Stir in chocolate chips, coconut, chopped pineapple and macadamia nuts. Drop by rounded tablespoonfuls onto ungreased baking sheets, spacing 2 inches apart.

5. Bake in heated 375° oven 10 to 12 minutes or until lightly golden. Cool cookies on baking sheets on wire racks 1 to 2 minutes. Transfer cookies to racks to cool completely.

No-Bake Marshmallow-Chip Clusters

Is it a candy? Or a cookie? All we know is that this jumble of marshmallows, peanuts, raisins, pretzels and chocolate chips is impossible to resist. Shown on page 55.

MAKES *about 3½ dozen clusters*

PREP *20 minutes*

REFRIGERATE *20 minutes*

3 tablespoons unsalted butter
4¼ cups mini-marshmallows
1 teaspoon vanilla
1½ cups broken-up pretzel sticks
¾ cup chopped peanuts
½ cup raisins
1 package (6 ounces) semisweet chocolate chips (1 cup)

1. Line 2 baking sheets with waxed paper.

2. Melt butter in a medium-size saucepan over medium heat. Stir in 3¼ cups marshmallows until melted. Remove from heat and stir in vanilla. Let cool slightly.

3. Mix pretzels, peanuts and raisins in a large bowl. Add marshmallow mixture. Stir in remaining marshmallows and chocolate chips until coated.

4. Spray hands with nonstick cooking spray. Using about 1 heaping tablespoonful at a time, shape clusters with your fingers. Roll mixture with hands into "haystacks"; place on prepared baking sheets. Refrigerate until firm, 20 minutes.

NOTE: *Store clusters in refrigerator, in a covered container.*

Butterscotch-Pecan Slices

Bake these the same day you prepare them or wait up to 3 days. Whichever way, you'll pop them in the oven for near-instant gratification.

MAKES *about 4 dozen cookies*
PREP *20 minutes*
REFRIGERATE *3 hours*
BAKE *at 350° for 10 to 12 minutes*

1¼ cups all-purpose flour
½ teaspoon baking powder
¼ teaspoon salt
6 tablespoons (¾ stick) unsalted butter
⅔ cup dark-brown sugar
1 egg
½ teaspoon vanilla
½ cup finely chopped pecans

1. Whisk together flour, baking powder and salt in a small bowl.

2. With a mixer on medium speed, beat butter and brown sugar in a medium-size bowl until creamy. Beat in egg and vanilla. Stir in pecans. Stir in flour mixture. Shape dough into two 11-inch-long logs; wrap in plastic wrap. Refrigerate 3 hours or up to 3 days, until well chilled.

3. Heat oven to 350°. Coat 2 baking sheets with nonstick cooking spray.

4. Cut dough into ¼-inch-thick slices. Place on prepared baking sheets, reshaping into rounds if necessary. Bake in heated 350° oven 10 to 12 minutes. Transfer cookies from baking sheets to wire racks to cool.

Almond Cookie Slices

Brew a pot of espresso and nibble at these long slim slices of crunchy almond goodness.

MAKES *3 dozen cookies*
PREP *20 minutes*
FREEZE *20 minutes*
BAKE *at 350° for 18 minutes*

Cookies

10 tablespoons (1¼ sticks) unsalted butter
⅓ cup honey
⅓ cup milk
¼ teaspoon almond extract
2½ cups blanched whole almonds, toasted
¾ cup packed light-brown sugar
3 cups all-purpose flour
1 teaspoon ground cinnamon
¾ teaspoon baking powder
½ teaspoon salt
¼ teaspoon baking soda

Almond Glaze

1 cup confectioners' sugar
½ teaspoon almond extract
6 teaspoons water or as needed

1. Prepare cookies: Melt butter in a small saucepan over medium heat. Stir in honey, milk and almond extract; set aside to cool.

2. Meanwhile, place 1¼ cups almonds and brown sugar in a food processor. Whirl just until nuts are texture of coarse meal.

3. Add butter mixture to processor. Whirl until smooth. Add flour, cinnamon, baking powder, salt and baking soda. Whirl just until mixture is combined. Scrape into a medium-size bowl. Stir in remaining 1¼ cups whole almonds.

4. Line a 9 x 9 x 2-inch-square cake pan with plastic wrap. Place dough in pan and pat to level. Place in freezer 20 minutes or until firm.

5. Meanwhile, heat oven to 350°. Lightly coat 2 baking sheets with nonstick cooking spray.

6. Lift plastic wrap out of pan to remove cookie mixture; slide mixture off plastic wrap onto a work surface. Cut cookie mixture into ¼-inch-wide slabs. Arrange slabs on prepared baking sheets, cut side down and spaced ½ inch apart.

7. Bake in heated 350° oven 18 minutes or just until golden. Cool cookies briefly on baking sheets on wire racks, then transfer to wire racks to cool completely.

8. Meanwhile, prepare glaze: Stir together confectioners' sugar and almond extract in a small bowl. Gradually stir in 6 teaspoons water or just enough to make a thin glaze. Drizzle glaze over cookies.

Chocolate Spritz Cookies

Unearth your cookie press—these melt-in-your-mouth rectangles with their elegant white chocolate edging are worth it.

MAKES *about 7½ dozen cookies*

PREP *10 minutes*

REFRIGERATE *10 minutes*

BAKE *at 375° for 5 to 7 minutes*

2 cups all-purpose flour
½ cup unsweetened cocoa powder
½ teaspoon salt
1 cup (2 sticks) unsalted butter, at room temperature
1 cup confectioners' sugar
1 egg yolk
6 ounces white baking chocolate
2 tablespoons vegetable oil

1. Sift flour, cocoa powder and salt into a medium-size bowl.

2. With a mixer on medium speed, beat together butter and sugar in a large bowl on medium speed until smooth and creamy. Beat in egg yolk. On low speed, beat in flour mixture until well combined. Cover; refrigerate 10 minutes.

3. Heat oven to 375°. Grease several baking sheets.

4. Spoon some of dough into a cookie press fitted with a bar-plate tip. Keep remaining dough refrigerated. Press dough onto a prepared baking sheet, making strips about the length of baking sheet and spaced 1 inch apart. Cut each strip into 2-inch lengths.

5. Bake in heated 375° oven 5 to 7 minutes or until firm. Remove from oven. With a pancake turner, immediately transfer cookies to wire racks to cool.

6. Continue with remaining dough, pressing out, cutting and baking.

7. Line a clean baking sheet with waxed paper. Heat chocolate and oil in a small saucepan over low heat until melted. Dip both ends of each cookie into chocolate, then place on paper; let set.

SPRITZ SUCCESS

Temperature is the key to successful spritz cookie dough. Too warm and the pressed cookies will lose their shape. Too cold and they will be difficult to press out. For best results, keep the dough refrigerated until you are ready to fill the press, put as much dough as possible into the press at one time, and then let the filled press stand at room temperature for several minutes before using.

PB Sandwich Cookies

There's peanut butter and marshmallow cream in every bite. Now the only question is: Do you eat the filling first?

MAKES *30 sandwich cookies*

PREP *30 minutes*

BAKE *at 375° for 8 to 10 minutes*

1⅓ cups all-purpose flour
½ teaspoon baking soda
½ teaspoon salt
½ cup granulated sugar
½ cup packed light-brown sugar
⅓ cup butter, at room temperature
2 eggs
1 tablespoon milk
1 teaspoon vanilla
1⅓ cups chunky peanut butter
¼ cup peanuts, finely chopped
1⅓ cups marshmallow cream

1. Heat oven to 375°.

2. Whisk together flour, baking soda and salt in a small bowl.

3. With a mixer on medium speed, beat sugars and butter in a medium-size bowl until blended. Beat in eggs, milk and vanilla. On low speed, gradually beat in flour mixture. Stir in ⅔ cup peanut butter.

4. Drop batter by rounded teaspoonfuls onto ungreased baking sheets, spacing 1½ inches apart. Top each with ⅛ teaspoon chopped peanuts.

5. Bake in heated 375° oven 8 to 10 minutes, until golden. Cool cookies 2 minutes on baking sheets. Transfer to racks to cool completely.

6. Turn cookies flat side up. Spoon about 2 teaspoons marshmallow cream onto half of the cookies. Spread about 1 teaspoon peanut butter onto each remaining cookie, then invert on top of a marshmallow cream-topped cookie.

Jumbo Chocolate Chip Cookies

Everything about these cookies is oversized— from the chunks of chocolate to the pecan pieces to the cookie itself!

MAKES *24 cookies*

PREP *20 minutes*

BAKE *at 325° for 15 to 17 minutes*

2¼ cups all-purpose flour
1 teaspoon baking soda
1 teaspoon salt
1 cup (2 sticks) unsalted butter or margarine, at room temperature
⅔ cup creamy peanut butter
1 cup granulated sugar
1 cup packed light-brown sugar
2 eggs
2 teaspoons vanilla
1 bag (12 ounces) semisweet chocolate chunks or 1 bag (10 ounces) oversized semisweet chocolate chips
1¼ cups coarsely chopped pecans

1. Heat oven to 325°.

2. Whisk together flour, baking soda and salt in a small bowl.

3. With a mixer on medium-high speed, beat butter, peanut butter and sugars in a large bowl 3 minutes, until light and fluffy. Beat in eggs and vanilla until blended. Stir in flour mixture until blended and a dough forms. Stir in chocolate chunks and pecans.

4. Using a ¼-cup measure, drop dough in slightly rounded mounds onto large ungreased baking sheets, spacing about 2 inches apart.

5. Bake in heated 325° oven 15 to 17 minutes or until golden brown around edges and lightly colored on top. Cool cookies on baking sheets on wire racks about 3 minutes. Transfer cookies to racks to cool completely.

Jumbo Chocolate Chip Cookies

White-Chocolate Mocha Cookies

For easy dividing, measure 2 tablespoons dough into an ice cream scoop for the first cookie; then judge the remainder by eye.

MAKES *about 15 cookies*

PREP *10 minutes*

BAKE *at 375° for about 12 minutes*

1¼ cups all-purpose flour
2 tablespoons unsweetened cocoa powder
½ teaspoon baking soda
½ cup (1 stick) butter, at room temperature
¾ cup packed light-brown sugar
1 teaspoon vanilla
¼ teaspoon salt
1 egg
1½ teaspoons instant espresso coffee powder
1 teaspoon boiling water
1 cup chopped walnuts or pecans
6 ounces white baking chocolate, coarsely chopped (1 cup)

1. Heat oven to 375°.

2. Whisk together flour, cocoa powder and baking soda in a small bowl.

3. With a mixer on medium speed, beat butter, sugar, vanilla and salt in a medium-size bowl 1 minute, until blended. Add egg; beat 1 minute.

4. Dissolve espresso powder in boiling water in a cup; stir into butter mixture. Stir in flour mixture. Stir in nuts and white chocolate.

5. Drop dough by rounded 2 tablespoonfuls onto ungreased baking sheets, spacing about 2 inches apart.

6. Bake in heated 375° oven about 12 minutes or until edges are golden and centers are set. Cool cookies on baking sheets on wire racks about 2 minutes. Transfer cookies to racks to cool.

Triple-Chocolate Cookies

Under a smooth exterior, treats await: toasted pecans, plus white and semisweet chocolate chips.

MAKES *2½ dozen cookies*

PREP *20 minutes* STAND *30 minutes*

BAKE *at 325° for 15 minutes*

2½ cups confectioners' sugar
½ cup unsweetened cocoa powder
3 tablespoons all-purpose flour
¼ teaspoon salt
4 egg whites
1 teaspoon vanilla
1 cup pecans, toasted, chopped
½ cup semisweet chocolate chips
½ cup white chocolate chips
Confectioners' sugar for dusting

1. Line baking sheets with aluminum foil; lightly coat with nonstick cooking spray.

2. Sift 1 cup confectioners' sugar, cocoa, flour and salt into medium-size bowl.

3. With a mixer on medium speed, beat egg whites in a medium-size bowl until foamy. Add remaining 1½ cups confectioners' sugar and vanilla; beat 1 minute, until soft peaks form. Add sifted cocoa mixture; beat 1 minute, until well blended. Stir in pecans and semisweet and white chocolate chips.

4. Drop dough by tablespoonfuls onto prepared baking sheets, spacing 1 inch apart. Dust lightly with confectioners' sugar. Let stand 30 minutes.

5. Meanwhile, heat oven to 325°.

6. Bake in heated 325° oven 15 minutes or until cookies are puffed and crackled, but still soft in center. Cool on baking sheets on wire racks 10 minutes. Transfer cookies to racks to cool completely. Store airtight at room temperature up to 1 week; freeze airtight 3 months.

Black-and-White Cookies

It's surprisingly simple to whip up this bakery classic: No rolling the dough or cutting it out—just drop it onto the baking sheet and spread into 2-inch rounds. All you need is a steady hand to spread the dual frostings evenly.

MAKES *fifteen 4-inch cookies*

PREP *30 minutes*

BAKE *at 350° for 15 minutes*

Cookies

- 2 cups all-purpose flour
- 1 teaspoon baking powder
- ½ teaspoon baking soda
- ½ teaspoon salt
- ⅔ cup butter or margarine, at room temperature
- ½ cup granulated sugar
- ½ cup packed light-brown sugar
- ⅓ cup buttermilk
- 1 egg
- 2 teaspoons vanilla

Icings

- 1 cup semisweet chocolate chips
- 1 tablespoon solid vegetable shortening
- 3 tablespoons milk
- 2½ cups confectioners' sugar
  Pinch salt

1. Prepare cookies: Position an oven rack in center of oven and a second rack in lower third. Heat oven to 350°.

2. Combine flour, baking powder, baking soda and salt on waxed paper. Beat together butter and sugars in a large bowl with a mixer on medium speed until creamy, about 2 minutes. Beat in buttermilk, egg and vanilla until well blended. On low speed, beat in flour mixture in 3 additions.

3. Drop batter by level ¼ cup onto 2 large ungreased baking sheets, spacing about 3 inches apart. Using a metal spatula, spread into 2-inch rounds.

4. Bake in heated 350° oven 8 minutes; switch positions of baking sheets. Bake another 7 to 9 minutes or until edges are lightly browned. Cool baking sheets on a wire rack 1 minute. Transfer cookies to rack to cool completely.

5. Meanwhile, prepare icings: For black (chocolate) icing, melt chocolate chips and shortening in top of a double boiler over barely simmering, not boiling, water, stirring until smooth. Let cool. For white icing, beat milk, confectioners' sugar and salt in a medium-size bowl until a spreading consistency, adding more milk if necessary; cover with plastic wrap.

6. Turn cooled cookies flat side up; brush off any crumbs. Spread 1 tablespoon white icing on half of each cookie. Let dry. Spread 2 teaspoons chocolate icing on other half of each cookie. Let dry. Store between sheets of waxed paper in a sealed container.

Double-Chocolate Chunky Cookies

Walnuts peek through chewy mounds that feature both semisweet and unsweetened chocolate.

Double-Chocolate Chunky Cookies

MAKES *22 cookies*
PREP *20 minutes*
MICROWAVE *2 minutes*
BAKE *at 350° for 9 minutes*

9 squares (1 ounce each) semisweet chocolate, chopped
3 squares (1 ounce each) unsweetened chocolate, chopped
½ cup (1 stick) butter or margarine, cut into small pieces
1 cup sugar
3 eggs
1 tablespoon instant espresso coffee powder or instant coffee powder
1 tablespoon vanilla
1 cup all-purpose flour
1½ teaspoons baking powder
1½ cups chopped walnuts

1. Heat oven to 350°. Coat several baking sheets with nonstick cooking spray.

2. Heat semisweet chocolate, unsweetened chocolate and butter in a medium-size microwave-safe bowl, covered, at 100% power 2 minutes. Uncover; stir until melted and smooth. Set aside to cool.

3. With a mixer on high speed, beat sugar, eggs, espresso powder and vanilla in a large bowl until light and fluffy.

4. Whisk together flour and baking powder in a small bowl; whisk into chocolate mixture. Whisk chocolate mixture into egg mixture. Stir in walnuts. Drop dough by slightly rounded 1½ tablespoonfuls onto prepared baking sheets, spacing about 2 inches apart.

5. Bake in heated 350° oven 9 minutes or until cookies are puffed and slightly crisped around edges. Cool on baking sheet on wire racks 1 minute. Transfer cookies to racks to cool completely.

Raspberry Brownies

These chewy squares get a hint of berry from both liqueur and jam.

MAKES *32 brownies*

PREP *20 minutes*

FREEZE *20 minutes*

BAKE *at 350° for 45 minutes*

1 cup (2 sticks) butter
4 squares (1 ounce each) unsweetened chocolate, chopped
4 eggs
1½ cups granulated sugar
1 teaspoon vanilla
2 tablespoons raspberry liqueur
½ teaspoon salt
1 cup all-purpose flour
1½ cups coarsely chopped walnuts
½ cup semisweet mini chocolate chips
1 cup raspberry preserves

1. Heat oven to 350°. Coat a 13 x 9 x 2-inch square baking pan with nonstick cooking spray.

2. Melt together butter and chocolate in top of a double boiler over barely simmering, not boiling, water, stirring until smooth. Set aside to cool.

3. Beat eggs and sugar in a large bowl until well combined, about 1 minute. Beat in vanilla, 1 tablespoon liqueur and salt. Stir in chocolate mixture. Stir in flour in 3 additions. Fold in walnuts and chocolate chips. Spread half of batter over bottom of prepared pan.

4. Mix together preserves and remaining 1 tablespoon liqueur in a small bowl. Spread over batter in pan. Place in freezer about 20 minutes or until preserves are firm.

5. Spread remaining batter over top of preserves. Bake brownies in heated 350° oven 45 minutes or until a wooden pick inserted in center comes out clean. Cool brownies in pan on a wire rack 15 minutes. Cut into 32 bars. Let cool completely.

Raspberry Brownies

Two-Tone Brownies

A thin layer of sweetened cream cheese hides underneath the rich, coffee-flavored chocolate frosting. Shown on page 55.

MAKES *16 brownies*

PREP *30 minutes*

BAKE *at 325° for about 25 minutes*

REFRIGERATE *3 hours or overnight*

Brownies

6   tablespoons (¾ stick) butter
3   squares (1 ounce each) unsweetened chocolate, chopped (½ cup)
1   tablespoon instant espresso coffee powder
1   cup granulated sugar
2   eggs, lightly beaten
1½ teaspoons vanilla
⅛   teaspoon salt
1   cup all-purpose flour
½   teaspoon ground cinnamon
1   cup (about 4 ounces) chopped walnuts

Cream Cheese Frosting

1   package (3 ounces) cream cheese, at room temperature
1   cup confectioners' sugar
½   teaspoon vanilla

Chocolate Frosting

¼   cup heavy cream
1   teaspoon instant espresso coffee powder
3   squares (1 ounce each) semisweet chocolate, chopped (½ cup)
1   tablespoon butter

1. Prepare brownies: Heat oven to 325°. Line an 8 x 8 x 2-inch square cake pan with aluminum foil, leaving an overhang on 2 opposite sides; coat with nonstick cooking spray.

2. Heat butter, chocolate and espresso powder in a medium-size saucepan over low heat, stirring until butter and chocolate are melted and mixture is smooth. Remove from heat. Whisk in sugar, then whisk in eggs, vanilla and salt until smooth. Stir in flour, cinnamon and walnuts. Scrape into prepared pan.

3. Bake in heated 325° oven about 25 minutes or until center of brownie is set. Let cool in pan on a wire rack.

4. Meanwhile, prepare Cream Cheese Frosting: With a mixer on medium speed, beat cream cheese, confectioners' sugar and vanilla in a small bowl 2 minutes, until fluffy. Spread over cooled brownie. Refrigerate just until set, about 1 hour.

5. Prepare Chocolate Frosting: Combine cream and espresso powder in a small saucepan; bring to simmering over medium heat. Add chocolate; remove from heat. Let stand 3 minutes. Add butter; stir until chocolate and butter are melted and mixture is smooth. Let stand 15 minutes, until frosting is slightly cool but still pourable. Pour over cream cheese frosting on brownie, spreading evenly. Refrigerate 2 hours or overnight.

6. Lift foil out of pan to remove brownie. Cut into 16 brownies.

Frosted Fudgy Brownies

Any richer and these would be illegal.

MAKES *3 dozen brownies*

PREP *20 minutes*

BAKE *at 350° for 30 minutes*

½ cup (1 stick) unsalted butter
3 squares (1 ounce each) unsweetened chocolate, chopped
2 eggs
1 cup granulated sugar
1 teaspoon vanilla
½ teaspoon salt
¾ cup all-purpose flour
½ cup coarsely chopped walnuts

Frosting

1 tablespoon unsalted butter
2 squares (1 ounce each) semisweet chocolate, chopped
¾ cup confectioners' sugar
4 teaspoons hot water

1. Heat oven to 350°. Coat an 8 x 8 x 2-inch square cake pan with nonstick cooking spray.

2. Melt butter and chocolate in a small saucepan over medium-low heat, stirring until smooth. Cool slightly.

3. With a mixer on medium speed, beat eggs, sugar, vanilla and salt in a medium-size bowl until fluffy. Stir in chocolate mixture. Fold in flour. Stir in walnuts. Spread batter in prepared pan.

4. Bake in heated 350° oven 30 minutes or until shiny and firm on top—do not overbake. Cool in pan on a wire rack.

5. Prepare frosting: Combine butter and chocolate in a small microwave safe bowl; heat at 100% power 1 minute; stir until melted. Stir in confectioners' sugar and hot water until spreadable. Frost brownies immediately (frosting will set quickly). Cut into 36 brownies.

Chocolate Dream Bars

What could be bad about a bar full of caramels and coconut, chocolate and pecans?

MAKES *48 bars*

PREP *25 minutes*

BAKE *crust at 350° for 8 minutes; bars at 350° for 20 minutes*

2½ cups chocolate graham cracker crumbs (about 2 packets, 11 crackers each)
½ cup (1 stick) unsalted butter, melted
1 cup heavy cream
30 individually wrapped caramels, unwrapped
2 cups sweetened flake coconut
1 package (12 ounces) semisweet chocolate chips (2 cups)
1 package (6 ounces) white chocolate chips (1 cup)
1 cup chopped pecans or walnuts
2 teaspoons vanilla

1. Heat oven to 350°. Line a 15½ x 10½ x 1-inch jelly-roll pan with aluminum foil.

2. Combine graham cracker crumbs and butter in a small bowl; mix well with fingers or a fork. Press evenly onto bottom of prepared pan. Bake in heated 350° oven 8 minutes. Transfer crust in pan to a wire rack to cool; leave oven on.

3. Bring cream to simmering in a small saucepan over medium heat. Add caramels; cook, stirring, until melted. Remove from heat; let stand 10 minutes.

4. Combine coconut, semisweet and white chocolate chips and pecans in a large bowl. Spoon evenly onto crust. Stir vanilla into caramel mixture. Drizzle over chocolate mixture.

5. Bake in heated 350° oven 20 minutes or until chocolate mixture is golden and bubbly. Transfer pan to a wire rack to cool. Cut into 48 bars. Refrigerate in covered plastic container up to 2 weeks.

Chocolate Raspberry Bars

Before cutting the bars, pipe straight lines of jam lengthwise on top; then drag a knife from side to side across the lines in alternate directions. That's all it takes to create the feathered pattern.

Chocolate Raspberry Bars; Milk-Chocolate Mocha Bars, *opposite*

MAKES *3 dozen bars*

PREP *20 minutes*

BAKE *at 375° for 20 minutes*

1 cup all-purpose flour
⅓ cup unsweetened cocoa powder
½ teaspoon baking soda
¼ teaspoon salt
1 stick (½ cup) unsalted butter, at room temperature
⅓ cup granulated sugar
⅓ cup packed light-brown sugar
1 egg
1 teaspoon vanilla
1 cup raspberry-flavored or semisweet chocolate chips
1 can (16 ounces) vanilla-flavored frosting
3 tablespoons seedless raspberry jam

1. Heat oven to 375°.

2. Sift flour, cocoa, baking soda and salt onto a piece of waxed paper.

3. With a mixer on medium-high speed, beat butter in a medium-size bowl until creamy. Add granulated sugar and brown sugar; beat until fluffy. Beat in egg. Beat in vanilla.

4. On low speed, beat in flour mixture. Fold in raspberry chips. Spread batter into an ungreased 13 x 9 x 2-inch baking pan.

5. Bake in heated 375° oven 20 minutes, until center is set. Transfer pan to a wire rack to cool completely.

6. When bar is completely cooled, spread with frosting. Stir jam in a small cup until smooth. Spoon into a small plastic food-storage bag; snip off a a corner of bag and pipe jam in straight lines lengthwise over top of frosting, spacing

about 1-inch apart. Place tip of a sharp knife in frosting and drag across pan, feathering lines. Repeat at 1-inch intervals, dragging in alternate directions. Refrigerate until frosting is set. Cut into 36 bars.

Milk-Chocolate Mocha Bars

If you find that this dough is too sticky to press into the baking pan, wrap your hand in plastic wrap, then smooth the mixture with your covered palm. Shown on opposite page.

MAKES *3 dozen bars*

PREP *20 minutes*

BAKE *at 350° for 20 to 25 minutes*

1 cup all-purpose flour
¼ cup unsweetened cocoa powder
2 tablespoons instant espresso coffee powder
½ teaspoon baking powder
¼ teaspoon salt
½ cup (1 stick) unsalted butter, at room temperature
½ cup packed dark-brown sugar
¼ cup granulated sugar
2 eggs
2 teaspoons vanilla
½ cup chopped pecans (optional)
1 package (6 ounces) milk chocolate chips (1 cup)

Mocha Frosting

3 tablespoons warm milk
1 tablespoon instant espresso coffee powder
1 box (1 pound) confectioners' sugar
½ cup (1 stick) unsalted butter, at room temperature
½ teaspoon vanilla
½ cup milk chocolate chips, for sprinkling

1. Heat oven to 350°. Coat a 13 x 9 x 2-inch baking pan with nonstick cooking spray.

2. Sift together flour, cocoa powder, espresso powder, baking powder and salt onto a piece of waxed paper.

3. With a mixer on medium-high speed, beat butter in a large bowl until smooth and creamy. Add brown sugar and granulated sugar and beat until light and fluffy. Add eggs, one at a time, beating well after each addition. Beat in vanilla.

4. On low speed, beat in flour mixture until well blended. Stir in pecans if using and chocolate chips until evenly distributed. Press evenly over bottom of prepared pan (mixture will be sticky).

5. Bake in heated 350° oven for 20 to 25 minutes or just until edges begin to pull away from sides of pan. Transfer pan to a wire rack to cool completely.

6. Meanwhile, prepare frosting: Stir together warm milk and espresso powder in a small bowl to dissolve powder. On medium speed, beat together confectioners' sugar, softened butter and vanilla in a medium-size bowl. Gradually beat in warm espresso mixture until frosting is smooth.

7. Spread frosting evenly over mocha bar; sprinkle chocolate chips on top. Refrigerate until frosting is set. Cut into 36 bars. Store, covered, in refrigerator.

Maple Bars

Pure maple syrup adds an unmistakable sweet note to easy, no-bake bars.

MAKES *4 dozen bars*

PREP *20 minutes*

REFRIGERATE *5 hours and 40 minutes*

Coconut-Graham Crust

1¼ cups graham cracker crumbs (about 1 packet, 11 crackers)
1¼ cups finely ground pecans
1¼ cups sweetened flake coconut
1¼ cups semisweet chocolate chips (7½ ounces)
6 tablespoons (¾ stick) unsalted butter, at room temperature

Maple-Cream Filling

3 cups confectioners' sugar
½ cup (1 stick) unsalted butter, at room temperature
⅓ cup pure maple syrup

Chocolate Topping

8 squares (1 ounce each) semisweet chocolate, chopped
1 cup heavy cream
2 ounces white baking chocolate, chopped

1. Prepare crust: Combine graham cracker crumbs, pecans, coconut, chocolate chips and butter in a medium-size bowl; mix well with fingers or a wooden spoon. Press evenly over bottom of a 13 x 9 x 2-inch baking dish. Refrigerate 30 minutes.

2. Prepare filling: With a mixer on medium speed, beat confectioners' sugar, butter and maple syrup in a medium-size bowl until smooth and creamy. Spread evenly over crust. Refrigerate until firm, about 2 hours.

3. Meanwhile, prepare topping: Combine semisweet chocolate and cream in a small saucepan. Cook over low heat, stirring until chocolate is melted and mixture is smooth. Remove from heat; set aside until room temperature, about 20 minutes. Pour over maple filling and spread evenly. Refrigerate until firm, about 3 hours.

4. Cut into twenty-four 2-inch squares; cut each square in half for 48 bars.

5. Melt white chocolate in a small saucepan over low heat. Cool slightly. Pour into a small plastic food-storage bag; snip off a corner of bag and drizzle chocolate in a swirl on top of each bar. Refrigerate until set, about 10 minutes. Store bars in refrigerator or freezer.

SYRUP GRADES

Maple syrup is graded according to color and flavor. Fancy or Grade AA is a very light amber color with a mild flavor; Grade B is dark amber with a hearty flavor, while Grade A falls in between. Be sure to refrigerate after opening.

Macaroon Squares

To give these coconutty squares a fancy finish, simply pipe with melted chocolate.

MAKES *24 squares*

PREP *10 minutes*

BAKE *at 350° for 35 minutes*

2 bags (7 ounces each) sweetened flake coconut
1 cup (4 ounces) unblanched almonds, ground
1 can (14 ounces) sweetened condensed milk
½ teaspoon vanilla
¼ teaspoon almond extract
2 eggs, lightly beaten
⅓ cup semisweet chocolate chips
Sweetened flake coconut for garnish (optional)
Chopped almonds for garnish (optional)

1. Heat oven to 350°. Line a 13 x 9 x 2-inch glass baking dish with aluminum foil. Coat foil generously with nonstick cooking spray.

2. Combine coconut and almonds in a medium-size bowl. Stir in condensed milk until dry ingredients are coated. Stir in vanilla, almond extract and eggs until well combined. Spread batter evenly in prepared baking dish.

3. Bake in heated 350° oven about 35 minutes or until center of macaroon is firm and edges start to brown slightly. Transfer dish to a wire rack; let cool about 20 minutes.

4. Invert macaroon onto a cutting board; carefully peel off foil. Let macaroon cool completely. Cut into 24 equal squares. Turn squares over.

5. Melt chocolate in top of a double boiler over barely simmering, not boiling, water. Spoon into a small plastic food-storage bag. Snip off a corner of bag and pipe chocolate over squares. Sprinkle coconut and chopped nuts on top if desired. Let stand until chocolate is firm.

Blueberry Bars

A cross between a cookie and a cheesecake—the best of both worlds! One tip for success: Always let cake cool completely before slicing into bars.

MAKES *30 bars*

PREP *15 minutes*

BAKE *crust at 350° for 12 to 15 minutes; bars at 300° for 25 to 30 minutes*

Cookie Crust

1¼ cups all-purpose flour
¼ cup sugar
2 eggs
¼ cup (½ stick) butter, at room temperature
1 teaspoon vanilla

Filling

2 packages (8 ounces each) cream cheese, at room temperature
½ cup sugar
1 tablespoon cornstarch
2 eggs
1 teaspoon vanilla
1 can (21 ounces) blueberry pie filling or topping

1. Prepare crust: Heat oven to 350°. Coat a 13 x 9 x 2-inch baking dish with nonstick cooking spray.

2. Mix flour and sugar in a large bowl. Add eggs, butter and vanilla; beat until a dough forms. Press dough over bottom of prepared dish.

3. Bake in heated 350° oven 12 to 15 minutes or until crust is firm. Transfer dish to a wire rack and let cool slightly.

4. Meanwhile, lower oven temperature to 300°.

5. Prepare filling: Beat cream cheese and sugar with a mixer on medium speed in a medium-size bowl until smooth and creamy, about 2 minutes. Add cornstarch, eggs and vanilla; beat 2 minutes or until well combined. Spread filling evenly over crust.

6. Bake in 300° oven 25 to 30 minutes or until center of filling is set. Transfer baking dish to a wire rack and let cool.

7. Spread pie filling evenly on cake top. Cut into 30 bars.

Conga Bars

Keep these on hand for after-school snacking, but don't be surprised if you find yourself sneaking a bite or two—they're too tempting to pass up.

Conga Bars

MAKES *3 dozen bars*

PREP *25 minutes*

BAKE *at 350° for 30 to 35 minutes*

Bars

2¼ cups all-purpose flour
2½ teaspoons baking powder
½ teaspoon salt
¾ cup (1½ sticks) unsalted butter or margarine, at room temperature
1 box (1 pound) light-brown sugar
3 eggs
1 teaspoon vanilla
1 package (6 ounces) chocolate chips (1 cup)
¼ cup coarsely chopped nuts, such as walnuts or pecans

Glaze

½ cup sifted confectioners' sugar
1½ to 3 teaspoons milk

1. Prepare bars: Heat oven to 350°. Lightly grease a 13 x 9 x 2-inch baking pan.

2. Sift together flour, baking powder and salt onto a sheet of waxed paper.

3. With a mixer on medium speed, beat butter and brown sugar in a large bowl until well blended. Add eggs, one at a time, beating well after each addition. On low speed, gradually beat in flour mixture until blended. Beat in vanilla. Stir in chocolate chips and nuts. Spread mixture evenly in prepared pan.

4. Bake in heated 350° oven 30 to 35 minutes or until a wooden pick inserted in center of cookie comes out clean. Transfer pan to a wire rack to cool completely.

5. Meanwhile, prepare glaze: In a small bowl, whisk together confectioners' sugar and enough milk to make a good drizzling consistency. (If cookie is not cool, cover glaze and set aside.) Drizzle glaze over cookie. Let stand until glaze hardens. Cut into 3 x 1-inch bars.

Chocolate-Orange Bites

Orange juice, rind and marmalade provide both a sweet and tart note that complements the intense chocolate frosting.

MAKES *4 dozen diamonds*

PREP *30 minutes*

BAKE *at 350° for 30 minutes*

REFRIGERATE *at least 1½ hours*

2   cups all-purpose flour
½   cup sugar
¼   teaspoon salt
1   cup (2 sticks) butter, chilled and cut into small pieces
1   cup orange juice
1   envelope unflavored gelatin
1   box (3.4 ounces) vanilla instant pudding-and-pie-filling mix
1   tablespoon grated orange rind
½   cup orange marmalade
½   cup heavy cream
5   squares (1 ounce each) semisweet chocolate, finely chopped
½   teaspoon vanilla
     Candied flowers for garnish (optional)

1. Heat oven to 350°. Line a 13 x 9 x 2-inch baking dish with aluminum foil, extending foil over sides.

2. Mix flour, sugar and salt in a large bowl. Cut butter into flour mixture with a pastry blender or 2 knives used scissor fashion until mixture resembles coarse meal. Press into bottom of prepared dish.

3. Bake in heated 350° oven 30 minutes or until edges of pastry are lightly browned. Let cool in baking dish on a wire rack 30 minutes.

4. Place ½ cup orange juice in a glass measure. Sprinkle gelatin over top. Let stand until softened, about 5 minutes. Microwave at 100% power 20 seconds. Stir to dissolve gelatin. (Or heat mixture in a small saucepan.) Let cool slightly.

5. Combine pudding mix, remaining ½ cup orange juice and orange rind in a medium-size bowl; mix until blended. Stir in gelatin mixture.

6. Using foil, lift pastry from baking dish and place on a baking sheet. Spread marmalade in a thin layer over pastry. Top with pudding mixture in an even layer. Refrigerate at least 30 minutes.

7. Bring cream to boiling in a small heavy saucepan. Remove from heat. Stir in chocolate until melted and mixture is smooth. Stir in vanilla. Let cool slightly. Pour over pudding layer; make a decorative pattern with a pastry comb or fork. Refrigerate at least 1 hour. Cut into diamond-shaped pieces. Garnish each piece with a candied flower if desired.

Cookies 101

On the surface, cookies may seem like the easiest option for bakers. But because the dough has so little moisture, minor problems can turn into major mistakes. Follow our tips to ensure dozens of perfect goodies, each and every time.

INGREDIENTS RULE

- If a batch of cookies crumbles, try this trick the next time you bake the recipe: Sprinkle a little water on the flour before you mix it with the other ingredients. The water will activate the gluten (a protein) in the flour, and this will help the cookies hold together.

- It's the amount of liquid (including butter, which liquefies as it melts) in a recipe that dictates whether the cookies spread during baking. There are several things you can do to minimize spread:

  a) Reduce the amount of liquid.

  b) Increase the amount of flour, or use bread flour, which absorbs more water, instead of all-purpose.

  c) Use shortening instead of some or all of the butter. Butter melts as soon as it meets the hot oven, but shortening holds its texture better, so cookies made with it keep their shape during baking.

  d) Chill the dough before putting the cookies into the oven. Very cold fat will take longer to melt, so the cookies won't be as likely to spread.

- The sweetener called for has a lot to do with texture. Cookies made with granulated sugar, little moisture and no acidic ingredients will be hard and crisp. Those made with brown sugar or honey absorb moisture and soften after baking. Corn syrup browns at a lower temperature than sugar; substituting even a tablespoon of it will give cookies a crisp surface.

- Recipes using egg for the liquid will be soft, rather than crisp. If a recipe is too crisp for your liking, try substituting cake flour for the all-purpose, or use shortening for part of the butter.

- If the dough is too acidic, the cookies may not brown during baking. Next time you make the recipe, add a little baking soda to neutralize the acid. Substituting corn syrup for a small amount of the sugar, and using bread flour instead of all-purpose also enhances browning.

ROLL THEM RIGHT

- Before rolling out chilled dough, sprinkle the work surface, disc of dough and rolling pin with a little flour.

- If you want the cookies to be light and puffy, lightly oil the work surface and rolling pin instead of sprinkling them with flour—the oil works just as well.

- Some people like to roll out dough between sheets of waxed paper. Though the dough may stick to the paper, it is easy to peel off the paper and adjust the dough.

- Gather dough scraps and reroll them as many times as you need to. Cookie dough has large amounts of sugar and fat, so, unlike pastry dough, it won't become as tough with repeated rolling.

PAN PICKS

- Heavy-duty aluminum baking sheets distribute heat evenly and reduce the risk that cookies will burn.

- Insulated baking trays (made with an air pocket between two sheets of metal) prevent cookies from burning but don't conduct heat as quickly as single sheet pans, so baking time may be longer.

- Dark metal baking sheets conduct heat very well, but there is a greater risk your cookies will burn.

TO GREASE OR NOT?

- Always grease the baking sheet if the recipe directs you to do so.

- If there is no indication of whether to grease the baking sheet, grease it. Some people mistakenly believe that greasing the pan will cause the cookies to spread during baking, but this is not the case—it is the amount of liquid and type of fat that cause cookies to spread.

- Even if you are using nonstick baking sheets, it is a good idea to grease them with nonstick cooking spray.

- Some bakers like to use flexible nonstick baking sheets, which are liners that you lay on the baking sheet. You can purchase them from a good baking supply vendor.

- Another alternative is to grease aluminum foil and use it to line baking sheets for easy cleanup. Parchment paper, available at good supermarkets, is even better.

IN AND OUT OF THE OVEN

- New electric ovens are computerized to heat evenly. If yours is of this type, you can put the oven racks at any level, and bake more than one sheet of cookies at a time.

- With an older, noncomputerized electric oven or a gas oven, place the oven rack in the middle position and bake 1 sheet at a time. It's a good idea also to rotate the baking sheet from back to front halfway through baking.

- If you decide to bake 2 sheets of cookies at one time, switch them between racks and rotate from back to front halfway through baking.

- Periodically check the accuracy of your oven thermostat with an oven thermometer.

- Always use a timer—cookies bake so quickly you don't want to forget them for even a minute.

- Cookies should be removed from the oven as soon as they begin to brown around the edges. If you wait until they're brown in the center, they'll be overdone.

- Most cookies will tear if you try to remove them from the baking sheet the minute they come out of the oven. Follow your recipe directions for removing cookies from the baking sheet so they can cool.

- If the recipe doesn't provide cooling information, place the baking sheet on a wire rack for 1 to 2 minutes to cool the cookies slightly, then transfer the cookies to the rack to cool completely.

- Cookies that contain egg are especially likely to stick to the baking sheet if they're left on it too long—so don't forget to remove them while still warm.

BAR COOKIE BRIEFING

- If you line the baking pan with aluminum foil, leaving an overhang at 2 opposite ends, you'll be able to lift out baked bars easily—without breaking.

- To press dough into the pan, first cover your hand with plastic wrap. You'll be able to gently smooth the surface without sticking.

- If baking in a glass pan, reduce the oven temperature by 25°.

- If your baking pan is not the size specified in the recipe, the baking time will differ. In a smaller pan, the dough will be thicker and take longer to bake. With a larger pan, the opposite is true, so check for doneness early.

- Be sure to let bar cookies cool completely before cutting. You'll have neater, crumb-free edges.

Mini-Chip Shortbreads

A drizzle of chocolate makes these melt-in-your-mouth triangles elegant enough for company.

Mini-Chip Shortbreads

MAKES *16 shortbreads*

PREP *20 minutes*

BAKE *at 325° for 25 minutes*

1¼ cups cake flour (not self-rising)
½ cup cornstarch
10 tablespoons (1¼ sticks) unsalted butter, at room temperature
¼ cup confectioners' sugar
2 tablespoons granulated sugar
¼ teaspoon salt
1 package (6 ounces) semisweet mini chocolate chips (1 cup)

1. Heat oven to 325°.

2. Whisk together flour and cornstarch in a small bowl.

3. With a mixer on medium-high speed, beat butter in a large bowl until smooth and creamy. Add confectioners' sugar, granulated sugar and salt; beat until very light colored and fluffy, 3 to 5 minutes.

4. With mixer running on low speed, slowly sift flour mixture over butter mixture; beat until a stiff dough forms. (Dough may separate, resembling coarse meal.)

5. Transfer dough to a lightly floured surface. Sprinkle ½ cup chocolate chips over dough; knead by hand until chips are evenly distributed. Divide dough in half.

6. Add extra flour to board. Pat each piece of dough into an 8-inch round. Using a spatula, carefully transfer to an ungreased baking sheet. Using a sharp knife, divide each round into 8 wedges, slicing completely through dough; do not pull wedges apart. Prick wedges with tines of a fork. Flute curved edges if desired.

7. Bake in heated 325° oven 25 minutes or until lightly golden. Immediately separate wedges and transfer to a wire rack to cool.

8. Melt remaining ½ cup chocolate chips in top of a double boiler over barely simmering (not boiling) water. Pour into a small plastic food-storage bag. Snip off a corner of bag and drizzle chocolate over shortbread.

Almond Shortbreads

A swirl of chocolate adds a festive air to these oh-so-scrumptious classics.

MAKES *2 dozen cookies*

PREP *15 minutes*

BAKE *at 350° for 12 to 14 minutes*

1¼ cups all-purpose flour
⅓ cup unblanched almonds, finely chopped
¼ teaspoon salt
½ cup (1 stick) butter, at room temperature
⅓ cup granulated sugar
1 teaspoon vanilla
1 teaspoon almond extract
½ cup semisweet chocolate chips
Confectioners' sugar for dusting

1. Heat oven to 350°. Lightly grease a large baking sheet.

2. Whisk together flour, almonds and salt in a small bowl.

3. With a mixer on medium speed, beat butter, sugar, vanilla and almond extract in a medium-size bowl until creamy and smooth, about 2 minutes. Stir in flour mixture.

4. Divide dough into fourths. On a greased baking sheet, pat or roll out each piece of dough into a 4½-inch round. Smooth edge. Press with tines of fork to make a pattern all around edge if desired. Using a sharp knife, divide each round into 6 wedges, slicing completely through dough; do not pull wedges apart.

5. Bake in heated 350° oven for 12 to 14 minutes or until lightly browned at edges. While still hot, recut rounds into wedges and remove to a wire rack to cool completely.

6. Melt chocolate chips in top of a double boiler over barely simmering (not boiling) water. Pour into a small plastic food-storage bag. Snip off a corner of bag and pipe chocolate over shortbread, making a swirled or random pattern as desired. Dust shortbread with confectioners' sugar.

SHORTBREAD SECRET

The shortbread recipes instruct you to cut the dough round into wedges before baking, but not to separate the pieces until they come out of the oven. This process will give you straight, even edges every time.

Chocolate-Dipped Almond Biscotti

For best results, don't dip until the cookie is completely cooled. You could also dip half the biscotti into white chocolate, half into bittersweet, and then decorate each with the alternate type.

MAKES *2 dozen biscotti*

PREP *20 minutes*

BAKE *at 375° for 15 to 18 minutes, then at 325° for 15 to 20 minutes*

1¼ cups all-purpose flour
1 teaspoon baking powder
¼ teaspoon salt
6 tablespoons (¾ stick) butter, at room temperature
½ cup sugar
1 whole egg
1 egg yolk
1 teaspoon grated orange rind
½ teaspoon vanilla
¼ teaspoon almond extract
1 cup slivered blanched almonds, toasted (see page 231) and coarsely chopped
8 squares (1 ounce each) bittersweet chocolate, chopped

1. Heat oven to 375°.

2. Whisk together flour, baking powder and salt in a small bowl. Beat butter and sugar in a medium-size bowl until creamy. Beat in egg, egg yolk, orange rind, vanilla and almond extract. Stir flour mixture into butter mixture. Stir in almonds.

3. Scrape dough onto an ungreased baking sheet. Shape into an 11 x 4-inch log. If dough is too soft to hold its shape, refrigerate until firm.

4. Bake in heated 375° oven 15 to 18 minutes or until lightly browned. Remove log to a cutting board. Lower oven temperature to 325°.

5. Let log stand until cool enough to handle, about 10 minutes.

6. Using a serrated knife, cut log crosswise on a slight angle into ½-inch-thick slices. Carefully transfer biscotti, cut side down, to a clean greased baking sheet.

7. Bake in heated 325° oven 15 to 20 minutes or until golden. Transfer biscotti to a wire rack to cool completely.

8. Line a baking sheet with waxed paper. Melt chocolate in top of a double boiler over barely simmering, not boiling, water, stirring until smooth. Remove pan from above water. One at a time, dip one end of each biscotti into chocolate, letting excess chocolate drip back into bowl, and then place on waxed-paper-lined baking sheet. Let stand in a cool place until chocolate is firm.

BISCOTTI HOW-TO'S

Bake log and let cool for 10 minutes. Then slice on the diagonal with a serrated knife.

After the second bake, cool. Dip into melted chocolate, letting excess drip back into bowl.

Fig-Lemon Biscotti

Baked first in a log, then in slices, biscotti are Italy's gift for dunking into coffee or dessert wine. Lemon and fig are a delightful departure from the more customary nut or anise flavorings.

MAKES *about 4 dozen biscotti*

PREP *20 minutes*

REFRIGERATE *several hours*

BAKE *at 350° for 40 minutes*

1½ cups all-purpose flour
½ teaspoon baking powder
¼ teaspoon salt
½ cup (1 stick) unsalted butter
¾ cup sugar
1 tablespoon grated lemon rind
1 egg
¼ teaspoon lemon extract
1 cup chopped dried figs
½ cup chopped walnuts

1. Heat oven to 350°. Lightly coat a baking sheet with nonstick cooking spray.

2. Whisk together flour, baking powder and salt in a small bowl; reserve.

3. With mixer on medium speed, beat butter, sugar, lemon rind, egg and lemon extract in a large bowl until blended. Stir in flour mixture, figs and walnuts. Divide dough in half. Shape each half into a 9-inch log on prepared baking sheet.

4. Bake until log is heated, about 25 minutes or until lightly golden. Transfer logs to wire racks. Cool 10 minutes.

5. Let logs stand until cool enough to handle, about 10 minutes. Transfer to a cutting board. Using a serrated knife, cut logs crosswise on a slight angle into ⅝-inch-thick slices. Transfer to a clean greased baking sheet, cut side down.

6. Bake in heated 350° oven 15 minutes. Transfer biscotti to a wire rack to cool completely.

Handwritten note on overlaid paper:
350°
25 then
15

📧 Time/Design®

Cookie Smarts

Chances are they'll be eaten long before they get stale. But here are tricks for keeping cookies fresh and sending them to loved ones.

STORAGE SAVVY

- Allow cookies to cool before putting them away.

- Store soft cookies at room temperature in a container with a tight-fitting lid. Use a decorated tin only if the seal is snug; otherwise, go for a resealable plastic bag.

- Store crisp cookies at room temperature in a container with a loose-fitting lid.

- Don't mix different varieties in one container. If you do, strongly flavored goodies will overpower milder ones.

- Keep cookies at room temperature for approximately 1 to 2 weeks.

- Or store in the freezer, then thaw for several hours before you plan to serve. But don't frost or sugar-coat cookies destined to be frozen; wait until defrosted, then proceed as desired.

PACK 'EM UP

Soft drop, bar and fruit cookies are among the best travelers; choose them to mail to far-flung family and friends.

- Use a metal container or decorative tin. Line the container with waxed paper or aluminum foil.

- Wrap cookies airtight. Wrap 2 drop cookies back to back, wrap bar cookies individually.

- Nest cookies securely in container, packing them close together to minimize shifting. Use crumpled foil or waxed paper as filler. The container should be so full that you have to use a little pressure to tape it shut. Place the container in a sturdy shipping box, cushioning it so it fits tightly.

Almond-Strawberry Tart, *page 104*

Maple-Walnut Pie, *page 93;* Pumpkin Chiffon Pie, *page 91*

Pies
and
Tarts

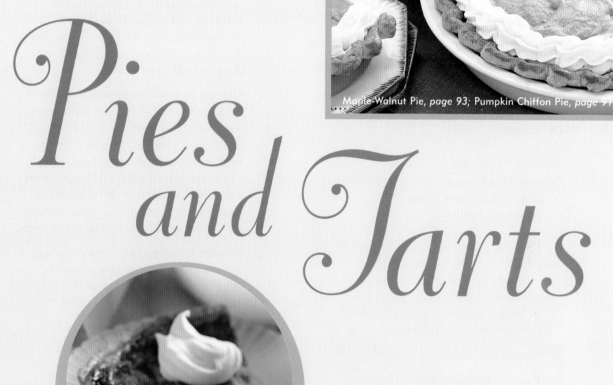

Rich 'n' Creamy Pear Pie, *page 96*

Chocolate Cream Pie

Nestled in a sweet pastry crust, this silky smooth filling is a chocolate lover's dream.

MAKES *8 servings*
PREP *30 minutes*
REFRIGERATE *3½ hours*
BAKE *crust at 425° for 25 minutes*
COOK *about 25 minutes*

Crust

Sweet Pie Pastry (recipe follows)

Chocolate Filling

2½ squares (1 ounce each) unsweetened chocolate
4 cups milk
1½ cups granulated sugar
⅔ cup cornstarch
¾ teaspoon salt
5 egg yolks
1½ teaspoons vanilla

Cream Topping

2 cups heavy cream
¼ cup confectioners' sugar
1½ teaspoons vanilla

1. Roll out pastry on a lightly floured surface to a 13-inch round. Fit pastry into a 9-inch pie plate, being careful not to stretch. Roll edge of pastry under to form a stand-up edge; flute edge. Refrigerate crust 30 minutes.

2. Meanwhile, heat oven to 425°.

3. Remove pie plate with pastry from refrigerator. Prick pastry all over with a fork. Line pastry shell with foil; fill with dried beans, rice or pie weights.

4. Bake pastry in heated 425° oven 15 minutes. Remove foil with beans. Continue to bake 8 to 10 minutes or until edge of pastry is golden brown. Cool completely on a wire rack.

5. Meanwhile, prepare filling: Heat chocolate and ½ cup milk in a small, heavy saucepan over low heat, stirring constantly, until chocolate melts. Combine sugar, cornstarch and salt in a large saucepan. Gradually stir in remaining 3½ cups milk until mixture is completely smooth.

6. Stir chocolate mixture into sugar-milk mixture. Cook over medium heat, stirring constantly, until mixture thickens and begins to bubble, 15 to 20 minutes; continue to cook another 2 to 3 minutes, stirring constantly. Remove saucepan from heat.

7. Using a fork, beat egg yolks slightly in a small bowl. Stir ½ cup hot milk mixture into yolks. Stir yolk mixture into milk mixture in saucepan. Cook over low heat, stirring constantly, 1 minute; do not overcook or eggs will begin to set up. Stir in vanilla. Pour into cooled pastry shell. Place plastic wrap directly on surface of filling. Refrigerate 3 hours.

8. Prepare topping: Just before serving, beat together cream, confectioners' sugar and vanilla in a small bowl until stiff peaks form. Spread topping over surface of pie.

Sweet Pie Pastry

Combine 1⅓ cups all-purpose flour, 2 tablespoons sugar and ½ teaspoon salt in a medium-size bowl. Using a pastry blender or 2 knives scissor fashion, cut ½ cup solid vegetable shortening, butter or margarine into flour mixture until coarse crumbs form. Gradually add 3 to 4 tablespoons cold water, tossing with a fork until mixture begins to come together. Shape into a ball.

Double Fudge Pie

Imagine a big gorgeous brownie baked inside a cocoa-laced crust. Who's got the milk?

MAKES *12 servings*

PREP *30 minutes*

BAKE *at 350° for 40 minutes*

Crust

1   cup all-purpose flour
1   teaspoon unsweetened cocoa powder
¼   teaspoon salt
3   tablespoons butter, chilled
3   tablespoons solid vegetable shortening, chilled
3   to 4 tablespoons ice water

Filling

½   cup (1 stick) unsalted butter
4   squares (1 ounce each) semisweet chocolate
¾   cup packed light-brown sugar
¼   cup water
2   eggs, separated
1   teaspoon vanilla
⅓   cup all-purpose flour
¼   teaspoon salt
1   cup chopped walnuts

1. Prepare crust: Mix flour, cocoa and salt in a medium-size bowl. Cut in butter and shortening with a pastry blender or 2 knives used scissor fashion until mixture resembles coarse meal.

2. Sprinkle water, 1 tablespoon at a time, over mixture, mixing lightly with a fork after each addition, until pastry is just moist enough to hold together.

3. Roll out pastry on a well-floured surface to a 13-inch round. Fit into a 9-inch pie plate. Trim overhang to 1 inch; flute edge into desired pattern (see page 89).

4. Heat oven to 350°.

5. Prepare filling: Melt butter and chocolate in a small saucepan over low heat, stirring until smooth. Transfer to a medium-size bowl; cool slightly. Stir in sugar and water. With a mixer on medium speed, beat in egg yolks and vanilla. Fold in flour and salt.

6. On medium-high speed and with clean beaters, beat egg whites in another medium-size bowl until soft peaks form. Fold into chocolate mixture until no white streaks remain. Fold in ½ cup walnuts. Spread into crust. Top with remaining ½ cup walnuts.

7. Bake in heated 350° oven 40 minutes or until filling is set. Transfer to a wire rack to cool completely.

FUDGE PIE HINTS

Gently fold beaten whites into chocolate mixture until no white streaks remain.

Tropical Chocolate-Banana Tart

Coconut, macadamia nuts and bananas team up to give this chocolate-rich tart its name.

Tropical Chocolate-Banana Tart

MAKES *12 servings*

PREP *30 minutes*

COOK *5 minutes*

REFRIGERATE *2 hours*

½ cup sweetened flake coconut
½ cup chopped macadamia nuts
¾ cup heavy cream
1 package (12 ounces) semisweet chocolate chips (2 cups)
2 medium ripe bananas
¼ cup confectioners' sugar
2 teaspoons lime juice
½ teaspoon coconut extract
1 package (8 ounces) cream cheese

1. Grease a 9-inch springform pan.

2. Lightly toast coconut and macadamias 2 minutes in a medium-size skillet over medium heat. Remove from heat.

3. Heat cream over medium heat just to boiling in a small saucepan. Remove from heat. Add chocolate chips and stir until melted and smooth. Add ½ cup coconut-macadamia mixture; reserve remainder. Set cream mixture aside 10 minutes, until slightly thickened. Pour into prepared pan. Refrigerate 1½ hours, until firm.

4. Slice bananas; arrange in pan in a single layer on top of chocolate.

5. Beat confectioners' sugar, lime juice and coconut extract into cream cheese. Spread over bananas, using a rubber spatula. Sprinkle remaining coconut-macadamia mixture around top edge, making a narrow border.

6. Chill tart 30 minutes. To serve, remove sides of pan; cut tart into slices.

Chocolate Candy Tarts

Chopped nuts and chocolate form individual tarts that showcase a fresh and candied ginger filling.

MAKES *14 tarts*

PREP *1 hour*

REFRIGERATE *3 hours*

COOK *5 minutes*

Ginger Filling

¼ cup sugar
3 tablespoons cornstarch
1 teaspoon grated fresh ginger
¼ teaspoon salt
2 cups milk

Chocolate Tart Shells

1 package (12 ounces) semisweet chocolate chips (2 cups)
2 tablespoons solid vegetable shortening
2 cups finely chopped nuts, such as walnuts

Topping

¾ cup semisweet chocolate chips
1 cup strawberries, hulled and quartered
2 tablespoons finely chopped candied ginger

1. Prepare filling: Combine sugar, cornstarch, fresh ginger and salt in a medium-size saucepan. Gradually add milk, blending until smooth. Cook over medium heat, stirring constantly, until mixture thickens and comes to boiling; cook, stirring continuously, 1 minute. Pour into a small bowl. Place a piece of plastic wrap directly on surface. Refrigerate several hours or until mixture is completely chilled.

2. Meanwhile, prepare tart shells: Cut fourteen 5-inch squares of aluminum foil. Invert fourteen 10-ounce baking pans or baking dishes on a work surface. Center a foil square over bottom of each dish and press to wrap against sides. Alternatively, use 4½ x 1¼-inch disposable foil pans, as-is or covered with foil squares.

3. Melt chocolate and shortening in top of a double boiler over barely simmering, not boiling, water, stirring until smooth. Stir in nuts. Let mixture cool slightly, about 15 minutes, being sure it remains spreadable.

4. Using a small metal spatula, carefully spread 2 tablespoons chocolate mixture over bottom and about ¼ inch down sides of each inverted foil-covered pan or dish. Refrigerate at least 30 minutes or until firm.

5. When filling is chilled and chocolate is firm, remove 1 chocolate-and-foil-covered dish from refrigerator; slip dish out of foil and carefully peel foil away from chocolate. Place chocolate shell, right side up, on a serving platter in refrigerator. Repeat for each shell.

6. Remove shells from refrigerator. Evenly spread level 2 tablespoons chilled filling into each shell. Return shells to refrigerator.

7. Prepare topping: Melt chocolate chips in top of a double boiler over barely simmering, not boiling, water, stirring until smooth. Remove from heat and cool slightly.

8. Meanwhile, arrange quartered strawberries on top of each tart filling. Sprinkle with candied ginger.

9. Pour melted chocolate into a small food-storage bag. Snip off a corner and pipe chocolate over tarts in a decorative pattern. Serve immediately.

EASY CHOCOLATE TART SHELLS

Spread 2 tablespoons chocolate mixture over bottom and about ¼ inch down sides of inverted foil-covered dish.

Piecrust Savvy

Making your own pie pastry is really not at all difficult. Here are simply the best recipes for single and double crusts—half butter for flavor and half vegetable shortening for flakiness. The dough can be made ahead and refrigerated, well wrapped, for up to 2 days or frozen for up to 1 month. Thaw frozen dough in refrigerator overnight.

SINGLE-CRUST PIE PASTRY

MAKES *one 9-inch crust*
PREP *20 minutes*
REFRIGERATE *30 minutes*

1¼ cups all-purpose flour
½ teaspoon salt
¼ cup (½ stick) cold unsalted butter, cut into small pieces
¼ cup solid vegetable shortening, chilled and cut into small pieces
3 to 4 tablespoons cold water

1. Mix flour and salt in a medium-size bowl.

2. Cut in butter and shortening with a pastry blender or 2 knives used scissor fashion until mixture resembles coarse meal.

3. Sprinkle cold water, 1 tablespoon at a time, over mixture, mixing lightly with a fork after each addition, until pastry is just moist enough to hold together.

4. Shape and flatten dough into a disc. Cover with plastic wrap. Refrigerate until well chilled, about 30 minutes. To blind-bake, see opposite.

DOUBLE-CRUST PIE PASTRY

MAKES *two 9-inch crusts*
PREP *20 minutes*
REFRIGERATE *30 minutes*

2½ cups all-purpose flour
1 teaspoon salt
½ cup (1 stick) cold unsalted butter, cut into small pieces
½ cup solid vegetable shortening, chilled and cut into small pieces
6 to 7 tablespoons cold water

1. Mix flour and salt in a medium-size bowl.

2. Cut in butter and shortening with a pastry blender or 2 knives used scissor fashion until mixture resembles coarse meal.

3. Sprinkle cold water, 1 tablespoon at a time, over mixture, mixing lightly with a fork after each addition, until pastry is just moist enough to hold together.

4. Divide pastry in half; shape each half into a disc. Cover with plastic wrap. Refrigerate until well chilled, about 30 minutes. To blind-bake, see box opposite.

PREPARING PIE PASTRY

1. With a pastry blender, cut butter and shortening into flour. Continue cutting until texture resembles coarse meal.

2. Slowly add ice water, a bit at a time, to flour mix. Combine with a fork.

3. Shape dough into 1 or 2 balls as directed in recipe, then press each ball into a disc. Wrap; chill 30 minutes.

4. On a lightly floured surface, roll chilled dough into a round 3 inches bigger than the top of your pie plate.

5. Carefully roll pastry around rolling pin so you can lift and transfer to pie plate without tearing.

6. Place rolled pastry over pie plate; gently unroll. Press pastry into plate without stretching.

TO FLUTE EDGE: Using both hands, pinch stand-up edge of pastry between thumbs and index fingers.

TO SCALLOP EDGE: Press stand-up edge of pastry with back of a spoon.

TO MAKE PIECRUST IN A FOOD PROCESSOR

Combine flour and salt in a food processor fitted with the steel blade. Pulse just to mix. Add butter and shortening. Whirl until mixture has texture of coarse meal, about 30 seconds. With machine running, add cold water in a slow and steady stream just until mixture begins to form a ball.

Proceed with step 4 of Single- or Double-Crust Pie Pastry recipe.

TO BLIND-BAKE A PIE SHELL

Heat oven to 400°. Roll out chilled pastry into a 12-inch round on a floured surface. Fit into a 9-inch pie plate. Fold excess dough under to form a stand-up edge; flute edge. Prick bottom with a fork. Line inside with aluminum foil. Fill with pie weights, raw rice or dried beans.

Bake in lower third of heated 400° oven 15 minutes. Carefully remove foil and weights. Return pie shell to oven 10 to 15 minutes or until light golden brown.

Remove pie shell from oven. Cool completely on a wire rack before filling.

Three-Nut Pie

An unbeatable trio of pecans, almonds and hazelnuts bake up in a cinnamon-accented filling.

Three-Nut Pie

MAKES *10 servings*
PREP *30 minutes*
REFRIGERATE *1 hour*
BAKE *at 325° for 50 minutes*

Crust

1¼ cups all-purpose flour
¼ teaspoon salt
⅓ cup solid vegetable shortening, chilled and cut into small pieces
1 tablespoon butter, chilled and cut into small pieces
3 to 4 tablespoons ice water
1 teaspoon cider vinegar

Nut Filling

¾ cup packed dark-brown sugar
¾ cup dark or light corn syrup
¼ cup (½ stick) butter
1½ teaspoons ground cinnamon
¼ teaspoon salt
⅛ teaspoon ground cloves
4 eggs
¾ cup slivered almonds
½ cup chopped hazelnuts
1 cup pecan halves

1. Prepare crust: Mix flour and salt in a medium-size bowl. Cut in shortening and butter with a pastry blender or 2 knives used scissor fashion until mixture resembles coarse crumbs.

2. Sprinkle ice water, 1 tablespoon at a time, and vinegar over flour mixture, mixing lightly with a fork after each addition, until pastry is just moist enough to hold together. Shape pastry into a ball and flatten into a 5-inch disc. Cover with plastic wrap. Refrigerate until thoroughly chilled, about 1 hour.

3. Heat oven to 325°.

4. Roll out pastry on a floured surface to an 11-inch round. Fit into a 9-inch pie plate. Fold overhanging pastry under to make an edge; press all around edge with tines of fork.

5. Prepare filling: Heat brown sugar, corn syrup, butter, cinnamon, salt and cloves in a medium-size saucepan over medium heat until butter is melted. Remove pan from heat; whisk in eggs, one at a time. Add almonds and hazelnuts. Pour into prepared crust. Arrange pecans on filling in concentric circles, beginning at outside and working toward center.

6. Bake in heated 325° oven 50 minutes or until golden brown and a knife inserted near center of filling comes out clean. Cool pie completely on a wire rack.

Pumpkin Chiffon Pie

After a big harvest dinner, you'll welcome this extra-light version of the seasonal classic. Shown on page 83.

MAKES *16 servings (two 9-inch pies)*

PREP *10 minutes*

COOK *10 to 14 minutes*

REFRIGERATE *overnight*

1   envelope unflavored gelatin
½   cup cold water
2   cups canned solid-pack pumpkin puree
1¾ cups packed dark-brown sugar
1   cup evaporated milk
2   egg yolks
½   teaspoon salt
½   teaspoon ground nutmeg
½   teaspoon ground cinnamon
¼   teaspoon ground ginger
¼   cup pasteurized liquid egg substitute
2   homemade or purchased pie shells (9-inch), blind-baked and cooled (recipe and method, page 89)
    Whipped cream for garnish (optional)

1. Sprinkle gelatin over cold water in a small saucepan; let stand 1 minute to soften. Stir over low heat until gelatin is dissolved, 1 minute. Remove from heat.

2. In a second small saucepan, stir together pumpkin, 1½ cups brown sugar, evaporated milk, egg yolks, salt, nutmeg, cinnamon and ginger. Cook over medium-low heat, stirring constantly, until mixture registers 160° on an instant-read thermometer, 10 to 13 minutes.

3. Stir gelatin mixture into pumpkin mixture. Pour into a medium-size bowl; refrigerate 90 minutes, until thickened.

4. With a mixer on medium speed, beat egg substitute in a second medium-size bowl until soft peaks form. Gradually beat in remaining ¼ cup sugar until firm peaks form. Fold into pumpkin mixture. Spoon mixture into prepared pie shells, dividing equally. Cover with plastic wrap and refrigerate overnight.

5. Serve pie garnished with whipped cream if desired.

SPICE SAVVY

Keep your spices away from the heat of the oven and out of direct light. Ground spices will keep their flavor for about 6 months—date the containers so you'll know when to discard.

Pecan-Sweet Potato Pie

Here is a perfect autumn finale; call it pecan pie — plus!

MAKES *10 servings*

PREP *25 minutes*

REFRIGERATE *1 hour*

BAKE *at 350° for 1 hour*

Crust

1¾ cups all-purpose flour
1 teaspoon salt
7 tablespoons solid vegetable shortening, chilled
¼ cup cold water

Filling

1 can (15¾ ounces) sweet potato, drained
4 eggs
⅓ cup packed dark-brown sugar
½ teaspoon ground allspice
½ cup dark corn syrup
⅓ cup granulated sugar
1 teaspoon vanilla
1¼ cups pecan halves

Whipped cream or vanilla ice cream for serving (optional)

1. Prepare crust: Mix flour and salt in a large bowl. Cut in shortening with a pastry blender or 2 knives used scissor fashion until mixture resembles coarse crumbs. Sprinkle cold water, 1 tablespoon at a time, over mixture, mixing lightly with a fork after each addition, until dough comes together. Loosely shape dough into a ball; cut into quarters. Shape 1 piece into a disc; wrap in plastic wrap. Shape remaining 3 pieces together into another disc; wrap. Refrigerate both discs 1 hour.

2. Line a baking sheet with waxed paper. Roll out smaller disc of dough on prepared baking sheet to a ¼-inch thickness. Using a 1¾-inch holly-leaf cutter, cut about 30 leaves into dough; lift and reserve scraps; place baking sheet with leaves in refrigerator. On a lightly floured surface, roll out larger disc of dough to a 12-inch round. Fit into a 9-inch pie plate, trimming dough even with edge of plate rim. Refrigerate pie plate with dough.

3. Gather dough scraps together on floured surface; roll out to a ¼-inch thickness. Using a 1¾-inch maple-leaf cutter, cut out about 12 maple leaves. Transfer leaves to baking sheet with holly leaves and refrigerate 30 minutes, until firm.

4. Remove piecrust and baking sheet with leaves from refrigerator. Dip a pastry brush into water; brush over a small section of crust edge. Arrange holly leaves, overlapping, along edge, moistening overlapping portions of leaves. Continue in this manner to arrange leaves all around crust edge. Set crust aside.

5. Heat oven to 350°.

6. Prepare filling: With mixer on medium high speed, beat sweet potato, 1 egg, dark-brown sugar and allspice in a medium-size bowl 2 to 3 minutes, until smooth. Scrape mixture into crust, spreading evenly.

7. Whisk together corn syrup, granulated sugar, vanilla and remaining 3 eggs in a clean medium-size bowl until well combined and smooth. Stir in pecans. Pour over sweet potato mixture in crust.

8. Arrange maple leaves decoratively on top of pecan mixture. Bake pie in heated 350° oven 1 hour or until filling is set and crust is lightly browned. Cool pie on a wire rack. Serve with whipped cream or vanilla ice cream if desired.

Maple-Walnut Pie

Decorate the center of the pie with baked pastry maple leaves, if you can. Shown on page 83.

MAKES *8 servings*

PREP *5 minutes*

BAKE *at 400° for 16 minutes, then at 300° for 35 minutes*

2 refrigerated ready-to-use piecrusts
3 eggs
¼ cup sugar
1 cup maple syrup
¼ cup (½ stick) unsalted butter, melted
1 tablespoon molasses
¼ teaspoon salt
1½ cups walnut pieces

1. Position oven rack in bottom third of oven. Heat oven to 400°.

2. Unfold 1 piecrust and fit into a 9-inch pie plate; crimp edge. Line crust with aluminum foil; fill with dried beans or rice. Unfold second crust onto a work surface. Using a 2- to 3-inch maple-leaf cutter, cut out 5 or 6 maple leaves. Place pie shell and leaf cutouts on a baking sheet.

3. Bake in heated 400° oven 6 minutes, until pastry is light brown. Transfer pie shell and leaf cutouts to a wire rack to cool. Leave oven on. Remove foil with beans from pie shell.

4. With a mixer on medium speed, beat eggs and sugar in a medium-size bowl 3 minutes, until blended and thick. Beat in syrup, butter, molasses and salt.

5. Spread walnuts evenly on bottom of piecrust. Pour egg mixture over walnuts.

6. Bake pie in heated 400° oven 10 minutes. Lower oven temperature to 300°. Bake pie 35 minutes or until filling is set in center. Transfer to a wire rack to cool. Arrange pastry leaves on top of filling.

Ruby Grape Tart

In a splendid switch from customary fruit toppers, ruby red grapes glisten on a layer of orange-flavored cream cheese.

MAKES *8 servings*

PREP *25 minutes*

BAKE *at 400° for 12 minutes*

1 refrigerated ready-to-use piecrust
1 package (8 ounces) cream cheese, at room temperature
¾ cup confectioners' sugar
2 teaspoons grated orange rind
1 tablespoon orange liqueur or orange juice
3 to 4 cups red seedless grapes
¼ cup currant jelly

1. Heat oven to 400°.

2. Unfold piecrust and fit into bottom and up sides of an 11-inch tart pan with a removable bottom. Trim edge of crust to extend ¼ inch above sides; fold to inside of tart, pressing to seal. Prick bottom of crust all over with a fork.

3. Place tart pan on a baking sheet. Bake in heated 400° oven 12 minutes or until crust is golden. Transfer to a wire rack to cool.

4. With a mixer on medium speed, beat cream cheese, sugar, orange rind and liqueur in a small bowl 2 minutes, until smooth. Spread cream cheese mixture evenly in crust. Arrange grapes on top, placing larger grapes at edge, smaller ones in center.

5. Heat jelly in a small saucepan over low heat until melted. Brush over tart. Refrigerate tart until jelly is set.

Peaches and Cream Tart

Use only the best ripe peaches as a luscious topping. Then enjoy the tart guilt-free: Each slice has only 180 calories and 5 grams of fat.

Peaches and Cream Tart

PREP *20 minutes*

BAKE *at 375° for 5 to 7 minutes*

COOK *3 minutes*

REFRIGERATE *2 hours 30 minutes*

Crust

1½	cups reduced-fat graham cracker crumbs (about 11 whole crackers)
6	tablespoons diet margarine
1	teaspoon ground cinnamon

Filling

¼	cup sugar
3	tablespoons all-purpose flour
1	envelope unflavored gelatin
¼	teaspoon salt
1½	cups skim milk
1	egg
1	teaspoon vanilla
½	cup frozen fat-free nondairy whipped topping, thawed
2	peaches, peeled, pitted and thinly sliced
2	tablespoons peach jam

1. Heat oven to 375°.

2. Prepare crust: Stir together graham cracker crumbs, margarine and cinnamon in a small bowl until blended. Press mixture evenly onto bottom and up sides of a 9-inch tart pan with a removable bottom.

3. Bake crust in heated 375° oven 5 to 7 minutes, until lightly colored. Transfer to a wire rack to cool.

4. Meanwhile, prepare filling: Whisk together sugar, flour, gelatin and salt in medium-size saucepan. Whisk in milk and egg. Cook over medium heat, stirring constantly, until mixture coats back of spoon, about 3 minutes; do not boil. Remove pan from heat. Stir in vanilla.

5. Place saucepan in a large bowl filled with ice cubes and water. Refrigerate until mixture mounds when dropped from a spoon, about 30 minutes.

6. Fold whipped topping into custard. Spoon filling into crust in pan. Refrigerate until firm, about 2 hours.

7. Arrange sliced peaches in concentric circles on top of tart. Heat jam in a small saucepan over low heat until melted. Brush over tart. Serve immediately or refrigerate until serving.

Pear Tartlets with Ginger Pastry Cream

Slice the pear as thinly as possible, then fan it out across the lush ginger cream.

MAKES *6 servings*

PREP *15 minutes*

COOK *4 to 5 minutes*

6   **frozen puff pastry shells (one 10-ounce box)**
½   **cup sugar**
2   **tablespoons cornstarch**
⅛   **teaspoon salt**
1   **cup milk**
1   **slice fresh ginger (⅛ inch thick), peeled**
2   **egg yolks**
1   **tablespoon butter**
½   **teaspoon vanilla**
½   **cup water**
1   **tablespoon lemon juice**
1   **ripe Anjou, Bartlett or Bosc pear**
3   **tablespoons apple jelly**

1. Bake pastry shells according to package directions. Cool completely on a wire rack; push down middle of each shell to form a cavity. Set aside.

2. Stir together sugar, cornstarch and salt in a small saucepan. Over medium-high heat, stir in milk. Add ginger; bring mixture to boiling, stirring constantly; cook 1 to 2 minutes or until thickened.

3. Beat egg yolks in a small bowl until light colored and thickened. Stir in a small amount of hot milk mixture. Stir yolk mixture into milk mixture in saucepan; cook, stirring constantly, over medium heat 2 minutes or until pastry cream thickens and registers 160° on an instant-read thermometer. Add butter and vanilla; stir until butter is melted.

4. Strain pastry cream through a fine-mesh sieve into a medium-size bowl. Place plastic wrap directly on surface. Refrigerate until cool.

5. Meanwhile, mix water and lemon juice in a small bowl. Peel pear. Cut in half lengthwise; core. Cut each half crosswise into thirds. Add to bowl.

6. Place each pastry shell on a dessert plate. Spoon pastry cream into shells, dividing equally. One at a time, slice each pear piece crosswise as thinly as possible; arrange in a fan on top of a tartlet.

7. Melt apple jelly in a small saucepan over medium heat. Brush over pears and pastry.

Rich 'n' Creamy Pear Pie

Best served warm with a generous dollop of freshly whipped cream. Shown on page 83.

MAKES *8 servings*

PREP *10 minutes*

BAKE *at 400° for 40 minutes*

1   refrigerated ready-to-use piecrust
1   egg white, lightly beaten
1   cup sour cream
2   whole eggs
⅓   cup granulated sugar
½   teaspoon vanilla
3   tablespoons light-brown sugar
3   tablespoons cake crumbs or graham cracker crumbs
1   tablespoon butter
2   ripe pears
    Whipped cream for garnish (optional)

1. Unfold piecrust; ease into a 9-inch tart pan with a removable bottom. Trim overhang. Brush bottom with egg white.

2. Place a baking sheet in oven. Heat oven to 400°.

3. Stir together sour cream, eggs, granulated sugar and vanilla in a small bowl. Crumble together brown sugar, cake crumbs and butter in another small bowl.

4. Peel, halve and core pears. Cut lengthwise into ¼-inch-thick slices. Arrange slices in piecrust in 2 concentric rings, overlapping slightly. Pour sour cream mixture over pears. Sprinkle with crumb mixture.

5. Bake tart on heated baking sheet in heated 400° oven 40 minutes or until cream is set and top is lightly golden.

6. Serve warm or at room temperature, garnished with whipped cream if desired.

Pear Tart Tatin

We were surprised, but canned pears worked better than fresh in this variation on the traditional French apple upside-down tart.

MAKES *8 servings*

PREP *10 minutes*

BAKE *at 425° for 25 minutes*

¼   cup plus 2 tablespoons packed dark-brown sugar
2   cans (15¼ ounces each) pear halves, in syrup, drained and blotted dry
    Single-Crust Pie Pastry (recipe, page 88)
¼   cup plus 2 tablespoons pecans, finely chopped

1. Heat oven to 425°.

2. Sprinkle ¼ cup brown sugar over bottom of a 10-inch nonstick skillet. Arrange 10 pear halves, cut side up, in a ring in skillet. Fill center with remaining pears. Sprinkle remaining 2 tablespoons sugar over pears.

3. Roll out dough on a lightly floured surface to an 11-inch round. Spread ¼ cup pecans evenly over crust. Using rolling pin, press nuts into crust. Be careful not to tear crust; if it should tear, pinch holes closed.

4. Gently lift crust and invert onto pears in skillet. Fold under edges of crust and tuck between pears and sides of skillet.

5. Bake in heated 425° oven 25 minutes or until crust is golden. Transfer skillet to a wire rack; let stand 15 minutes or until pan is cool enough to handle. Invert a serving platter on top of skillet; flip tart onto platter. Sprinkle remaining 2 tablespoons pecans on top and serve warm or at room temperature.

NOTE: *Tart can be made several hours ahead. Flip onto serving platter and let stand, loosely covered, at room temperature.*

Streusel-Topped Apple Sour Cream Pie

Be ready with a sheet of foil to place over the streusel topping if it starts to brown too quickly—you don't want anything to spoil the balance of nutty-sweet crumbles and bubbly apple slices.

MAKES *10 servings*
PREP *25 minutes*
COOK *12 to 15 minutes*
BAKE *at 375° for 50 to 60 minutes*
STAND *4 hours*

Streusel

1   cup chopped walnuts
¾   cup packed dark-brown sugar
½   cup all-purpose flour
1   teaspoon ground cinnamon
⅛   teaspoon salt
6   tablespoons (¾ stick) unsalted butter, cut into pieces and chilled

Pie

2   tablespoons unsalted butter
3   pounds baking apples, such as Granny Smith, peeled, cored and sliced into eighths
1   cup granulated sugar
1   teaspoon vanilla
¾   cup sour cream
1   egg, lightly beaten
¼   cup all-purpose flour
⅛   teaspoon salt
⅛   teaspoon ground nutmeg
1   deep-dish 9-inch frozen pie shell, thawed

1. Prepare streusel: Whisk together walnuts, brown sugar, flour, cinnamon and salt. With fingertips, rub butter into flour mixture until crumbly.

2. Heat oven to 375°.

3. Prepare pie: Melt butter in a large heavy saucepan over medium heat. Stir in apples. Stir in ½ cup granulated sugar; cook, stirring frequently, 12 to 15 minutes, until apples are barely tender. Stir in ½ teaspoon vanilla. Remove from heat; set aside to cool.

4. In a medium-size bowl, stir together sour cream, egg, remaining ½ cup granulated sugar, flour, remaining ½ teaspoon vanilla, salt and nutmeg.

5. Drain apples in a colander; fold into sour cream mixture. Spoon into pie shell; tilt shell slightly so liquid flows evenly around apples. Sprinkle streusel over top. Place pie on a baking sheet.

6. Bake in heated 375° oven 50 to 60 minutes, until apples are fork-tender. Check pie after baking 30 minutes; tent loosely with aluminum foil if topping is browning quickly. Transfer pie to a wire rack and let stand at least 4 hours before serving.

NOTE: *Pie can be made a day ahead, covered, and refrigerated. Let stand at room temperature at least an hour before serving.*

Cran-Apple Pie

Savor all the flavors of fall under one crust! For extra oomph, add ½ teaspoon cinnamon to the flour when you mix the pastry.

MAKES *12 servings*

PREP *1 hour*

BAKE *at 425° for 15 minutes, then at 400° for 40 to 45 minutes*

1   cup fresh or frozen cranberries, chopped
½   cup apple juice
½   cup granulated sugar
½   teaspoon grated orange rind
    Double-Crust Pie Pastry (recipe, page 88)
8   McIntosh apples (about 2½ pounds)
½   cup packed light-brown sugar
3   tablespoons cornstarch
    Pinch ground cinnamon
    Pinch ground cloves
1   egg yolk
1   tablespoon milk

1. Combine cranberries, apple juice, 3 tablespoons granulated sugar and orange rind in a small saucepan. Bring to simmering over high heat; lower heat; simmer, stirring occasionally, 12 minutes or until consistency of cranberry sauce. Let cool.

2. Heat oven to 425°.

3. For bottom crust, roll out 1 disc of pie pastry on a floured surface to a 13-inch round. Fit into a 9-inch pie plate. Smooth pastry over bottom and up sides of plate. Trim off excess dough.

4. Peel and core apples; cut each crosswise into eight ½-inch-thick slices. Combine with ¼ cup granulated sugar, brown sugar, cornstarch, cinnamon and cloves in a large bowl. Add cooled cranberry mixture and egg yolk; stir well to mix. Scrape into prepared crust. Spread apples, mounding high in center; do not pack down.

5. Roll out remaining disc of pastry to a 13-inch round. Place over filling. Trim dough, leaving a ¾-inch overhang. Fold top crust under bottom crust; press to seal; flute edge. Cut 10 vents in top. Brush crust with milk; sprinkle with remaining 1 tablespoon granulated sugar.

6. Place pie on a baking sheet. Bake in heated 425° oven 15 minutes. Lower oven temperature to 400°. Bake 40 to 45 minutes or until golden brown. (Check pie after 30 minutes; if crust is browning too quickly, tent edges loosely with strips of foil.) Remove to a wire rack; cool at least 40 minutes.

BEST BAKING APPLES

Choose Granny Smith and Rome for their crisp, tart taste. McIntosh and Golden Delicious have a tender, juicy sweetness. Other baking apple options: sweet-tart Jonagold, sweet, juicy Fuji and Empire—a cross between McIntosh and Red Delicious.

Cran-Apple Pie

Lemon Meringue Pie

Star of diners across America, this tart treat with its billowing meringue satisfies every time. For easiest cutting, plan to have the completed pie come out of the oven 3 hours before serving.

MAKES *8 servings*

PREP *35 minutes*

REFRIGERATE *1½ hours*

COOK *18 minutes*

BAKE *crust at 425° for about 23 minutes; pie at 325° for about 33 minutes*

Crust

Sweet Pie Pastry (recipe, page 84)

Lemon Filling

3	to 4 large lemons
1¾	cups sugar
¾	cup cornstarch
¼	teaspoon salt
2¼	cups water
6	eggs, separated
2	tablespoons butter or margarine

Meringue

6	egg whites from filling above plus 2 more whites
½	teaspoon cream of tartar
¾	cup sugar

1. Roll out pastry on a lightly floured surface to a 13-inch round. Fit pastry into a 9-inch pie plate, being careful not to stretch. Roll edge of pastry under to form a stand-up edge; flute edge. Refrigerate crust 30 minutes.

2. Meanwhile, heat oven to 425°.

3. Remove pie plate with pastry from refrigerator. Prick pastry all over with a fork. Line pastry shell with foil; fill with dried beans, rice or pie weights.

4. Bake pastry in heated 425° oven 15 minutes. Remove foil with beans. Continue to bake 8 to 10 minutes or until edge of pastry is golden brown. Cool completely on a wire rack.

5. Prepare filling: Grate 2 tablespoons rind and squeeze ¾ cup juice from lemons. Combine sugar, cornstarch and salt in a large saucepan. Gradually stir in water and lemon juice until mixture is completely smooth. Cook over medium heat, stirring constantly, until mixture thickens and bubbles, 15 to 20 minutes. Then cook another 2 to 3 minutes, stirring constantly. Remove from heat.

6. Using a fork, beat egg yolks slightly in a small bowl. Quickly stir ½ cup hot lemon mixture into yolks. Stir yolk mixture into remaining lemon mixture in saucepan. Cook over low heat, stirring constantly, 1 minute; do not overcook or eggs will begin to set up.

7. Remove saucepan from heat. Stir in butter until melted. Stir in lemon rind. Pour filling into cooled pastry shell.

8. Place oven rack in lower third of oven. Heat oven to 325°.

9. Prepare meringue: With a mixer on low speed, beat 8 egg whites and cream of tartar in a large bowl until foamy. On high speed, slowly beat in ¾ cup sugar, 1 tablespoon at a time, until stiff peaks form, about 3 minutes. Spoon meringue over pie filling, spreading evenly and sealing meringue to edge of crust to prevent shrinkage. Swirl meringue into peaks.

10. Bake pie in lower third of heated 325° oven 30 minutes or until an instant-read thermometer inserted in meringue registers 140°. Bake 3 minutes longer; meringue should be golden brown. Let cool on a wire rack at room temperature up to 2 hours. Refrigerate 1 hour before slicing (longer chilling makes the meringue difficult to cut).

Lemony Fruit Tart

Who says a tart has to be round? Our striking rectangle is easy to arrange and really shows off the rows of kiwi—it's easy to slice, too.

MAKES *8 servings*

PREP *30 minutes*

REFRIGERATE *30 minutes*

COOK *10 minutes*

BAKE *at 450° for about 18 minutes*

Crust

1½ cups all-purpose flour
½   teaspoon salt
⅓   cup butter, cut into small pieces and chilled
¼   cup solid vegetable shortening
4   to 5 tablespoons ice water

Filling

¾   cup heavy cream
3   tablespoons confectioners' sugar
2   tablespoons prepared lemon curd
1   teaspoon grated lemon rind

Topping

4   kiwi, peeled and thinly sliced into rounds
8   red seedless grapes
¼   cup pasteurized egg whites
1   tablespoon granulated sugar

1. Prepare crust: Whisk together flour and salt in a medium-size bowl. Cut in butter and shortening with a pastry blender or 2 knives used scissor fashion until mixture resembles coarse crumbs.

2. Sprinkle water, 1 tablespoon at a time, over mixture, mixing lightly with a fork after each addition, until pastry is just moist enough to hold together. Gather pastry into ball and press into a disc. Wrap in plastic wrap; refrigerate 30 minutes.

3. Heat oven to 450°.

4. Place pastry between 2 sheets of plastic wrap on a work surface. Roll out pastry to a 13 x 8½-inch rectangle to fit an 11 x 7-inch pan (see note). Fit pastry into pan, discarding plastic wrap and folding under any excess dough. Prick bottom lightly all over with a fork. Line crust with foil; fill with dried beans or pie weights.

5. Bake in heated 450° oven 8 minutes. Remove foil and weights. Bake 8 to 10 minutes longer, until crust is golden. Cool crust completely in pan on a wire rack.

6. Prepare filling: Meanwhile, with mixer on medium-high speed, beat cream and confectioners' sugar in a medium-size bowl until stiff peaks form. Fold in lemon curd and lemon rind. Spread filling evenly over bottom of cooled crust.

7. Prepare topping: Arrange kiwi slices in crosswise rows on top of filling, overlapping slightly. Dip each grape into egg white, letting excess drip off, then dip into sugar; arrange on top of tart. Serve slightly chilled or at room temperature.

NOTE: *For a round tart, use a 9-inch tart pan with a removable bottom. Roll out crust into an 11-inch round. Bake as for rectangular tart.*

Lemon Pie

After a hearty meal, there's something refreshing about a citrusy dessert. Here, a garnish of toasted slivered almonds adds an elegance and pleasing crunch in contrast to the silky custard.

Lemon Pie

MAKES *10 servings*

PREP *10 minutes*

BAKE *at 350° for 20 to 25 minutes*

1   cup sugar
2   tablespoons all-purpose flour
4   eggs
1   tablespoon grated lemon rind
6   tablespoons lemon juice (from 3 lemons)
½   cup (1 stick) butter, melted
½   teaspoon vanilla
¼   teaspoon almond extract
1   frozen 9-inch deep-dish pie shell
¼   cup slivered almonds, toasted
    (see page 231)

1. Position oven rack in lower third of oven. Heat oven to 350°.

2. Whisk together sugar and flour in a small bowl. Break eggs into a medium-size bowl; add sugar mixture. With a mixer on medium speed, beat until light in color and slightly thickened, about 3 minutes.

3. Stir in lemon rind, lemon juice, butter, vanilla and almond extract. Pour into pie shell.

4. Bake in lower third of heated 350° oven 20 to 25 minutes or until filling is set and lightly browned. Sprinkle toasted almonds over top of the pie. Transfer pie to a wire rack to cool.

Strawberry Rhubarb Pie

Sugar and a little nutmeg are all you need to gussy up these classic harbingers of spring.

MAKES *8 servings*

PREP *10 minutes*

BAKE *at 400° for 50 minutes*

2 **refrigerated ready-to-use piecrusts**
1 **pint (2 cups) strawberries, hulled and quartered**
3 **cups fresh or thawed cut rhubarb (1-inch pieces)**
1 **cup sugar**
⅓ **cup cornstarch**
⅛ **teaspoon salt**
⅛ **teaspoon ground nutmeg**

1. Heat oven to 400°. Unfold 1 piecrust and fit into a 9-inch glass pie plate.

2. Place strawberries, rhubarb, sugar, cornstarch, salt and nutmeg in a large bowl; stir gently to combine—do not crush strawberries or rhubarb.

3. Unfold second piecrust on a lightly floured surface and flatten slightly with a rolling pin. Using a paring knife or cookie cutter, cut out six 1-inch strawberry shapes in a ring around center of crust. Cut out leaf shapes from the strawberry cutouts; reserve the leaves on a sheet of waxed paper.

4. Spoon strawberry filling into crust-lined pie plate. Place second piecrust on top. Fold edge of top piecrust under edge of bottom piecrust; crimp edges of crusts together to seal. Using a little water as glue, arrange piecrust leaves in a ring on crust, inside strawberry cutouts.

5. Bake in heated 400° oven 50 minutes or until crust is golden and filling is bubbly. If edges of crust brown too quickly, cover them with strips of aluminum foil. Transfer pie to a wire rack and cool completely.

Strawberry Rhubarb Pie

Almond-Strawberry Tart

Only the very best springtime berries need apply. Shown on page 82.

MAKES *8 servings*

PREP *25 minutes*

BAKE *at 375° for 20 minutes*

REFRIGERATE *1 hour*

¾ cup plus 2 tablespoons all-purpose flour
⅓ cup slivered almonds, ground or very finely chopped
3 tablespoons sugar
⅛ teaspoon salt
6 tablespoons (¾ stick) unsalted butter or margarine, chilled
1 egg yolk, slightly beaten
2 to 3 tablespoons water
1 box (3.4 ounces) vanilla instant pudding-and-pie-filling mix
1¾ cups sour cream
½ teaspoon almond extract
5 cups strawberries, hulled
¼ cup strawberry jelly
¼ cup sliced almonds, lightly toasted (see page 231)

1. Heat oven to 375°.

2. Combine flour, ground almonds, sugar and salt in a medium-size bowl. Cut in butter with a pastry blender or two knives used scissor fashion until mixture resembles coarse crumbs. Add egg yolk and water; toss with a fork until mixture comes together; shape into a disc.

3. Press dough onto bottom and up sides of a 9 x 1-inch fluted tart pan with a removable bottom, making sides even with top edge of pan. Line pastry with aluminum foil; fill with dried beans, rice or pie weights.

4. Bake in heated 375° oven 15 minutes. Remove foil with weights; return crust to oven. Bake 5 minutes or until lightly golden. Transfer to a wire rack to cool 10 minutes. Remove sides of pan. Cool crust completely on rack.

5. Prepare pudding-and-pie-filling mix according to package directions for pie, substituting sour cream for milk and adding almond extract. Spread pudding in bottom of prepared pie shell. Cover with plastic wrap and refrigerate at least 1 hour.

6. Arrange whole strawberries, hulled end down, on top of pudding.

7. Melt jelly in small saucepan over low heat. Brush carefully over strawberries. Sprinkle toasted almonds on top. Let tart stand at room temperature until ready to serve, up to 2 hours.

TART TECHNIQUE

Fit rolled pastry into tart pan. To make sides even with top edge of pan, press pastry gently over edge, then roll a rolling pin around the top. The excess pastry will be neatly cut off by the pan edge.

Checkerboard Strawberry Pie

Talk about a showstopper! Carry this to the table for oohs and ahhs, then wait for the applause when everyone tastes the amazing blend of berries and white chocolate.

MAKES *8 servings*

PREP *25 minutes*

COOK *5 to 6 minutes*

STAND *2 hours*

REFRIGERATE *4 hours*

Chocolate Crust

1¼ cups graham cracker crumbs (about 10 whole graham crackers)
2 tablespoons unsweetened cocoa powder
2 tablespoons confectioners' sugar
5 tablespoons butter, melted

Filling

¼ cup granulated sugar
3 tablespoons cornstarch
1½ cups milk
1 package (6 ounces) white chocolate chips (1 cup)
1 teaspoon vanilla
3 drops red food coloring
1 container (12 ounces) frozen nondairy topping, thawed
2 cups chopped strawberries (about 1½ pints whole strawberries)

Decoration

6 strawberries
6 striped chocolate kisses, wrapping removed

1. Prepare crust: Mix graham cracker crumbs, cocoa powder and confectioners' sugar in a medium-size bowl. Stir in melted butter until well mixed. Press mixture over bottom and up sides of a 9-inch glass pie plate. Cover and place in freezer until ready to fill.

2. Prepare filling: Mix sugar and cornstarch in a medium-size saucepan. Place over medium heat; gradually stir in milk. Cook over medium-high heat, stirring constantly, until mixture thickens and comes to a boil, about 5 minutes. Remove from heat. Add chocolate chips, vanilla and food coloring, stirring until chocolate is melted and mixture is smooth. Transfer to a large bowl; cover surface directly with plastic wrap. Cool to room temperature, about 2 hours.

3. When cool, whisk chocolate mixture until smooth. Reserve 1 cup whipped topping and fold remainder into chocolate mixture.

4. Spread half of chocolate filling over bottom of prepared crust. Top with chopped strawberries. Spread remaining chocolate filling over strawberries. Refrigerate at least 4 hours.

5. Prepare decoration: Spoon reserved cup whipped topping into a pastry bag fitted with a large star tip. Make a grid over top of pie, piping 1 line across center in 1 direction, 1 line on each side of center line, and then repeating to pipe 3 lines at a right angle to first 3 lines. Pipe a decorative border around edge of pie. Arrange whole strawberries in alternate squares on top of pie. Arrange kisses in remaining alternate squares.

Plum Galette

All it takes is plums, pecans and brown sugar to turn a round of pastry into a rustic masterpiece.

Plum Galette

MAKES *12 servings*

PREP *20 minutes*

BAKE *at 375° for 35 to 40 minutes*

1   box (11 ounces) piecrust mix
3   tablespoons plus ⅓ cup packed brown sugar
⅔   cup chopped pecans
1¼   pounds plums
1   tablespoon all-purpose flour

1. Heat oven to 375°.

2. Combine piecrust mix, 3 tablespoons brown sugar and ⅓ cup pecans in a medium-size bowl. Stir in amount of water recommended on crust box for making a double-crust pie; continue stirring until ingredients come together to form a ball of dough.

3. Roll out dough on a lightly floured surface to a 13-inch round. Loosely roll dough back onto rolling pin; unroll onto an ungreased large baking sheet.

4. Prepare filling: Halve and pit plums; cut each half into 4 slices. Toss slices in a medium-size bowl with remaining ⅓ cup brown sugar, remaining ⅓ cup pecans and flour. Mound filling onto center of dough, leaving a 2-inch border. Spoon any sugar mixture left in bowl on top of filling. Fold border up over filling, working all the way around.

5. Bake in heated 375° oven 35 to 40 minutes, until filling is hot and crust is golden. Cool galette on baking sheet on a wire rack. Serve slightly warm.

Coconut-Strawberry Tartlets

Look for light coconut milk to flavor the filling along with sweetened flake and coconut extract. It's a veritable coconut extravaganza.

MAKES *12 servings* PREP *25 minutes*
BAKE *at 400° for 12 minutes*
COOK *12 to 15 minutes*
REFRIGERATE *30 minutes*

6 frozen pastry tart shells (one 10-ounce package), thawed
1 egg
1 tablespoon water
1 package (3½ ounces) vanilla pudding-and-pie-filling mix (not instant)
1 can (14 ounces) light coconut milk
⅓ cup sweetened flake coconut, chopped
¼ teaspoon coconut extract
2 to 3 pints small or medium strawberries (48 berries), hulled
½ cup strawberry jelly, melted

1. Heat oven to 400°.

2. On a lightly floured surface, roll out each tart shell into a 6-inch round. Mix egg with 1 tablespoon water in a cup. Brush egg wash onto edge of each tart shell, then fold up edge to form a lip. Prick center of each shell with a fork. Place on a baking sheet.

3. Bake in heated 400° oven about 12 minutes, until golden. Remove from oven; gently press down center of shells if puffed up. Cool on a wire rack.

4. Meanwhile, whisk together pudding-and-pie-filling mix and coconut milk in a small saucepan. Stir in flake coconut. Cook according to pudding package directions 12 to 15 minutes, until thickened. Remove from heat. Stir in coconut extract. Press plastic wrap onto surface of pudding. Refrigerate about 30 minutes, until cool to the touch.

5. To assemble, spoon pudding into tart shells, dividing equally. Place strawberries, hulled end down, over pudding. Lightly glaze strawberries with melted strawberry jelly. To serve, cut tarts in half.

Coconut-Strawberry Tartlets

Mocha Crepes with White Chocolate Ganache

Each bite offers at least a few irresistible mini chips adrift in a pool of white chocolate.

MAKES *16 servings*
PREP *20 minutes*
COOK *1 hour 20 minutes*
REFRIGERATE *about 1½ hours*

Crepes

1¼ cups all-purpose flour
2 tablespoons unsweetened cocoa powder
2 tablespoons sugar
1 tablespoon instant espresso coffee powder
½ teaspoon baking powder
½ teaspoon salt
2 cups milk
2 tablespoons butter or margarine, melted
2 eggs
1 teaspoon vanilla

White Chocolate Ganache

2 cups heavy cream
2 boxes (6 ounces each) white baking chocolate, finely chopped
¼ cup coffee-flavored liqueur
½ cup mini chocolate chips

Raspberry Puree

2 packages (10 ounces each) frozen raspberries in syrup, thawed
3 tablespoons cornstarch

Fresh raspberries for garnish (optional)

1. Prepare crepes: Combine flour, cocoa powder, sugar, espresso powder, baking powder and salt in a medium-size bowl. Add milk, butter, eggs and vanilla; beat on low speed until blended. Beat on medium-low just until smooth.

2. Coat an 8-inch nonstick skillet with nonstick cooking spray. Heat over medium heat until a drop of water sizzles. Pour 2 heaping tablespoons batter into skillet and rotate skillet until a film of batter covers bottom. Cook until surface of crepe begins to dry, 2 to 3 minutes. Run a spatula around edge to loosen. Turn over; cook until bottom is lightly browned, about 2 minutes. Remove crepe. Repeat with remaining batter. Stack crepes alternately with sheets of waxed paper and keep covered (see note, below).

3. Prepare ganache: Bring cream to boiling in a heavy medium-size saucepan over medium-high heat. Remove from heat. Stir in white chocolate until melted and smooth. Stir in liqueur. Pour into a bowl, straining through a sieve. Refrigerate 30 minutes, stirring occasionally.

4. Using a whisk or an electric mixer on low speed, beat chocolate mixture just until fluffy, 30 seconds. Refrigerate until chilled, about 1 hour. Then beat on high until thickened, about 30 seconds (do not overbeat). Fold in mini chips. Refrigerate until ready to fill crepes.

5. Meanwhile, prepare puree: Press berries and their liquid through a fine sieve into a small saucepan; discard seeds. Stir in cornstarch; simmer, stirring, until thickened, 1 to 2 minutes. Refrigerate until ready to fill crepes.

6. Just before serving, spoon about 3 tablespoons ganache down center of each crepe. Fold 2 opposite sides over filling. Spoon about 1 tablespoon puree onto each plate; top with a filled crepe. Garnish with fresh raspberries, if desired.

NOTE: *Crepes can be made ahead. Stack alternately with sheets of waxed paper; wrap in plastic. Refrigerate several days, or freeze up to 1 month. To use, thaw unwrapped at room temperature 3 hours.*

Festive Napoleons

Light-as-air layers of crisp phyllo stack prettily with a choice of fillings—raspberries and kiwi, mandarin oranges or chocolate chips.

MAKES *6 Napoleons*

PREP *30 minutes*

BAKE *at 375° for 8 to 10 minutes*

7 sheets phyllo dough, thawed if frozen
2 tablespoons butter, melted
½ pound cream cheese
½ cup sour cream
¼ cup granulated sugar
½ teaspoon vanilla
1 tablespoon raspberry jam
3 kiwi, peeled, sliced ¼ inch thick
1 pint raspberries, halved
1½ teaspoons confectioners' sugar for dusting

1. Heat oven to 375°. Coat 2 baking sheets with cooking spray.

2. Unfold phyllo sheets on a work surface. Cover with plastic wrap and a clean kitchen towel. Keeping unused sheets covered as you work to prevent them from drying out, remove 1 sheet from stack and lay flat. Brush sheet lightly with butter. Repeat with remaining phyllo sheets, buttering each and stacking; leave top sheet unbuttered. Cut stacked sheets lengthwise into thirds and then crosswise into sixths, making 18 rectangles. Place on baking sheets.

3. Bake in heated 375° oven 8 to 10 minutes, until slightly colored. Transfer phyllo rectangles from baking sheet to a wire rack to cool.

4. Meanwhile, with a mixer on medium speed, beat cream cheese, sour cream, sugar and vanilla in a medium-size bowl until light and fluffy. Stir in jam.

5. Spread 1 rounded tablespoon cream cheese mixture over each of 12 phyllo rectangles. Arrange kiwi slices on 6 cheese-topped rectangles; arrange raspberries on remaining cheese-topped rectangles.

6. Place a raspberry rectangle on top of each kiwi rectangle, then top each with a plain rectangle. Dust tops with confectioners' sugar.

Chocolate Chip Napoleons

Prepare Festive Napoleons, omitting jam, kiwi and berries and stirring in 2 tablespoons mini chocolate chips in step 4. Melt 2 ounces semisweet chocolate; drizzle on top of assembled Napoleons.

Mandarin Orange Napoleons

Prepare Festive Napoleons, substituting ¼ teaspoon almond extract for jam and one 11-ounce can mandarin orange segments for kiwi and berries. Drain oranges before arranging on cheese-topped rectangles.

Strawberry-Rhubarb Pockets

The classic springtime duo, wrapped in little packages of puff pastry.

Strawberry-Rhubarb Pockets

MAKES *8 pockets*

PREP *20 minutes*

BAKE *at 400° for 15 to 20 minutes*

1 **pint strawberries, hulled and coarsely chopped**
1¼ **cups fresh or thawed cut rhubarb (½-inch pieces)**
¾ **cup sugar**
1 **teaspoon fresh lemon juice**
2 **tablespoons cornstarch**
1 **package (17¼ ounces) puff pastry sheets, thawed**
Confectioners' sugar for dusting

1. Heat oven to 400°. Coat 8 cups in a standard 12-muffin pan with nonstick cooking spray.

2. Combine strawberries, rhubarb, sugar, lemon juice and cornstarch in medium-size saucepan. Cook over medium-high heat 10 minutes. Reduce heat to medium; cook 2 minutes, until liquid is thickened, clear and bubbly. Let cool slightly.

3. Open pastry sheets on a work surface. Cut each sheet into 4 equal squares. Gently press center of 1 square into bottom of a prepared muffin cup. Spoon in about ¼ cup fruit mixture. Fold 2 opposite corners of pastry over filling; repeat with remaining 2 corners; brush top with water to seal. Repeat with remaining pastry and filling.

4. Bake in heated 400° oven 15 to 20 minutes, until tops are puffed and golden brown. Cool pockets in pan on a wire rack 10 minutes, then remove from pan to a wire rack; cool 5 to 10 minutes. Dust with confectioners' sugar.

Apricot-Cheese Turnovers

Filled with a delectable blend of cheese and fruit, these turnovers are delicious plain or drizzled with a bit of raspberry puree.

MAKES *8 turnovers*

PREP *25 minutes*

BAKE *at 350° for 25 minutes*

Single-Crust Pie Pastry (recipe, page 88)
1   package (8 ounces) cream cheese
½   package (7.5-ounce size) farmer's cheese
½   cup sugar
¼   teaspoon ground cinnamon
1   teaspoon vanilla
1   egg white
½   cup dried apricot halves, chopped
1   whole egg, lightly beaten
     Sugar for sprinkling
1   package (10 ounces) frozen raspberries
     in light syrup, thawed

Apricot-Cheese Turnovers

1. Cut pastry into 8 pieces. On a floured surface, roll out each piece to a 6-inch round. Place pastry on baking sheets; cover; refrigerate until chilled.

2. Meanwhile, with a mixer on medium speed, beat cream cheese, farmer's cheese, sugar, cinnamon and vanilla in a medium-size bowl. Beat in egg white until blended. Stir in apricots.

3. Heat oven to 350°. Coat 2 baking sheets with nonstick cooking spray.

4. Remove pastry from refrigerator. Working with one pastry round at a time, brush beaten egg around edge, forming a 1-inch border; spoon scant ⅓ cup filling in center; fold pastry in half over filling and crimp edges. Place turnovers on prepared baking sheets. Brush with egg; sprinkle sugar on top.

5. Bake in heated 350° oven 25 minutes, until golden. Cool on wire racks.

6. Meanwhile, place raspberries in a food processor; whirl to puree. To remove seeds, press through a fine-mesh sieve. Refrigerate until ready to serve. Drizzle raspberry puree over pastries as desired.

Éclairs

These mouth-watering eclairs made their debut in a 1978 article featuring "Wickedly Delicious Pastries" and have been a frequent reader request ever since.

MAKES *12 eclairs*

PREP *30 minutes*

COOK *9 minutes*

REFRIGERATE *custard 2 hours*

BAKE *puffs at 425° for 35 minutes; let stand 10 minutes*

Vanilla Custard

2½ cups milk
5 egg yolks
¾ cup sugar
⅔ cup sifted all-purpose flour
2 tablespoons butter or margarine
1 tablespoon vanilla
Heavy cream or milk, as needed

Cream Puff Dough

1 cup water
½ cup (1 stick) butter or margarine, cut into small pieces
1 teaspoon sugar
¼ teaspoon salt
1 cup sifted all-purpose flour
4 whole eggs

Glaze

1 square (1 ounce) unsweetened chocolate
1 tablespoon butter or margarine
2 tablespoons water
1 cup confectioners' sugar
1 teaspoon vanilla
2 squares (1 ounce each) white baking chocolate (optional)

1. Prepare custard: Heat milk in a large heavy saucepan over medium heat until small bubbles appear around edge.

2. Beat egg yolks and sugar in a large bowl about 3 minutes, until pale yellow and thick. Beat in flour. Gradually beat in hot milk. Pour mixture back into saucepan. Cook, stirring, over medium-high heat until mixture comes to boiling and thickens. Lower heat; cook, stirring, 2 minutes or until very thick (mixture will be lumpy at first, but lumps will disappear). Remove from heat.

3. Stir in butter and vanilla until butter is melted. Place waxed paper directly on surface. Refrigerate at least 2 hours.

4. Meanwhile, prepare dough: Heat water, butter, sugar and salt in a medium-size saucepan over medium heat to a full, rolling boil.

5. Add flour all at once; stir vigorously with a wooden spoon until mixture forms a thick, smooth ball that leaves sides of pan clean, about 1 minute. Continue to cook, stirring, another 2 minutes.

6. Remove saucepan from heat. Add eggs, one at a time, beating well after each addition with a wooden spoon until dough is shiny and smooth, about 30 seconds.

7. Heat oven to 425°.

8. Attach a large plain tip to a pastry bag (or use bag without tip); spoon dough into bag. Press dough out onto ungreased baking sheets, making 12 strips, each 4 or 5 inches long and 1 inch wide; space strips 1½ inches apart. Or use a spoon to shape dough into strips.

9. Bake in heated 425° oven 35 minutes or until dough is puffed and golden brown. Turn oven off; let puffs sit in oven, with door slightly ajar, 10 minutes. Transfer puffs to wire a rack to cool completely.

10. When puffs are cooled and custard is gelled, fit a pastry bag with a small plain tip and fill with custard. (If chilled custard mixture is too stiff, stir in 2 to 4 tablespoons heavy cream or milk, 1 tablespoon at a time.)

11. Make a small hole in one end of each puff with tip of a knife. Press filling through hole into each puff. Or split puffs lengthwise, spoon filling in, and replace tops.

12. Prepare glaze: Place chocolate, butter and water in top of a double boiler over barely simmering, not boiling, water; stir until chocolate and butter are melted and smooth. Remove from heat. Stir in confectioners' sugar and vanilla. Spread warm glaze over eclairs. Let stand until glaze is firm.

13. If desired, melt white chocolate in same manner and drizzle over tops.

ECLAIRS MADE EASY

Bring butter mixture to a full rolling boil. Pour flour all at once into saucepan.

Stir vigorously until mixture clumps and leaves side of pan; cook, stirring, 2 minutes.

Remove pan from heat; add eggs, one at a time, stirring well after each addition.

Mini Butterscotch Phyllo Cups

Prebaked shells cradle sweetened cream cheese and a pecan half for divine little pick-me-ups.

MAKES *30 mini cups*

PREP *20 minutes*

COOK *5 minutes*

REFRIGERATE *about 1 hour*

½ **cup butterscotch chips**
2 **tablespoons milk**
6 **ounces cream cheese, at room temperature, cut into chunks**
2 **packages prebaked phyllo cups (30 cups total)**
⅔ **cup semisweet chocolate chips**
30 **pecan halves**

1. Melt butterscotch chips and 1 tablespoon milk in top of a double boiler over barely simmering, not boiling, water, stirring until smooth. Whisk in cream cheese, a few chunks at a time, and whisk until smooth. Divide mixture among phyllo cups, using about 1 teaspoon filling per cup. Place cups on a baking sheet and refrigerate about 1 hour, until chilled.

2. In a clean double-boiler top, melt chocolate chips and remaining 1 tablespoon milk as before. Spoon into a pastry bag fitted with a medium-large round tip. One at a time, pipe a large dot of chocolate on top of filling in each phyllo cup and then press a pecan half onto each dot.

3. Refrigerate cups 10 minutes, until chocolate is relatively firm to the touch. Remove cups from refrigerator 10 to 15 minutes before serving for optimum flavor of filling.

Apple Pandowdy, page 120

Fruit Treats

Fruit Compote, *page 137*

Cherry Streusel Delights, *page 121*

Banana Baked Apples

For all the pleasure of a baked apple but none of the fat, turn to our version—a filling of bananas, apricots and raisins replaces all the usual butter.

MAKES *4 servings*

PREP *20 minutes*

BAKE *at 350° for 1 hour*

2   cups apple cider
4   dried apricots or pitted prunes, finely chopped
3   tablespoons raisins
4   large, firm, tart apples, such as Granny Smith
¼   cup fat-free wheat-and-barley nugget cereal or other crunchy cereal
3   tablespoons light-brown sugar
½   teaspoon ground cinnamon
1   banana
2   tablespoons orange liqueur
2   tablespoons maple syrup
2   teaspoons cornstarch

1. Warm cider in a small saucepan. Remove from heat; add apricots and raisins. Let stand 15 minutes to soften.

2. Using a large melon baller or an apple corer, core each apple, starting at the top and making a hole about 1 inch in diameter but not cutting through bottom.

3. Heat oven to 350°.

4. Remove apricots and raisins from pan using a slotted spoon and transfer to a medium-size bowl, reserving cider. Add cereal, brown sugar and cinnamon to apricots and raisins. Chop banana. Stir banana and 1 tablespoon liqueur into fruit mixture. Spoon mixture into apples, packing firmly and mounding generously on top.

5. Place apples in a small glass baking dish. With a wooden skewer, deeply pierce sides and top of apples, taking care holes do not cut completely through bottom. Using a teaspoon, drizzle syrup over top and sides of apples, filling holes. Add reserved cider to baking dish.

6. Bake apples in heated 350° oven until they are soft and filling is lightly browned, about 1 hour. If filling browns too quickly, cover loosely with aluminum foil.

7. Transfer apples to serving bowls. Strain pan juices into a small saucepan. Heat to boiling. Dissolve cornstarch in remaining 1 tablespoon liqueur in a cup; whisk into saucepan. Return sauce to boiling. Pour over apples. Serve at once.

START-TO-FINISH BANANA BAKED APPLES

Using a large melon baller or an apple corer, core each apple; do not cut through bottom.

Spoon banana mixture into apples, packing firmly and mounding generously on top.

With a wooden skewer, pierce sides and top of apples, taking care holes do not cut completely through bottom.

Apple-Custard Enchiladas

No one will guess this dessert has fewer than 200 calories a serving and a mere 2 grams of fat. Thank nonfat tortillas and milk. Shown on page 126.

MAKES *8 servings*
PREP *15 minutes*
COOK *17 minutes*
BAKE *at 350° for 10 to 12 minutes*

Custard

1½ cups nonfat milk
¼ cup granulated sugar
2 tablespoons cornstarch
   Pinch salt
1 egg
¼ teaspoon vanilla

Filling

¼ cup boiling water
2 tablespoons sweetened dried cranberries, chopped
1 tablespoon butter
2 large Golden Delicious or other sweet apples, peeled, cored and sliced (2¼ cups)
¾ teaspoon ground cinnamon
   Pinch ground nutmeg
2 tablespoons packed dark-brown sugar
2 tablespoons water
½ teaspoon granulated sugar

8 nonfat flour tortillas (6-inch)

1. Heat oven to 350°.

2. Prepare custard: Bring milk to boiling in a small saucepan over medium heat. Meanwhile, whisk together sugar, cornstarch, salt and egg in a small bowl. Whisk a small amount of hot milk into cornstarch mixture; then stir cornstarch mixture into milk in saucepan. Lower heat to medium-low; cook milk mixture, stirring, until thickened, about 6 minutes. Remove saucepan from heat. Stir in vanilla. Cover saucepan and set aside.

3. Prepare filling: Bring water to boiling in a small saucepan. Add cranberries. Remove from heat; let stand 5 to 10 minutes, until cranberries are plump.

4. Meanwhile, melt butter in a 10-inch skillet over medium heat. Add apples, ½ teaspoon cinnamon and nutmeg; cook, stirring occasionally, until apples are softened, 7 to 10 minutes. Stir in brown sugar; cook, stirring, until apples are coated and thickened slightly, about 2 minutes. Remove skillet from heat.

5. Drain cranberries; stir half into apple mixture in skillet.

6. Mix water and granulated sugar in a small bowl. Place tortillas on a work surface. Brush each with sugar water; spoon ¼ cup apple mixture onto center; top with 2 tablespoons custard. Roll up tortillas; place seam side down in a 12 x 7-inch glass baking dish. Sprinkle remaining ¼ teaspoon cinnamon over top. Cover dish tightly with aluminum foil. Reserve remaining custard and cranberries for serving.

7. Bake enchiladas in heated 350° oven 10 to 12 minutes or until light golden brown. Serve warm; spoon reserved custard over each serving and sprinkle reserved cranberries on top.

Apple Dumplings

Season Granny Smith apples with cinnamon, brown sugar and a smidgen of apricot marmalade, wrap in a coat of pastry and bake—then enjoy their homey goodness.

MAKES *8 servings*

PREP *25 minutes*

REFRIGERATE *1 hour*

BAKE *at 400° for 30 to 35 minutes*

2½ cups all-purpose flour
 1 tablespoon baking powder
 ½ teaspoon salt
 ½ cup (1 stick) cold unsalted butter, cut into small pieces
 ¼ cup solid vegetable shortening, cut into small pieces and chilled
 ½ to ¾ cup milk
 4 small Granny Smith apples
 4 cinnamon sticks (2- to 3-inch)
 2 teaspoons apricot marmalade
 ¼ cup granulated sugar
 ¼ cup packed light-brown sugar
     Milk for brushing
     Granulated sugar for sprinkling

1. Whisk together flour, baking powder and salt in a large bowl. Cut in butter and shortening with a pastry blender or 2 knives used scissor fashion until mixture resembles coarse meal.

2. Stir in enough milk to make a soft dough. Turn out dough onto a lightly floured surface. Gently knead a few times; do not overwork. Shape into a disc; wrap in plastic wrap; refrigerate at least 30 minutes.

3. Peel apples. Using a large melon baller or an apple corer, core each apple, starting at the top and making a hole about 1 inch in diameter but not cutting through bottom.

4. Grease a baking sheet. Divide dough into 4 equal pieces. Roll out 1 piece on a lightly floured surface to a 10-inch square.

5. Place an apple in center of pastry square. Insert 1 cinnamon stick in hollow; spoon in ½ teaspoon marmalade, 1 tablespoon granulated sugar and 1 tablespoon brown sugar. Lightly brush exposed surface of pastry with water. Repeat with remaining apples.

6. Fold up pastry, smoothing over apple, pressing folds to seal and gathering corners together at top; twist corners decoratively to make a tight seal. (Or trim excess dough and use to decorate top.) Repeat with remaining pieces of dough and apples. Place dumplings on prepared baking sheet. Refrigerate at least 30 minutes.

7. Heat oven to 400°.

8. Remove baking sheet with dumplings from refrigerator. Brush each dumpling with milk; sprinkle granulated sugar on top. Bake in heated 400° oven 30 to 35 minutes or until pastry is golden brown.

9. Serve dumplings warm or at room temperature. Remove cinnamon sticks and cut each dumpling in half vertically.

APPLE DUMPLING WRAP-UP

Insert cinnamon stick in hollow center of apple; spoon in marmalade and sugars.

Lightly brush exposed surface of pastry with water.

Apple and Apricot Betty

According to Southern lore, kitchen servants were often referred to as Betty. This type of dessert—with alternating layers of fruit and buttered cake or cookie crumbs—is one they frequently prepared.

MAKES *8 servings*

PREP *15 minutes*

BAKE *at 400° for about 35 minutes*

Apple and Apricot Betty

3   cups pound cake crumbs (from about a half of a pound cake, broken or whirled in a food processor)

¼   cup (½ stick) unsalted butter, melted

¼   teaspoon salt

3   to 4 medium McIntosh apples, peeled, cored and thinly sliced (4 cups)

7   to 8 fresh apricots, peeled, pitted and cut into quarters (2 cups) (see note, below)

½   cup packed brown sugar

½   cup sliced almonds

2   tablespoons grated orange rind

2   tablespoons unsalted butter, cut into small pieces

1. Heat oven to 400°.

2. Mix pound cake crumbs, melted butter and salt in a medium-size bowl.

3. Mix apples, apricots, sugar, almonds and orange rind in another medium-size bowl.

4. Sprinkle one-fourth of crumb mixture evenly onto bottom of a shallow 2½-quart baking dish. Spoon one-third of fruit mixture evenly on top. Continue to add alternating layers of crumbs and fruit, ending with a final layer of crumbs. Dot butter on top.

5. Cover dish with lid or aluminum foil. Bake in heated 400° oven 30 minutes. Uncover; bake 5 minutes or until topping is browned and apples are tender.

NOTE: *2 cups peach slices can be substituted for apricots.*

Apple Pandowdy

In this old-timey preparation, cooked apples are baked under a biscuit or pastry crust. In early American kitchens, the crust was broken up—according to legend, this was known as dowdying—and pressed back into the fruit just before it finished baking. Shown on page 114.

MAKES *8 servings*

PREP *15 minutes*

BAKE *at 400° for 35 minutes*

Dough

1   cup all-purpose flour
¼   cup sugar
1   teaspoon baking powder
¼   teaspoon salt
½   cup (1 stick) unsalted butter, cut into small pieces
¼   cup water

Filling

7   small apples, peeled, cored and thinly sliced (6 cups)
2   tablespoons lemon juice
2   tablespoons all-purpose flour
1   teaspoon ground cinnamon
½   cup maple syrup
1   tablespoon unsalted butter, cut into small pieces
1   tablespoon sugar
    Heavy cream for serving (optional)

1. Heat oven to 400°. Butter a shallow 2½-quart baking dish.

2. Prepare dough: Whisk together flour, sugar, baking powder and salt in a medium-size bowl. Cut in butter with a pastry blender or 2 knives used scissor fashion until mixture resembles coarse crumbs. Add water, stirring just to moisten.

3. Prepare filling: Combine apples and lemon juice in a large bowl and toss to coat. Sprinkle with flour and cinnamon; toss to coat. Transfer to a large skillet.

Stir in maple syrup. Cook over medium heat, stirring occasionally, until heated through, 3 to 4 minutes.

4. Spoon apple mixture into prepared baking dish. Dot with butter. Drop dough by rounded tablespoonfuls over apples. Sprinkle sugar on top.

5. Bake in heated 400° oven 35 minutes, until topping is golden brown, breaking up crust into large pieces with a spoon after 15 minutes. If topping browns too quickly, cover loosely with aluminum foil.

6. To serve, spoon warm pandowdy into dessert bowls; pour cream over top if desired.

Cran-Apple Strudel

You save on calories and fat here since there's no butter—but we promise you won't miss it. Between the layers of phyllo, there's just a spritz or two of nonstick cooking spray.

MAKES *8 servings*

PREP *20 minutes*

BAKE *at 350° for 35 to 40 minutes*

2   cups diced, peeled Golden Delicious apples (2 small apples)
½   cup low-fat granola
½   cup maple syrup
¼   cup cranberries
¼   cup golden raisins, chopped
1   tablespoon lemon juice
1   teaspoon cornstarch
½   teaspoon ground cinnamon
¼   teaspoon ground nutmeg
6   sheets phyllo dough, thawed if frozen
1   teaspoon confectioners' sugar for sprinkling
½   teaspoon ground cinnamon for sprinkling

1. Heat oven to 350°. Coat a 15½ x 10½ x 1-inch jelly-roll pan with nonstick cooking spray.

2. Combine apples, granola, maple syrup, cranberries, raisins, lemon juice, cornstarch, cinnamon and nutmeg in a medium-size bowl and mix well. Cover; let stand 15 minutes.

3. Meanwhile, lay 1 phyllo sheet on a flat surface with a long side facing you. Coat with cooking spray. Top with another sheet; coat. Continue until all phyllo sheets are in a stack and coated with spray.

4. Spoon a 2-inch-wide strip of granola mixture lengthwise onto phyllo, leaving a 1-inch border of phyllo at both short ends and on the long side farthest from you. Fold border at short ends over filling; roll up phyllo into a log starting with the long side closest to you. Place, seam side down, on prepared pan.

5. Bake strudel in heated 350° oven 35 to 40 minutes, until golden. Cool on pan on a wire rack. Sprinkle with sugar and cinnamon.

Cherry Streusel Delights

Make this tantalizing cross between a bar cookie and a piece of cake during the short Bing cherry season—and savor summer. Shown on page 115.

MAKES *8 servings*

PREP *25 minutes*

BAKE *at 350° for 50 minutes*

6   tablespoons (¾ stick) butter, at room temperature
⅓   cup packed light-brown sugar
1   egg
1   teaspoon vanilla
1   cup all-purpose flour
½   teaspoon baking powder
    Pinch salt

Streusel Topping

¾   cup all-purpose flour
¾   cup packed light-brown sugar
½   cup (1 stick) butter, cut into small pieces

1¼   pounds Bing cherries, stemmed and pitted (4 cups)

1. Heat oven to 350°. Coat an 8 x 8 x 2-inch square glass baking dish with nonstick cooking spray.

2. Beat together butter and brown sugar in a medium-size bowl until creamy. Stir in egg and vanilla.

3. Mix flour, baking powder and salt in a small bowl. Stir flour mixture into butter mixture to make a dough. Pat dough evenly into bottom of prepared baking dish.

4. Prepare topping: In same bowl, mix flour and brown sugar. Using a pastry blender, fork or fingertips, work in butter until mixture holds together.

5. Spoon cherries on top of dough in baking dish. Sprinkle streusel over top.

6. Bake in heated 350° oven 50 minutes or until topping is golden brown. Cool in pan 10 minutes. Cut into rectangles. Serve warm, at room temperature or chilled.

Blueberry Buckle

Ideal with a cup of hot or iced java, this is a classic buckle—a single-layer cake baked with fruit folded into the batter or on top. With a layer of streusel added over all, the top-heavy cake tends to fall—or buckle.

Blueberry Buckle

MAKES *8 servings*

PREP *15 minutes*

BAKE *at 350° for 55 to 60 minutes*

Streusel Topping

1 cup firmly packed dark-brown sugar
⅔ cup all-purpose flour
1 teaspoon ground cinnamon
½ teaspoon ground nutmeg
½ cup (1 stick) cold unsalted butter, cut into small pieces

Cake

2 cups cake flour (not self-rising)
2 teaspoons baking powder
½ teaspoon salt
½ cup (1 stick) unsalted butter, at room temperature
½ cup granulated sugar
1 egg
1 teaspoon vanilla
½ cup milk
1 pint blueberries (about 2 cups)
Confectioners' sugar for dusting

1. Heat oven to 350°. Butter a 9-inch tube pan with a removable bottom; dust with flour.

2. Prepare topping: Mix sugar, flour, cinnamon and nutmeg in a medium-size bowl. Cut in butter with a pastry blender or 2 knives used scissor fashion until mixture resembles coarse crumbs.

3. Prepare cake: Whisk together flour, baking powder and salt in a small bowl.

4. With a mixer on medium speed, beat butter in a large bowl until creamy. Add granulated sugar; beat until fluffy. Beat in egg and vanilla. On low speed, beat flour mixture into butter mixture in 3 additions, alternating with milk and ending with flour mixture; beat well after each addition.

5. Spread half of batter into prepared pan. Cover with berries. Drop remaining batter by tablespoonfuls over berries. Spoon streusel mixture evenly on top.

6. Bake in heated 350° oven 55 to 60 minutes, until topping is deep golden brown. Remove pan to a wire rack to cool slightly. Remove sides of pan. Dust confectioners' sugar over top of buckle.

Blueberry-Nectarine Crisp

No blueberries? Try raspberries. And peaches could sub for the nectarines. This is the height of versatility.

MAKES *8 servings*

PREP *10 minutes*

BAKE *at 375° for 50 to 60 minutes*

5 large nectarines (1½ pounds), pitted and cut into eighths
1 pint blueberries (about 2 cups)
½ cup granulated sugar
4 teaspoons lemon juice
1 tablespoon cornstarch
1 cup all-purpose flour
½ cup packed light-brown sugar
½ cup (1 stick) unsalted butter, cut into small pieces

1. Heat oven to 375°.

2. Toss nectarines, blueberries, granulated sugar, lemon juice and cornstarch in a large bowl. Spoon fruit mixture into an 8 x 8 x 2-inch square baking dish.

3. In same bowl, mix flour and brown sugar. With fingertips, mix butter into flour mixture until crumbly. Sprinkle over top of fruit.

4. Bake in heated 375° oven 50 to 60 minutes or until bubbly and browned.

Peaches and Cream Un-pie

Nestle ripe fruit slices in a soothing, custard filling and presto—the flavors of pie without the work of a crust.

MAKES *8 servings*

PREP *15 minutes*

BAKE *at 375° for 50 to 60 minutes*

1½ cups sour cream
4 eggs
¾ cup plus 2 tablespoons granulated sugar
½ cup all-purpose flour
2 teaspoons vanilla
⅛ to ¼ teaspoon almond extract
Pinch salt
5 large peaches (1½ pounds), halved, pitted and cut into 2-inch-thick slices
Confectioners' sugar for dusting (optional)

1. Heat oven to 375°. Butter a 2- to 2½-quart shallow baking dish.

2. With a mixer on medium speed, beat together sour cream and eggs in a medium-size bowl until smooth. On low speed, gradually beat in ¾ cup granulated sugar, flour, vanilla, almond extract and salt until mixture is well blended and smooth.

3. Pour batter into prepared dish. Top with peach slices, overlapping to cover batter. Sprinkle top with remaining 2 tablespoons granulated sugar.

4. Bake in heated 375° oven 50 to 60 minutes or until a wooden pick inserted in center comes out clean. Dust with confectioners' sugar if desired. Serve warm.

Peach-Raspberry Betty with Pecans

Make it easy on yourself and jumpstart the topping with crushed vanilla wafer cookies. Just blend them with chopped pecans and brown sugar. Yum.

MAKES *8 servings*

PREP *20 minutes*

BAKE *at 350° for 1 hour*

5   large peaches (1½ pounds), peeled, pitted and cut into 2-inch-thick slices
1   pint raspberries (about 2¼ cups)
⅓   cup granulated sugar
1½   cups crushed vanilla wafer cookies (38 cookies)
½   cup chopped pecans
¼   cup packed light-brown sugar
½   cup (1 stick) butter, melted
2   tablespoons butter, cut into small pieces

1. Heat oven to 350°.

2. Toss peaches, raspberries and granulated sugar in a large bowl.

3. Combine crushed cookies, pecans and brown sugar in a medium-size bowl. Pour melted butter on top; toss until mixture is well blended and evenly moistened.

4. Sprinkle one-third of cookie mixture evenly over bottom of an ungreased 6-cup soufflé dish. Spoon half of fruit mixture on top. Sprinkle with half of remaining cookie mixture. Spoon the remaining fruit mixture on top and then sprinkle with remaining cookie mixture. Dot evenly with 2 tablespoons butter.

5. Bake in heated 350° oven 1 hour or until top is golden and fruit is bubbling. Serve warm.

Pear-Cherry Crisp

Show off fall's fabulous pears in an easy-on-the-cook crisp—the name comes from the topping of butter, sugar, flour and rolled oats that gets crisp when it's baked.

MAKES *6 servings*

PREP *10 minutes*

BAKE *at 375° for 30 to 35 minutes*

4   Bartlett, Anjou or Bosc pears, peeled, cored and cut into 1-inch chunks
¾   cup dried cherries
¼   cup white grape juice
1   tablespoon fresh lemon juice
½   cup old-fashioned rolled oats
¼   cup packed light-brown sugar
¼   cup packed dark-brown sugar
1   teaspoon ground cinnamon
     Pinch ground nutmeg
¼   cup (½ stick) butter, cut into small pieces
     Vanilla ice cream for serving (optional)

1. Heat oven to 375°. Coat a 9 x 9 x 2-inch square glass baking dish with nonstick cooking spray.

2. Place pears, cherries, grape juice and lemon juice in a small bowl; toss to coat evenly.

3. Combine oats, brown sugars, cinnamon and nutmeg in a small bowl. Cut in butter with a pastry blender or 2 knives used scissor fashion until mixture resembles coarse crumbs.

4. Spoon pear mixture into prepared baking dish, spreading evenly. Sprinkle oat mixture over top.

5. Bake in heated 375° oven 30 to 35 minutes or until filling starts to bubble and pears are fork-tender. If top browns too quickly, cover loosely with aluminum foil. Transfer to a wire rack; let stand 15 to 20 minutes. Serve with vanilla ice cream if desired.

Poached Pears

French chefs have been poaching pears in wine for years; this recipe shows how easy it is! Pears should be ripe, but not overly so.

MAKES *4 servings*

PREP *15 minutes*

POACH *12 to 15 minutes.*

Pear Preparation

1½ cups water
1 tablespoon lemon juice
4 Bartlett, Bosc or Anjou pears

Poaching Liquid

1½ cups granulated sugar
10 black peppercorns
2 whole cloves
1 sliver (1 x ¼ inch) fresh ginger, peeled
1 cup white grape juice
1 cup dry white wine
1 cup water
⅓ cup lemon juice

Sauce and Whipped Cream

1 box (10 ounces) frozen raspberries in syrup, thawed
½ cup heavy cream
1 tablespoon confectioners' sugar

1. Prepare pears: Mix water and lemon juice in a small bowl. One at a time, peel pears lengthwise; remove end, core and seeds from bottom using a melon baller, leaving a cavity. Place pears in lemon-water in bowl. (Lemon juice keeps pears from turning brown before you are ready to cook them.)

2. Prepare poaching liquid: Combine granulated sugar, peppercorns, cloves, ginger, grape juice, wine, water and lemon juice in a medium-size saucepan and stir to dissolve sugar. Bring to boiling over medium heat.

3. Lay pears on their side in poaching liquid in saucepan. Cover pan and return liquid to boiling. Lower heat to medium-low; simmer 12 to 15 minutes or until thickest part of pears is knife-tender. Using a slotted spoon, carefully remove pears to a plate to cool.

4. Prepare sauce and whipped cream: Place raspberries in a food processor or blender; whirl to puree. To remove seeds, place a fine-mesh sieve over a small bowl and press through raspberry puree with the back of a wooden spoon; discard seeds. With a mixer on medium-high speed, beat cream and confectioners' sugar in a medium-size bowl until firm (not stiff) peaks form.

5. To serve, ladle an equal amount of raspberry sauce onto each of 4 dessert plates, spreading into a round on each. Spoon whipped cream into a pastry bag fitted with star tip. On each plate, pipe a ring of whipped cream on top of sauce, leaving a 1-inch border. Place a pear in center of whipped cream.

NOTE: *Leftover poaching liquid can be used for a refreshing drink over ice, or cook down to a syrup to use in desserts.*

Spiced Pear Potpie

On a cool winter's night, bake pears topped with a biscuit crust for classic comfort food. You'll be pleased to know this recipe is deliciously low in fat.

Spiced Pear Potpie; Apple-Custard Enchiladas, *page 117*

MAKES *8 servings*

PREP *20 minutes*

BAKE *at 400° for 20 minutes, then at 350° for 25 to 35 minutes*

1½ tablespoons cornstarch
1 teaspoon ground cinnamon
½ teaspoon ground ginger
  Pinch ground cloves
6 ripe pears, peeled, cored and sliced lengthwise
⅓ cup packed light-brown sugar
2 tablespoons granulated sugar
1 cup reduced-fat biscuit mix
½ cup nonfat milk
1 egg
  Vanilla low-fat yogurt for serving (optional)

1. Heat oven to 400°. Grease an 8 x 8 x 2-inch square baking dish.

2. Whisk together cornstarch, cinnamon, ginger and cloves in a small bowl. Combine pears, brown sugar and 1½ tablespoons granulated sugar in a large bowl. Sprinkle cinnamon mixture over pear mixture; toss to combine. Pour into prepared dish.

3. Stir together biscuit mix, milk and egg in a medium-size bowl. Pour evenly over fruit mixture in dish. Sprinkle remaining ½ tablespoon sugar on top.

4. Bake in heated 400° oven 20 minutes. Lower oven temperature to 350°. Bake 25 to 30 minutes, until filling is bubbly and topping is golden. Serve warm with vanilla yogurt if desired.

Strawberry-Rhubarb Crumble

Strawberries and rhubarb are a traditional couple—updated here with an appealing topping of oats, sugar and pecans. Vanilla ice cream wouldn't be a bad addition, either.

MAKES *8 servings*

PREP *20 minutes*

BAKE *at 375° for 45 minutes*

1½ pints strawberries, hulled and cut into chunks (about 3 cups)
2½ cups cut rhubarb (1-inch pieces, about 5 stalks)
2 tablespoons lemon juice
1 cup granulated sugar
¼ cup cornstarch

Topping

1 cup old-fashioned or quick-cooking oats (not instant)
1 cup all-purpose flour
½ cup firmly packed dark-brown sugar
½ cup chopped pecans
½ cup (1 stick) cold unsalted butter, cut into small pieces
1 teaspoon ground cinnamon

1. Heat oven to 375°. Butter a 10-inch deep-dish pie plate.

2. Stir strawberries, rhubarb and lemon juice in a large bowl until well mixed. Whisk together sugar and cornstarch in a small bowl. Add to strawberry mixture; toss gently to coat fruit. Spoon evenly into prepared pie plate.

3. Prepare topping: Place oats, flour, brown sugar, pecans, butter and cinnamon in a food processor. Whirl just until combined and still crumbly; do not over-process. Sprinkle crumb mixture evenly over fruit in pie plate.

4. Bake in heated 375° oven until topping is golden brown, about 35 minutes. Cover loosely with aluminum foil. Bake 10 minutes longer or until heated through and bubbly. Serve warm.

Strawberry-Rhubarb Crumble

Biscuit-Topped Strawberry-Apricot Bake

Don't worry if the fruit juices bubble up and over the side of the pie plate—that shows the dessert is homemade. Protect your oven by placing a baking sheet under the pie plate before cooking.

MAKES *8 servings*

PREP *20 minutes*

BAKE *at 375° for 60 minutes*

Fruit

½ cup sugar
1 tablespoon cornstarch
1 tablespoon grated orange rind
1½ pints strawberries, hulled and quartered (about 3¼ cups)
3 apricots, halved, pitted and cut into eighths

Biscuit Topping

1¼ cups buttermilk baking mix
¼ cup plus 1 teaspoon sugar
1½ teaspoons grated orange rind
⅓ cup milk
2 tablespoons butter, melted

1. Heat oven to 375°.

2. Prepare fruit: With a fork, mix sugar, cornstarch and orange rind in a small bowl until well blended. Mix strawberries and apricots in a 10-inch glass pie plate. Sprinkle sugar mixture evenly over fruit; gently toss fruit to coat evenly.

3. Prepare topping: Combine baking mix, ¼ cup sugar and orange rind in a medium-size bowl until well blended. Stir in milk and melted butter with a fork until dry ingredients are moistened.

4. Using rounded tablespoonfuls, drop dough onto fruit, forming a ring about

1 inch inside edge of pie plate. Sprinkle dough with remaining 1 teaspoon sugar. Place pie plate on a baking sheet to catch any drips.

5. Bake in heated 375° oven 60 minutes or until topping is browned and fruit is bubbly in center. If topping begins to brown too much, cover with aluminum foil. Let cool 30 minutes before serving.

Strawberry-Chocolate Shortcake

Each tower of this luscious dessert is stacked so high that it serves two! How much more fun could shortcake be?

MAKES *8 servings*

PREP *30 minutes*

BAKE *at 425° for 12 minutes*

1 pint strawberries, hulled and sliced (about 2 cups)
½ pint raspberries (1 cup)
1 cup sugar

Chocolate Shortcake

2 cups all-purpose flour
½ cup unsweetened cocoa powder
1 tablespoon baking powder
½ teaspoon salt
6 tablespoons (¾ stick) unsalted butter, cut into bits and chilled
½ cup milk
1 teaspoon vanilla
1 cup heavy cream, whipped
Fresh mint sprigs, for garnish
Hot fudge sauce for serving (optional)

1. Heat oven to 425°.

2. Place strawberries and raspberries in a medium-size bowl. Gently stir in ¼ cup sugar; toss to coat. Let stand 20 minutes, stirring occasionally.

3. Meanwhile, prepare shortcake: Combine flour, cocoa powder, remaining ¾ cup sugar, baking powder and salt in a large bowl. Cut in butter with a pastry blender or 2 knives used scissor fashion until mixture resembles coarse crumbs. Slowly add milk and vanilla, tossing with a fork, until mixture just comes together.

4. Turn out dough onto a lightly floured surface. Knead lightly about 10 times. Pat or roll dough to a ¾-inch thickness. Using a fluted 4-inch-round cookie cutter and gathering and rerolling dough scraps as necessary, cut out 4 shortcakes. Place shortcakes about 1 inch apart on an ungreased baking sheet.

5. Bake in heated 425° oven 12 minutes or until a wooden pick inserted in center of shortcakes comes out clean. Transfer shortcakes to a wire rack to cool completely.

6. To serve, cut each shortcake in half horizontally. Place bottom halves on a serving platter. Spoon some juice from strawberry mixture over bottoms. Spoon strawberry mixture on each bottom half, reserving a few berries for garnish. Spoon about ½ cup whipped cream over each. Cover each with a top half. Garnish with fruit and mint. Drizzle with fudge sauce if desired. Cut each in half for 2 servings.

Almond-Stuffed Strawberries

Take chocolate-dipped berries to a new level—stuff 'em! A honey-sweet mix of cream cheese, almond extract and chopped almond fills the centers most magnificently.

MAKES *12 serving*

PREP *15 minutes*

REFRIGERATE *10 minutes*

12 strawberries, rinsed
¾ cup semisweet chocolate chips
1 package (3 ounces) cream cheese
2 tablespoons honey
¼ teaspoon almond extract
1 tablespoon chopped almonds

1. Using a paring knife, halve berries lengthwise, cutting through the leafy hull as well. Using knife tip, remove center core from each half; dry berries on a layer of paper toweling.

2. Place chocolate chips in a small microwave-safe bowl; microwave at 100% power 60 seconds to melt; stir.

3. Line a baking sheet with waxed paper. Holding a berry by its hull, dip into chocolate, covering bottom half. Place on lined baking sheet. Repeat with other berries. Refrigerate 10 minutes.

4. Beat together cream cheese, honey and almond extract in a small bowl. Spoon into a pastry bag fitted with a small tip. Pipe mixture into berries. Sprinkle with almonds.

Three-Fruit Shortcake

With blueberries baked into the cake and then teamed with strawberries, kiwi and whipped cream for the filling, what's not to love?

MAKES *8 servings*

PREP *20 minutes*

BAKE *at 425° for 15 to 20 minutes*

Shortcake

- 2 cups all-purpose flour
- ¼ cup sugar
- 2 teaspoons baking powder
- ½ teaspoon baking soda
- ½ teaspoon ground cinnamon
- ½ teaspoon salt
- ¼ cup (½ stick) cold unsalted butter, cut into small pieces and chilled
- ⅔ cup buttermilk
- 1 egg
- ½ pint blueberries (1 cup)
- 2 teaspoons grated lemon rind

Filling

- 1½ pints strawberries, hulled and sliced (about 3 cups)
- ½ cup blueberries
- 2 kiwi, peeled and sliced
- 2 tablespoons sugar
- 1 cup heavy cream

1. Heat oven to 425°.

2. Prepare shortcake: Sift together flour, sugar, baking powder, baking soda, cinnamon and salt into a large bowl. Cut in butter with a pastry blender or 2 knives used scissor fashion until mixture resembles coarse crumbs.

3. Whisk together buttermilk and egg in a medium-size bowl. Stir in blueberries and lemon rind. Gently fold buttermilk mixture into flour mixture just until evenly moistened. Turn out dough onto a lightly floured board and knead very lightly 7 or 8 times, being careful not to crush the blueberries and adding a little flour to keep dough from sticking.

4. Shape dough into a ¾-inch-thick disc on an ungreased baking sheet. Using a knife, score disc deeply to divide into 8 equal wedges without cutting all the way through.

5. Bake shortcake in heated 425° oven 15 to 20 minutes or until lightly golden. Remove to a wire rack to cool slightly.

6. Meanwhile, prepare filling: Toss together strawberries, blueberries, kiwi and sugar in a large bowl. With a mixer on medium-high speed, whip cream in a medium-size bowl until firm but not stiff peaks form.

7. To serve, separate shortcake wedges and split each horizontally in half. Fill with berry mixture and whipped cream.

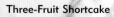
Three-Fruit Shortcake

Phyllo Cups with Strawberries and Custard Sauce

Here is an inviting combo of tastes and textures—crispy phyllo, soothing custard, fresh juicy berries and a drizzle of melted chocolate that's sure to please!

MAKES *4 servings*

PREP *30 minutes*

REFRIGERATE *1 hour*

BAKE *at 375° for 10 to 12 minutes*

Custard Sauce

2 egg yolks
2 tablespoons sugar
1 cup low-fat milk (1%)
½ teaspoon vanilla

4 sheets phyllo dough, thawed if frozen
2 pints strawberries, hulled and halved (about 4 cups)
3 tablespoons sugar
2 squares (1 ounce each) semisweet chocolate
Confectioners' sugar for dusting

1. Prepare sauce: Whisk together egg yolks and sugar in a small heatproof bowl until pale yellow. Bring milk to boiling in a small saucepan over high heat. Slowly add to egg yolk mixture, whisking, then pour mixture back into saucepan. Cook over low heat, stirring, until mixture thickens and coats back of spoon, about 10 minutes; do not boil or mixture may curdle. Remove from heat. Stir in vanilla. Refrigerate custard sauce 1 hour.

2. Meanwhile, lay 1 phyllo sheet on a flat surface with long side facing you. Coat with cooking spray. Top with another sheet; coat. Continue until all phyllo sheets are in a stack and coated with spray. Cut stack lengthwise in fourths, then crosswise in fourths again for a total of 16 stacks of small phyllo rectangles. Cover phyllo with moist paper toweling to prevent drying out.

3. Heat oven to 375°. Lightly coat four 10-ounce custard cups with nonstick cooking spray.

4. Lightly coat each of the 4 phyllo sheets in 1 stack with nonstick cooking spray. Gently press stack into 1 prepared cup, placing a short end of stack in middle of cup bottom and draping stack up and over side. Repeat with 3 more stacks to line entire cup, coating each with spray and placing at a right angle to previous stack. Bend overhanging dough upright. Repeat to line remaining cups with remaining phyllo. Place lined cups on a baking sheet.

5. Bake in heated 375° oven 10 to 12 minutes or until phyllo is crisp and golden. Transfer custard cups to a wire rack to cool completely.

6. Meanwhile, combine berries and sugar in a large bowl. Let stand 20 minutes, stirring occasionally. Melt chocolate in top of a double boiler over barely simmering, not boiling water, stirring until smooth.

7. To serve, lift phyllo cups out of custard cups; place each on a dessert plate. Spoon 2 tablespoons custard sauce evenly around each phyllo cup and 2 tablespoons into each cup. Spoon berries into cups, dividing equally. Drizzle melted chocolate on top; dust with confectioners' sugar.

Fruit Facts

Though many of the fruits called for in these recipes are available year 'round, summer or fall is when they show off their sweetness. To choose, start with a sniff test—you should immediately smell a distinctive fragrance that signals the specific fruit.

APPLES

Select firm, unblemished fruit. Sweetness varies among types, and each type has a distinctive flavor. McIntosh, Granny Smith, Golden Delicious, Empire, Jonagold and Rome are all good for baking and cooking.

APRICOTS

Look for plump, firm, yellow-to-orange-colored fruit with no brown spots.

BANANAS

Go for plump fruit with vibrant, intact skin. Bananas will ripen if left out at room temperature; turn them occasionally.

BERRIES

All types of berries should be plump, firm, unblemished and free of mildew. Pick strawberries that have a deep crimson hue; caps should be green and fresh-looking. Never choose strawberries with white shoulders or a greenish hue; they won't ripen off the vine. Berries can be used interchangeably but, of course, the recipe will taste and look different depending upon the fruit used. Berries are usually sold by the ½ pint, pint or quart; the container may hold slightly more than the strict cup equivalent. In most cases, this won't affect the outcome of a dessert recipe.

CHERRIES

Reach for the largest, glossiest, firmest fruit that has the greenest stems. Avoid any that are missing their stems.

NECTARINES AND PEACHES

Choose firm fruit with no soft, brown areas. Look for a yellow background with red blush. Use these fruits interchangeably.

PEARS

Make sure a pear is ripe by pressing gently with your thumb near the base of the stem; the flesh of the pear should yield slightly. Avoid bruised fruit. Anjou, Bartlett and Bosc are the best types for baking and cooking.

PLUMS

Buy firm, slightly resilient fruit that is plump with no soft or dark spots. Plums range from red, blue and purple to yellow and green.

STORAGE TIPS

- If apricots, peaches, pears, nectarines and plums are not quite ripe, place in a brown paper bag; do not crowd. Place bag on a counter, out of sunlight. Add an apple or banana to speed the ripening process.

- Store apricots, cherries, peaches, nectarines and plums, unwashed, in a perforated plastic bag in the refrigerator crisper.

- Ripe bananas can be refrigerated, but their skins will turn black.

- Keep apples and pears in perforated bags in the refrigerator or a dry cool place— ideally 32° to 40°.

- Berries are best eaten right away, but they will keep in the refrigerator for a few days. First discard any bruised or moldy fruit to prevent rot from spreading. Wrap unwashed berries loosely. When ready to use strawberries, wash them with caps still on to prevent water from penetrating flesh.

- To freeze berries, arrange them, unwashed, in a single layer on a baking sheet; freeze 2 hours until solid. Place in freezer bag, press out excess air; seal. Use within 2 months. Frozen berries retain flavor, but some, especially strawberries, lose texture and will be better cooked than raw.

Berry-Orange Grunt

Instead of baking like a cobbler, this dessert is steamed on the stovetop, so the topping is soft, like a dumpling. The cooking fruit supposedly makes a grunting noise.

Berry-Orange Grunt

MAKES *8 servings* PREP *15 minutes*
COOK *25 minutes*

Fruit

4   cups berries (blueberries, raspberries and/or blackberries)
1   cup sugar
¼   cup frozen orange juice concentrate, thawed
1   teaspoon grated orange rind

Dumplings

1   cup all-purpose flour
¼   cup sugar
2   teaspoons grated orange rind
1   teaspoon baking powder
½   teaspoon baking soda
¼   teaspoon salt
¼   teaspoon ground nutmeg
¾   cup buttermilk
2   tablespoons unsalted butter, melted

Vanilla ice cream for serving (optional)

1. Prepare fruit: In a 9- or 10-inch skillet with a tight-fitting lid, stir together berries, sugar, orange juice concentrate and orange rind until well mixed. Simmer, uncovered, 2 to 3 minutes.

2. Prepare dumplings: Whisk together flour, sugar, orange rind, baking powder, baking soda, salt and nutmeg in a large bowl. Mix buttermilk and melted butter in a small bowl. Add to flour mixture, stirring until flour mixture is moistened and forms a loose dough.

3. Dollop dough in small mounds onto fruit in skillet. Cover tightly; cook over medium heat without lifting lid 15 minutes. Then check dumplings for firmness; if they are not set, replace cover and cook 5 minutes longer.

4. To serve, scoop dumplings into dessert bowls, spoon fruit over each serving and top with ice cream if desired.

Mixed-Berry Cornmeal Cobbler

Cornmeal adds a different—yet welcome—texture to the biscuit topping.

MAKES *8 servings*

PREP *15 minutes*

BAKE *at 350° for 1 hour 20 minutes*

1   pint blueberries (2 cups)
1   pint raspberries (2 cups)
1   pint strawberries, hulled and halved (about 2 cups)
½   cup sugar
3   tablespoons cornstarch

Topping

⅓   cup sugar
¼   cup (½ stick) butter, at room temperature
1   egg
1   teaspoon vanilla
⅔   cup all-purpose flour
⅓   cup yellow cornmeal
2   teaspoons baking powder
¼   teaspoon salt
¼   cup milk

1. Heat oven to 350°.

2. Toss blueberries, raspberries, strawberries, sugar and cornstarch in a large bowl until well mixed. Spoon into an ungreased 8 x 8 x 2-inch square baking dish, spreading evenly.

3. Prepare topping: In same bowl, beat together sugar and butter on medium speed until light and fluffy, about 3 minutes. Beat in egg and vanilla until well blended.

4. Mix together flour, cornmeal, baking powder and salt in a small bowl.

5. Add half of flour mixture to butter mixture. On low speed, beat just until combined. Beat in milk, then remaining flour mixture. Drop dough by large spoonfuls onto berries in baking dish.

6. Bake in heated 350° oven 1 hour and 20 minutes or until top is golden and fruit is bubbly. Serve warm.

Mixed-Berry Cornmeal Cobbler

Meringue Berry Boxes

Tuck 4 kinds of berries inside these perky meringue boxes and watch the compliments roll in. The meringue boxes can be made up to 2 days in advance; store airtight at room temperature.

MAKES *8 servings*

PREP *20 minutes*

BAKE *at 250° for 50 minutes*

7   **egg whites, at room temperature**
½   **teaspoon cream of tartar**
1½ **cups sugar**

Filling

½   **pint strawberries, hulled and cut into chunks (about 1 cup)**
½   **pint blueberries (1 cup)**
½   **pint blackberries (1 cup)**
½   **pint raspberries (1 cup)**
¼   **cup sugar**
2   **tablespoons orange juice**

1. Heat oven to 250°. Line 2 baking sheets with aluminum foil.

2. With a mixer on medium speed, beat egg whites and cream of tarter in a large bowl until soft peaks form. Gradually add sugar, a few tablespoons at a time, beating constantly until fully incorporated, 7 to 10 minutes; meringue should form peaks that are glossy and stiff, with no grainy sugar granules.

3. Transfer meringue to a large pastry bag fitted with a ¼-inch round tip. Pipe box outlines onto prepared baking sheets, piping sixteen 2½-inch squares and eight 2½-inch circles. Fill in outlines with a small amount of meringue, spreading with a spatula.

4. To make box bottoms, one at a time, build "sides" on 8 squares and all circles by piping a continuous stream of meringue around perimeter of each. Do not pipe higher than 1¼ inches, or sides may fall over.

5. To make tops for square boxes, pipe a dollop for a handle onto center of each of the 8 remaining squares.

6. Bake meringues in heated 250° oven 50 minutes, until firm; do not allow to brown. Cool completely on baking sheets on wire racks. Then gently peel boxes and tops from foil. If meringues stick to foil, cut foil around each, lift each meringue and then carefully peel off foil.

7. Prepare filling: Stir together strawberries, blueberries, blackberries, raspberries, sugar and orange juice in a large bowl until well mixed.

8. To serve, place 1 square box and 1 round box on each dessert plate. Fill each with ¼ cup berry mixture. Top square box with a lid, or prop lid on side.

MERINGUE MAGIC

Make meringue when the weather is dry. When it is humid, the sugar absorbs moisture from the air, which will make the meringue weep or turn soft or sticky. Store meringue in airtight containers at room temperature up to several weeks; don't refrigerate or freeze.

Mixed Berry Gratin

For a colorful finale that's ready to eat in less than 15 minutes, consider this gratin of three berries flavored with the distinctive tastes of brown sugar and nutmeg.

MAKES 6 *servings*

PREP 5 *minutes*

BROIL *about 8 minutes*

1   pint strawberries, hulled; halved if large (about 2 cups)
½   pint raspberries (1 cup)
½   pint blueberries (1 cup)
1⅓ cups shortbread cookie crumbs (about 20 shortbread cookies)
¼   cup packed dark-brown sugar
⅛   teaspoon ground nutmeg
½   cup heavy cream
1   tablespoon confectioners' sugar
¼   teaspoon vanilla
¼   cup frozen liquid cholesterol-free egg substitute, thawed

1. Place all berries on paper toweling; blot dry. Toss berries together in a medium-size bowl.

2. Heat oven to broil. Position oven rack 8 inches from heat source.

3. Butter a 10-inch-square flameproof dish. Sprinkle cookie crumbs evenly onto bottom of dish. Arrange berries evenly over crumbs. Sprinkle with brown sugar and nutmeg.

4. With a mixer on medium speed, beat cream, confectioners' sugar and vanilla in a small bowl until soft peaks form. Gently fold in egg substitute.

5. Broil berries 6 minutes or until slightly softened. Remove baking dish from oven. Adjust position of oven rack to 4 inches from heat. Scrape cream mixture evenly over berries in dish; broil until lightly golden, 1 to 2 minutes. Serve immediately.

Fruit Compote

This recipe offers a triple blessing—you can prepare it in advance, the flavors meld deliciously if it stands awhile before you serve it, and a serving has only 200 calories. Spoon it over nonfat vanilla yogurt to make a totally fat-free creamy dessert. Shown on page 115.

MAKES 12 *servings*

PREP 10 *minutes*

COOK *about 20 minutes*

1   cup water
    Grated rind of 1 lemon
2   tablespoons fresh lemon juice (from 1 lemon)
¼   cup sugar
1   cup dried apricots (about 6 ounces)
1   cup pitted prunes with lemon essence (about 6 ounces)
½   cup golden raisins
½   cup dried cherries or dried cranberries
1   navel orange
1   cinnamon stick (2- to 3-inch)
2   tablespoons orange-flavored liqueur
1   quart nonfat vanilla yogurt for serving (optional)

1. Combine water, lemon rind, lemon juice and sugar in a small saucepan. Add apricots, prunes, raisins and cherries.

2. Cut orange in half lengthwise, then slice crosswise into semicircles. Cut semicircles in half. Gently stir into dried fruit mixture in saucepan until well mixed. Add cinnamon stick. Cover; simmer 10 minutes. Add liqueur; simmer, uncovered, 5 minutes.

3. If desired, serve warm over nonfat vanilla yogurt. Or transfer to a nonmetallic container, cover and refrigerate up to 1 week.

Breakfast Twist Bread, *page 157*

Double Blueberry Coffee Cake, *page 149*

Sweet Breads

Cheese-Filled Crowns, *page 152*

Cherry-Nut Mini Loaves

Dried fruit lends texture and a touch of tart flavor that is mellowed by brandy.

MAKES *3 mini loaves (8 slices each)*

PREP *15 minutes*

BAKE *at 350° for 30 to 40 minutes*

1 package (3 ounces) dried tart cherries (¾ cup)
½ cup brandy
2¼ cups all-purpose flour
1 teaspoon baking soda
1 teaspoon baking powder
½ teaspoon salt
½ teaspoon ground allspice
2 eggs
¾ cup granulated sugar
¼ cup packed light-brown sugar
½ cup buttermilk
¼ cup vegetable oil
¾ cup walnuts, coarsely chopped
Confectioners' sugar for dusting (optional)

1. Heat cherries and brandy in a small saucepan over low heat just until mixture starts to simmer. Remove from heat; let stand 5 minutes to allow cherries to soften.

2. Heat oven to 350°. Coat 3 mini loaf pans, 6 x 3 x 2 inches each, with nonstick cooking spray (see note, right).

3. Mix together flour, baking soda, baking powder, salt and allspice in a large bowl.

4. With a mixer on high speed, beat eggs, granulated sugar and brown sugar in a medium-size bowl until well blended. On low speed, beat in buttermilk and oil.

5. Stir egg mixture into flour mixture until moistened and batter just comes together—do not overmix. Fold in walnuts and cherries with soaking liquid. Divide batter equally among prepared pans.

6. Bake in heated 350° oven 30 to 40 minutes or until a wooden pick inserted in centers comes out clean. Let loaves cool in pans on a wire rack 10 minutes. Turn out onto rack to cool completely.

7. Dust loaves with confectioners' sugar if desired.

NOTE: *Make one 9 x 5 x 3-inch loaf. Bake in heated 350° oven about 1 hour or until a wooden pick inserted in center comes out clean.*

Streusel-Topped Banana Bread

Don't throw out that overripe banana; whip up our quick bread instead. Baked with a streusel topping, it will remind you how good homemade banana bread can be.

MAKES *3 mini loaves (8 slices each)*

PREP *10 minutes*

BAKE *at 350° for 30 minutes*

1½ cups all-purpose flour
1½ teaspoons baking powder
¾ teaspoon baking soda
¼ teaspoon salt
¼ teaspoon ground nutmeg
¼ teaspoon ground cinnamon
1 cup mashed bananas (3 small overripe bananas, about 1 pound)
2 eggs
⅓ cup granulated sugar
¼ cup (½ stick) butter, melted

Streusel Topping

½ cup all-purpose flour
½ cup packed light-brown sugar
¼ cup (½ stick) butter, softened
½ teaspoon ground nutmeg
½ teaspoon ground cinnamon

1. Heat oven to 350°. Grease three 5¾ x 3¼ x 2-inch mini loaf pans.

2. Whisk together flour, baking powder, baking soda, salt, nutmeg and cinnamon in a small bowl.

3. With a mixer on medium-high speed, beat bananas, eggs, granulated sugar and butter in a large bowl until smooth. On low speed, gradually beat in flour mixture. Divide batter equally among prepared pans.

4. Prepare topping: Mix together flour, brown sugar, butter, nutmeg and cinnamon in a small bowl with a fork until crumbly. Sprinkle over batter in pan.

5. Bake in heated 350° oven 30 minutes or until a wooden pick inserted in centers comes out clean. If streusel browns too quickly, cover loosely with aluminum foil. Cool breads in pans on wire rack 10 minutes. Turn out onto rack to cool completely.

Sweet-Potato Loaf

An orange-flavored drizzle gives this quick bread an elegant gloss.

MAKES *2 loaves (12 slices each)*

PREP *30 minutes*

BAKE *at 350° for 65 to 70 minutes*

3½ cups all-purpose flour
4 teaspoons baking powder
2 teaspoons salt
2 cans (15.75 ounces each) sweet potatoes, drained and mashed
2 cups packed light-brown sugar
½ cup (1 stick) butter, melted
2 eggs
2 tablespoons grated orange rind
½ cup orange juice
1½ cups pecans, chopped
1½ cups golden raisins

Glaze

½ cup confectioners' sugar
½ teaspoon grated orange rind
1½ to 3 teaspoons orange juice

1. Heat oven to 350°. Grease two 8½ x 4½ x 2¼-inch loaf pans; dust with flour.

2. Whisk together flour, baking powder and salt in a medium-size bowl.

3. Stir together sweet potatoes, brown sugar, butter, eggs and orange rind in a large bowl.

4. With a mixer on low speed, beat flour mixture into sweet potato mixture in 3 additions, alternating with orange juice and ending with flour mixture; beat until well blended. Stir in pecans and raisins. Spread batter into prepared pans, dividing equally.

5. Bake in heated 350° oven 65 to 70 minutes or until a wooden pick inserted in centers comes out clean. Let loaves cool in pans on wire racks 15 minutes. Turn out onto racks to cool completely.

6. Prepare glaze: Whisk together sugar, orange rind and orange juice in a small bowl until smooth. Drizzle over top of loaves.

STORING NUTS

Since nuts contain a fair amount of fat, they can turn rancid over time. Shelled nuts will keep for several weeks in a tightly covered container in a cool, dark place; they can be frozen for up to several months. Unsalted nuts will stay fresh longer than salted ones. Unshelled nuts can be kept even longer—up to a year in the freezer.

Banana-Coconut Loaf

Two delightful tastes of the tropics come together in one sweetly decadent loaf.

Banana-Coconut Loaf

MAKES *1 loaf (12 slices)*
PREP *15 minutes*
BAKE *at 350° for 1 hour 10 minutes*

2 cups all-purpose flour
1 teaspoon baking powder
1 teaspoon ground cinnamon
½ teaspoon baking soda
½ teaspoon salt
2 eggs
¾ cup sugar
1 cup mashed banana (3 small overripe bananas, about 1 pound)
½ cup vegetable oil
¼ cup buttermilk
1 teaspoon vanilla
⅔ cup shredded sweetened flake coconut
½ cup pecan halves
½ cup semisweet chocolate chips

1. Heat oven to 350°. Coat a 9 x 5 x 3-inch loaf pan with nonstick cooking spray.

2. Mix flour, baking powder, cinnamon, baking soda and salt in a large bowl.

3. Beat eggs and sugar in a medium-size bowl on high speed until blended. On low speed, beat in banana, oil, buttermilk and vanilla.

4. Stir egg mixture into flour mixture until moistened and batter just comes together—do not overmix.

5. Fold in ⅓ cup coconut, nuts and chocolate chips. Pour into prepared pan. Sprinkle with remaining ⅓ cup coconut.

6. Bake in heated 350° oven 1 hour 10 minutes or until a wooden pick inserted in center comes out almost clean. Let loaf cool in pan on a wire rack 10 minutes. Turn out onto rack to cool completely.

Strawberry Tea Loaf

Berry good: a slice of quick bread studded with strawberries and macadamia nuts, smeared with berry-flavored cream cheese.

MAKES *1 loaf (12 slices)*

PREP *20 minutes*

BAKE *at 350° for 60 minutes*

1⅔ cups strawberries, hulled and coarsely chopped

1 container (8 ounces) whipped cream cheese

2 tablespoons confectioners' sugar

2 cups all-purpose flour

¾ cup granulated sugar

1½ teaspoons baking powder

½ teaspoon baking soda

½ teaspoon salt

2 eggs

⅓ cup butter or margarine, melted

⅓ cup cranberry-strawberry juice

2 teaspoons grated lemon rind

¾ cup macadamia nuts, coarsely chopped and toasted (see page 231)

1. With a fork, mash 2 tablespoons strawberries in a small bowl. Add cream cheese and confectioners' sugar; stir until combined. Refrigerate.

2. Heat oven to 350°. Grease a 9 x 5 x 3-inch loaf pan; dust with flour.

3. Whisk together flour, granulated sugar, baking powder, baking soda and salt in a large bowl.

4. Beat eggs slightly in a small bowl; stir in melted butter, fruit juice and lemon rind. Add egg mixture to flour mixture, stirring until no traces of flour remain. Stir in remaining berries and nuts. Scrape batter into prepared pan.

5. Bake in heated 350° oven 60 minutes, until a wooden pick inserted in center comes out clean; if loaf browns too quickly, cover loosely with aluminum foil.

6. Let loaf cool in pan on a wire rack 10 minutes. Turn out onto rack to cool completely. Cut into slices; serve with strawberry-cream cheese mixture.

Strawberry Tea Loaf

Date-Nut Bread

Rich and dense, and perfect with tea, this bread can also be made in mini loaf pans for lunch bags or gift-giving—cut baking time to 30 minutes if you do this.

MAKES *1 loaf (12 slices)*

PREP *20 minutes*

BAKE *350° for 1 hour*

1 package (8 ounces) pitted dates, coarsely chopped
1 cup boiling water
2 cups all-purpose flour
1 teaspoon baking soda
½ teaspoon baking powder
½ teaspoon salt
¼ teaspoon ground cinnamon
¼ teaspoon ground allspice
1 egg, lightly beaten
⅔ cup sugar
1 tablespoon butter, melted
½ teaspoon vanilla
½ cup coarsely chopped walnuts

1. Combine dates and boiling water in a small bowl; let cool to room temperature.

2. Heat oven to 350°. Grease a 9 x 5 x 3-inch loaf pan.

3. Whisk together flour, baking soda, baking powder, salt, cinnamon and allspice in a medium-size bowl.

4. With a mixer on medium speed, beat egg, sugar, butter and vanilla in a large bowl. Add flour mixture and beat just until dry ingredients are moistened. Add date mixture, beating until well combined. Add nuts. Scrape batter into prepared pan.

5. Bake in heated 350° oven 1 hour, until a wooden pick inserted in center comes out clean. Let loaf cool in pan on a wire rack 10 minutes. Turn out from onto rack to cool completely.

Chocolate-Zucchini Loaf

Zucchini plants have a way of multiplying. When your garden overflows, try this new chocolatey twist on the usual bread.

MAKES *1 loaf (12 slices)*

PREP *15 minutes*

BAKE *at 350° for 60 to 65 minutes*

1¾ cups all-purpose flour
½ cup granulated sugar
¼ cup packed light-brown sugar
3 tablespoons unsweetened cocoa powder
¾ teaspoon baking powder
½ teaspoon baking soda
½ teaspoon salt
2 eggs
¾ cup vegetable oil
1 teaspoon vanilla
1 cup coarsely grated zucchini (about 3½ ounces)
½ cup semisweet mini chocolate chips
Confectioners' sugar for dusting

1. Heat oven to 350°. Coat a 3½ x 4½ x 2⅝-inch loaf pan with nonstick cooking spray.

2. Sift together flour, sugars, cocoa powder, baking powder, baking soda and salt into a large bowl.

3. Beat eggs, oil and vanilla in a medium-size bowl until well combined. Stir in zucchini.

4. Stir egg mixture into flour mixture until moistened and a stiff batter just comes together—do not overmix. Fold in chocolate chips. Spoon batter into prepared pan.

5. Bake in heated 350° oven 60 to 65 minutes or until a wooden pick inserted in center of loaf comes out clean. Let cool in pan on a wire rack 10 minutes. Turn out onto rack to cool completely. Before serving, dust with confectioners' sugar.

Pumpkin-Pecan Mini Loaves

A topping of luxurious pecans and brown sugar puts the finishing touch on yummy quick breads that remind us of Thanksgiving. They're perfect for brunch.

MAKES *3 mini loaves (8 slices each)*

PREP *15 minutes*

BAKE *at 375° for 28 minutes*

2½ cups all-purpose flour
2 teaspoons pumpkin pie spice
1 teaspoon baking powder
1 teaspoon baking soda
½ teaspoon salt
2 eggs
½ cup granulated sugar
¼ cup packed light-brown sugar
1 cup canned pumpkin puree (not pie filling)
½ cup buttermilk
¼ cup vegetable oil
1 teaspoon vanilla
½ cup pecans, coarsely chopped

Topping

⅓ cup packed light-brown sugar
⅓ cup pecans, finely chopped
¼ cup (½ stick) butter, at room temperature
¼ cup all-purpose flour

1. Heat oven to 375°. Coat three 6 x 3 x 2-inch mini loaf pans with nonstick cooking spray.

2. Whisk together flour, pumpkin pie spice, baking powder, baking soda and salt in a large bowl.

3. Beat eggs and sugars in a separate large bowl on high speed. On medium speed, beat in pumpkin, then buttermilk, oil and vanilla until smooth.

4. Stir egg mixture into flour mixture until moistened and batter just comes together—do not overmix. Fold in pecans. Spoon batter into prepared pans, dividing equally.

5. Prepare topping: Using a fork or your fingertips, mix brown sugar, pecans, butter and flour in a small bowl until crumbly. Sprinkle topping on batter in pans, dividing equally.

6. Bake in heated 375° oven 28 to 30 minutes or until a wooden pick inserted in centers comes out clean. Transfer pans to a wire rack; cool loaves in pans 5 minutes. Gently lift loaves out of pans; cool completely on racks.

PUMPKIN MUFFIN POINTERS

After mixing wet ingredients into dry ingredients, fold in chopped pecans.

For topping, use your fingertips to blend sugar, finely chopped pecans, butter and flour until crumbly.

Almond-Plum Coffee Cake

Use a springform pan so that this pretty-as-a-picture cake can be removed easily for display!

Almond-Plum Coffee Cake

MAKES *8 servings* PREP *20 minutes*
BAKE *at 350° for about 1 hour*

1½ cups all-purpose flour
2 teaspoons baking powder
¼ teaspoon salt
¾ cup granulated sugar
½ cup blanched whole almonds
½ cup (1 stick) butter, cut into 8 pieces, at room temperature,
2 eggs
1 teaspoon vanilla
½ cup milk
1 teaspoon grated orange rind

Topping

5 to 6 large plums (1¼ pounds), pitted and cut into eighths (3 cups)
¼ cup granulated sugar
2 tablespoons butter, cut into small pieces
Confectioners' sugar for dusting (optional)

1. Heat oven to 350°. Butter and flour a 9-inch springform pan.

2. Whisk together flour, baking powder and salt in a medium-size bowl.

3. Place sugar and almonds in a food processor. Whirl until finely ground. Add butter to processor. Whirl to combine. Add eggs and vanilla; whirl to combine.

4. Add milk to mixture in processor; whirl until blended. Add flour mixture; whirl until well blended and smooth. Add orange rind; whirl to blend. Scrape batter into prepared pan, spreading evenly.

5. Assemble topping: Arrange plum slices on batter, overlapping in a decorative pattern. Sprinkle granulated sugar over plums. Dot with butter.

6. Bake in heated 350° oven about 1 hour or until top is lightly browned and a wooden pick inserted in center comes out clean. Dust with confectioners' sugar if desired. Cool in pan on a wire rack; remove sides of pan before serving.

Streusel-Topped Apple Cake

Apple-cinnamon flavored yogurt provides moistness, and apple juice and chopped Granny Smiths give a healthy apple accent.

MAKES *16 servings*

PREP *20 minutes*

BAKE *at 350° for 50 minutes*

2½ cups all-purpose flour
2 teaspoons baking powder
½ teaspoon baking soda
¼ teaspoon salt
¼ teaspoon ground cinnamon
⅛ teaspoon ground nutmeg
⅛ teaspoon ground cardamom
½ cup (1 stick) butter, at room temperature
1¼ cups granulated sugar
3 eggs
1 container (8 ounces) apple-cinnamon low-fat yogurt
⅓ cup apple juice
1 teaspoon vanilla
2 Granny Smith apples (1 pound), peeled, cored and coarsely chopped
½ cup chopped walnuts (optional)

Topping

¾ cup all-purpose flour
⅓ cup packed light-brown sugar
½ teaspoon ground cinnamon
⅓ cup butter, at room temperature
¼ cup chopped walnuts (optional)

1. Heat oven to 350°. Coat a 13 x 9 x 2-inch baking pan with nonstick cooking spray.

2. Whisk flour, baking powder, baking soda, salt, cinnamon, nutmeg and cardamom in a small bowl.

3. With a mixer on medium speed, beat butter and granulated sugar in a large bowl until smooth and creamy, 2 minutes. Beat in eggs, one at a time, beating well after each addition. Mix yogurt, apple juice and vanilla in a small bowl.

4. On low speed, beat flour mixture into butter mixture in 3 additions, alternating with yogurt mixture and ending with flour. Stir in apples and walnuts if desired. Spread batter in prepared pan.

5. Prepare topping: Mix flour, brown sugar and cinnamon in a small bowl. Work butter in with fingers until pea-size pieces form. Add nuts if desired. Sprinkle over batter.

6. Bake in heated 350° oven 50 minutes or until a wooden pick inserted in center comes out clean. Transfer pan to a wire rack to cool. Serve cake slightly warm.

Orange Loaf

Sunny, citrusy tang—just right for tea.

MAKES *12 servings* PREP *10 minutes*

BAKE *at 350° for 35 minutes*

COOK *5 minutes*

1¾ cups all-purpose flour
⅓ cup sugar
1 tablespoon baking powder
¾ teaspoon salt
3 tablespoons unsalted butter, cut into small pieces and well chilled
1½ tablespoons poppy seeds
1½ tablespoons grated orange rind
¼ cup vegetable oil
1 egg
½ cup milk
¼ cup orange juice
1½ teaspoons orange extract

Glaze

2 tablespoons honey
2 tablespoons orange juice
2 teaspoons lemon juice

1. Heat oven to 350°. Coat a 6-cup bundt pan with nonstick cooking spray.

2. Combine flour, sugar, baking powder and salt in a large bowl. Cut in butter until mixture resembles fine crumbs. Stir in poppy seeds and orange rind.

3. Lightly beat together oil, egg, milk, orange juice and orange extract in a small bowl. Stir into flour mixture until just blended. Spoon batter into prepared pan.

4. Bake in heated 350° oven 35 minutes or until golden and a wooden pick inserted in center comes out clean. Remove from pan to a wire rack.

5. Meanwhile, prepare glaze: Combine honey, orange juice and lemon juice in a small saucepan; bring to boiling over medium-high heat. Adjust heat to low; cook until slightly thickened, about 5 minutes. Remove from heat and let glaze cool. Brush over top of baked loaf.

Yogurt Coffee Cake

Extra egg whites plus yogurt make this coffee cake especially light and airy.

MAKES *12 servings*

PREP *20 minutes*

BAKE *at 350° for 50 to 55 minutes*

COOL *15 minutes*

¾ cup chopped pecans
½ cup firmly packed light-brown sugar
1½ teaspoons ground cinnamon
2½ cups all-purpose flour
1½ teaspoons baking powder
1½ teaspoons baking soda
½ teaspoon salt
½ cup (1 stick) butter or margarine, at room temperature
1 cup granulated sugar
3 whole eggs
3 egg whites
1½ cups plain low-fat yogurt
1½ teaspoons vanilla

1. Heat oven to 350°. Grease a 10-inch (12-cup) bundt pan.

2. Combine pecans, brown sugar and cinnamon in a small bowl.

3. Whisk flour, baking powder, baking soda and salt in a medium-size bowl.

4. With a mixer on medium speed, beat butter and granulated sugar in a large bowl until light and fluffy. Add eggs and egg whites, one at a time, beating well after each addition. Beat flour mixture into egg mixture in 3 additions, alternating with yogurt and ending with flour mixture. Beat in vanilla.

5. Spread half of batter into prepared pan. Sprinkle evenly with half of pecan mixture. Spoon remaining batter over top, spreading carefully, and sprinkle with remaining pecan mixture.

6. Bake in heated 350° oven 50 to 55 minutes or until top is golden brown and a wooden pick inserted in center of cake comes out clean.

7. Cool cake in pan on a wire rack 15 minutes. Run a knife around edges of cake at pan sides and center; invert cake onto a plate, then invert onto another rack so crumb layer is on top. Let cool completely or serve warm.

Double Blueberry Coffee Cake

Lemonade adds zip to our tender, blueberry-laced cake; a blueberry sauce tops it off. Shown on page 139.

MAKES *12 servings*

PREP *20 minutes*

COOK *5 to 7 minutes*

BAKE *at 350° for 45 to 50 minutes*

3 cups cake flour (not self-rising)
2½ teaspoons baking powder
¼ teaspoon salt
1¼ cups (2½ sticks) unsalted butter, at room temperature
1¾ cups sugar
4 eggs
1 tablespoon grated lemon rind
2 teaspoons vanilla
1 cup lemonade
1½ cups blueberries

Blueberry Sauce

1 cup blueberries
¼ cup sugar
2 teaspoons cornstarch
¼ cup water

Blueberries for garnish (optional)

1. Heat oven to 350°. Coat a 10-inch (12-cup) bundt pan with nonstick cooking spray.

2. Sift together cake flour, baking powder and salt onto a piece of waxed paper.

3. With a mixer on medium speed, beat butter in a medium-size bowl until smooth. Beat in sugar until light and fluffy, 2 to 3 minutes. Beat in eggs, one at a time, beating well after each addition. Beat in lemon rind and vanilla.

4. Beat flour mixture into butter mixture in 3 additions, alternating with lemonade and ending with flour mixture. Fold in blueberries. Scrape batter into prepared pan.

5. Bake in heated 350° oven 45 to 50 minutes or until top is golden and a wooden pick inserted in center of cake comes out clean. Transfer cake in pan to a wire rack; let cool completely, 1 hour. Run a knife around edges of cake at pan sides and center and invert cake onto a serving dish.

6. Meanwhile, prepare sauce: Combine blueberries, sugar, cornstarch and water in a medium-size saucepan. Cook over medium heat until sugar is dissolved, liquid is no longer cloudy and blueberries begin to burst, 5 to 7 minutes. Transfer mixture to a food processor or blender. Whirl to a smooth puree.

7. To serve, cut cake into slices and drizzle with warm or room-temperature blueberry sauce; garnish with blueberries if desired.

Chocolate and Peanut Butter Bread

Chocolate and Peanut Butter Bread

Wrap mini chocolate-peanut butter cups in balls of dough; then stack them high in a baking pan for a towering taste treat.

MAKES *1 round loaf (24 slices)*

PREP *25 minutes*

RISE *1¾ hours*

BAKE *at 375° for 30 to 35 minutes*

¾ cup warm water (105° to 115°)
2 teaspoons plus ⅓ cup sugar
2 envelopes (¼ ounce each) active dry yeast
2 tablespoons butter, at room temperature
¼ cup smooth peanut butter
1 egg
3 to 3¼ cups bread flour
1 teaspoon salt
26 mini chocolate-peanut butter cups
1 tablespoon milk

1. Mix together warm water and 2 teaspoons sugar in a small bowl. Sprinkle yeast over top. Let stand until foamy, 5 to 10 minutes.

2. Mix together butter, peanut butter, egg, 2 cups flour, salt and remaining ⅓ cup sugar in a large bowl. Add yeast mixture. Beat with a mixer on medium speed 3 minutes or until well combined. Stir in 1 cup flour or more as needed for dough to come together.

3. Turn out dough onto a lightly floured surface. Knead until smooth and elastic, about 8 minutes, adding more flour as needed to prevent sticking. Place in a greased bowl, turning to coat. Cover with a clean kitchen towel or plastic wrap. Let rise in a warm place about 1¾ hours, until doubled in volume.

4. Punch down dough. Let rest 5 minutes. Turn out onto a floured surface. Gently roll or pat into a 9-inch square. With a sharp knife or pizza cutter, cut into 36 equal squares (6 across by 6 down).

5. Unwrap 18 mini peanut butter cups. Cut each in half. Grease a 6-cup bundt pan or 9-inch round layer-cake pan.

6. Enclose each peanut butter cup half in a dough square, pinching dough edges together to seal and form a ball. Place balls, smooth side down, in bottom of prepared pan; add balls in layers until all are used.

7. Place pan in cold oven. Turn oven on to 375°. Bake bread 30 to 35 minutes or until top is golden and puffed. Immediately remove bread from pan; cool on a wire rack.

8. Meanwhile, unwrap remaining 8 mini peanut butter cups. Melt in a small saucepan over very low heat. Stir in milk until smooth. Drizzle over bread.

9. To serve, cut bread into slices or pull pieces apart.

CHOCOLATE–PEANUT BUTTER BREAD HOW-TO'S

Enclose each filling piece in a dough square, pinching dough edges together to seal.

Place dough balls, smooth side down, in pan, making layers until all balls are used.

Cheese-Filled Crowns

Roll up the dough like a jelly roll, then slice and bake in muffin cups. Voilà. Perfect puffs filled with berry-flavored cream cheese. Shown on page 139.

MAKES *16 crowns*
PREP *25 minutes*
RISE *1¼ hours*
REFRIGERATE *15 minutes*
BAKE *at 350° for 15 to 20 minutes*

Dough

- ½ cup warm water (105° to 115°)
- 2 teaspoons plus ¼ cup maple syrup
- 2 envelopes (¼ ounce each) active dry yeast
- 6 tablespoons butter, melted
- 1 whole egg
- ¼ cup sweetened dried cranberries, chopped
- 3 to 3¼ cups bread flour
- 1½ teaspoons salt

Filling

- 4 ounces berry-flavored cream cheese (½ cup)
- 1 tablespoon berry preserves
- 3 tablespoons all-purpose flour
- 1 egg yolk
- 1 teaspoon vanilla
   Pinch ground nutmeg
- ¼ cup chopped pecans

Topping

- 1 teaspoon sugar
- ¼ teaspoon ground cinnamon

1. Prepare dough: Mix warm water and 2 teaspoons maple syrup in a small bowl. Sprinkle yeast over top. Let stand until foamy, 5 to 10 minutes.

2. Combine remaining ¼ cup maple syrup, butter, egg, cranberries, 2 cups flour and salt in a large bowl. Add yeast mixture. Beat with mixer on medium speed 3 minutes or until well combined. Stir in enough of remaining flour to make a soft dough.

3. Turn out dough onto a lightly floured surface. Knead until smooth and elastic, 5 to 8 minutes, adding more flour as needed to prevent sticking. Place in a greased large bowl, turning to coat. Cover with a clean kitchen towel or plastic wrap. Let rise in a warm place until doubled in volume, about 1¼ hours.

4. Punch down dough. Let rest 5 minutes.

5. Meanwhile, prepare filling: Beat cream cheese, preserves, flour, egg yolk, vanilla and nutmeg in a small bowl until smooth.

6. Turn out dough onto a floured surface. Using a floured rolling pin, roll out dough to a 16 x 11-inch rectangle. Spread filling over dough, leaving a 1-inch border. Sprinkle with pecans. Roll up from a long side. Cover with greased plastic wrap. Refrigerate 15 minutes to firm slightly.

7. Meanwhile, grease 16 cups in two standard 12-muffin pans.

8. Cut chilled roll into 16 equal slices. Place each slice, cut side up, in a greased muffin cup. Using kitchen shears held point down, cut each slice into quarters; spread dough pieces apart with your fingertips. Cover pans. Let rise until doubled in volume, 25 to 30 minutes.

9. Heat oven to 350°.

10. Prepare topping: Mix sugar and cinnamon. Sprinkle over crowns.

11. Bake in heated 350° oven 15 to 20 minutes or until golden brown. Transfer pan to a wire rack to cool slightly, about 10 minutes. Remove crowns from pan and serve warm.

Spiced Doughnuts

Make these on a lazy Saturday when you can take the time, and enjoy them that same day (as if you would have any leftovers!).

MAKES *20 doughnuts and 20 holes*

PREP *25 minutes*

REFRIGERATE *1 hour*

COOK *about 40 minutes*

Doughnuts

3¾ cups all-purpose flour
¾ cup granulated sugar
¼ cup packed light-brown sugar
¾ cup buttermilk
2 eggs
2 tablespoons solid vegetable shortening
2 teaspoons baking powder
1 teaspoon baking soda
1 teaspoon ground cinnamon
½ teaspoon ground nutmeg
½ teaspoon salt
¼ teaspoon ground allspice
¼ teaspoon ground cloves
  Vegetable oil for frying

Toppings *(optional)*

Sugar & Spice Mix (recipe follows)
Brown sugar
Granulated sugar
Confectioners' Sugar Glaze
(recipe follows)
Finely chopped nuts
Toasted coconut (see page 231)

1. Place 2 cups flour, sugars, buttermilk, eggs, shortening, baking powder, baking soda, cinnamon, nutmeg, salt, allspice and cloves in a large bowl. With a mixer on low speed, beat just until smooth, constantly scraping sides of bowl, about 1 minute. Increase speed to medium; beat 1 minute.

2. On low speed, beat in remaining 1¾ cups flour. Cover bowl tightly with plastic wrap; refrigerate 1 hour.

3. Pour oil into a deep-fat fryer to a depth of 3 to 4 inches (or use saucepan deep enough to allow 5 to 6 inches between top of oil and top of pan). Heat over medium-high heat, until temperature registers 370° on a deep-fat thermometer.

4. On a lightly floured surface, roll out dough to ½-inch thickness. Using a floured 3-inch doughnut cutter, or 3-inch and ¾-inch plain round cookie cutters, and gathering and rerolling scraps as necessary, cut out 20 doughnuts and 20 doughnut holes.

5. Using a metal slotted spoon, place doughnut holes in hot oil; as they rise to surface, turn frequently until evenly golden, 3 to 4 minutes. Remove holes with spoon to paper toweling to drain. Repeat with doughnuts, frying 2 or 3 at a time.

6. Let cool completely on paper toweling, turning once. If desired, coat with toppings: Place each sugar topping in a separate plastic food storage bag; add doughnuts, one at a time, and shake to coat. Or spread glaze over doughnuts, then sprinkle nuts or coconut on top.

Sugar & Spice Mix

Whisk together ½ cup granulated sugar, ½ teaspoon ground cinnamon, ¼ teaspoon ground nutmeg, ⅛ teaspoon ground allspice and ⅛ teaspoon ground cloves in a small bowl.

Confectioners' Sugar Glaze

Whisk together 1 cup confectioners' sugar and 1 to 2 tablespoons milk in a small bowl until well blended and a good glazing consistency.

Old-Fashioned Crumb Cake

Looking for the best-ever crumb cake? This yeasty version as a serious contender: Lots of crumbs, tender cake—it has it all.

MAKES *16 servings*

PREP *30 minutes* RISE *2½ to 3 hours*

BAKE *at 375° for 30 minutes*

¼ cup milk
¼ cup granulated sugar
⅓ cup solid vegetable shortening
½ teaspoon salt
¼ cup warm water (105° to 115°)
1 envelope active dry yeast
2 eggs, lightly beaten
2½ cups all-purpose flour

Topping

2 cups all-purpose flour
1 cup packed light-brown sugar
1 teaspoon ground cinnamon
¼ teaspoon ground nutmeg
¼ teaspoon salt
1 cup (2 sticks) butter, melted
¼ cup confectioners' sugar for dusting

1. Heat milk, sugar, shortening and salt in a small saucepan over medium heat just until shortening is melted. Let cool until lukewarm.

2. Meanwhile, pour warm water into a large bowl. Sprinkle yeast over top; let stand until foamy, about 5 minutes. Stir to dissolve yeast. Add cooled milk mixture, eggs and ½ cup flour. Beat with a wooden spoon until smooth. Stir in remaining flour until dough comes together. Turn out onto a floured surface. Knead 5 minutes or until smooth and silky.

3. Place dough in a greased large bowl, turning to coat. Cover; let rise in a warm place until doubled in volume, 1½ to 2 hours.

4. Coat a 13 x 9 x 2-inch baking pan with nonstick cooking spray. Punch down dough and press into pan; cover with plastic wrap. Let rise 1 hour or until almost doubled in volume.

5. Heat oven to 375°.

6. Prepare topping: Whisk flour, brown sugar, cinnamon, nutmeg and salt in a medium-size bowl. Stir in melted butter until mixture is crumbly. Crumble topping evenly over dough in pan.

7. Bake cake in heated 375° oven 30 minutes or until a knife inserted in center comes out clean and crumbs are lightly brown and crisp. Cool in pan on a wire rack 30 minutes. Sprinkle with confectioners' sugar. Cut into 16 squares. Serve warm or at room temperature.

Sticky Buns

As they bake, sticky buns send aloft an utterly irresistible aroma of caramelizing brown sugar.

MAKES *15 buns*

PREP *20 minutes* RISE *2¼ hours*

BAKE *at 350° for 25 to 28 minutes*

Dough

½ cup milk
¼ cup (½ stick) unsalted butter, cut into small pieces
2 tablespoons packed dark-brown sugar
2 tablespoons granulated sugar
½ teaspoon salt
1 envelope active dry yeast
½ cup warm water (105° to 115°)
2 eggs, lightly beaten
2 tablespoons sour cream
4⅓ cups all-purpose flour

Filling

¼ cup (½ stick) unsalted butter, at room
    temperature
½ cup packed dark-brown sugar
· ½ cup chopped pecans
½ teaspoon ground cinnamon

Topping

5 tablespoons unsalted butter, melted
4½ tablespoons packed dark-brown sugar
¾ cup maple syrup
¾ cup pecan halves

1. Prepare dough: Heat milk in a small
   saucepan over medium heat until
   steaming. Add butter, stirring until
   melted. Stir in sugars and salt. Remove
   from heat; let cool to lukewarm.

2. Sprinkle yeast over warm water in a
   medium-size bowl; let stand until foamy,
   about 5 minutes. Stir to dissolve yeast.

3. Stir eggs, sour cream and milk mixture
   into yeast mixture. Stir in 2 cups flour
   until well blended and smooth. Stir in
   2 more cups flour; knead until dough
   comes together.

4. Turn out dough on a lightly floured
   surface; knead until smooth and elastic,
   adding as much of remaining ⅓ cup
   flour as needed to prevent sticking.
   Place dough in a buttered bowl, turning
   to coat. Cover; let rise in a warm place,
   away from drafts, until doubled in
   volume, about 1½ hours.

5. Meanwhile, prepare filling: Mix butter,
   sugar, pecans and cinnamon in a small
   bowl. Set aside.

6. Prepare topping: Place melted butter in
   a 13 x 9 x 2-inch baking pan and brush
   sides with enough butter to coat. Add
   brown sugar and maple syrup to butter
   remaining in pan bottom; stir to dissolve
   sugar and spread mixture over bottom.
   Scatter pecans evenly on top.

7. Punch down dough; shape into a ball.
   Roll out on a lightly floured surface into
   a 24 x 10-inch rectangle. Brush with
   remaining 1 tablespoon melted butter.
   Scatter filling evenly over dough, leaving
   a 1-inch border all around.

8. Starting from a long side, roll up dough,
   jelly-roll style. Using a sharp knife, cut
   dough crosswise into 15 slices, about
   1½ inches each. Arrange slices, cut side
   up and rolled sides touching, on top
   of pecans in baking pan.

9. Coat a sheet of waxed paper with
   nonstick cooking spray; place, coated
   side down, over dough slices. Let rise
   in a warm place, until doubled in
   volume about 45 minutes.

10. Heat oven to 350°. Remove waxed
    paper from buns. Bake 25 to
    28 minutes, until golden brown. If
    buns start to brown too quickly, cover
    loosely with aluminum foil.

11. Run a knife around edges of pan to
    loosen buns. Invert a jelly-roll pan over
    top of pan; invert baking pan along
    with jelly-roll pan; shake gently. Place
    jelly roll pan on a wire rack. Lift off
    baking pan, letting topping drip over
    buns; scrape off any topping that sticks
    to bottom of pan. Separate buns and
    serve immediately.

STICKY BUNS HOW-TO'S

Starting from a long
side, roll up dough
jelly-roll style.

Cut dough into slices,
and arrange, cut-side
up and rolled sides
touching, on top of
pecan mixture.

Bread Baking Secrets

Don't let fear keep you from making homemade coffee cakes and other yeast-raised sweets. Our tips make the process worry-free and leave you to enjoy the heady aromas coming from the oven.

THE LOWDOWN ON YEAST

This so-called magic ingredient comes in several varieties. Here is a helpful primer:

- Active dry yeast is generally dissolved in warm water (105° to 110°, comfortably warm to the touch) and then added to other ingredients. It can also be used in the same way as fast-acting yeast.

- Fast-acting yeast is generally mixed dry with other ingredients. The liquid added to these must be very warm (120° to 130°) but not hot enough to burn your skin.

- Instant (bread machine) yeast should not be dissolved before use. Follow the instructions on the label.

- Store yeast at a cool temperature or in the refrigerator and use before the expiration date marked on the envelope.

BAKER'S TRICK

- Dough will be easier to braid or twist if you let it rest a few minutes first. Divide it and form into rough logs or rectangles as indicated, give it a few minutes, and then refine the shape and complete the recipe.

PREPARING DOUGH

1. Sprinkle yeast over warm water in a cup or mixing bowl as indicated in recipe. Let stand until foamy, about 5 minutes.

2. Mix dough, then shape into a ball and transfer to a floured work surface. To knead, press with heel of your hand, stretching dough away.

3. Fold dough back on itself. Rotate a quarter-turn and knead again. Repeat, folding, turning, and kneading until dough is smooth and elastic.

4. Place dough in a lightly greased bowl; cover and let rise as directed. To test if dough is risen, press top lightly with a fingertip. If it leaves an indentation, dough is ready to be punched down and shaped.

TO ROLL OUT DOUGH: On a floured surface, shape dough into a rectangle with your hands, then, using a rolling pin, roll it to the dimensions specified in recipe.

TO ROLL UP DOUGH: After spreading or sprinkling filling over dough, use both hands to roll dough into a log.

Breakfast Twist Bread

Take any humdrum morning up a notch with a scrumptious fruit-and-chocolate-filled loaf. Shown on page 138.

MAKES *12 servings*

PREP *20 minutes*

RISE *about 1¼ hours*

BAKE *at 350° for 25 minutes*

1 envelope active dry yeast
¼ cup warm water (105° to 115°)
¼ cup granulated sugar
½ teaspoon salt
¼ cup (½ stick) butter, melted
1 whole egg
¼ cup milk
½ teaspoon vanilla
2½ cups all-purpose flour
¾ cup dried-fruit bits
2 tablespoons mini chocolate chips
2 tablespoons chopped hazelnuts or walnuts
2 tablespoons brown sugar
2 tablespoons butter

Topping

2 tablespoons all-purpose flour
2 tablespoons granulated sugar
¼ teaspoon ground cinnamon
1 tablespoon butter, at room temperature
2 tablespoons chopped hazelnuts or walnuts
1 egg white, lightly beaten, for brushing

1. Sprinkle yeast over warm water in a small bowl. Let stand until foamy, about 5 minutes.

2. Whisk together granulated sugar, salt, butter, egg, milk and vanilla in a medium-size bowl. Stir in 1 cup flour. Stir in yeast mixture. With a wooden spoon, beat in enough of remaining flour for dough to hold together. (Dough will be soft.)

3. Turn out dough onto a generously floured surface. Knead until smooth and elastic, about 5 minutes. Transfer to a greased bowl, turning to coat. Cover with a clean kitchen towel or plastic wrap. Let rise in a warm place until doubled in volume, about 1 hour.

4. Combine fruit bits, chocolate chips and nuts in a small bowl. Heat brown sugar and butter in small saucepan until melted and well combined. Stir into fruit mixture.

5. Punch down dough; turn out onto a work surface. Divide dough in half. Roll out 1 piece into a 14 x 8-inch rectangle. Sprinkle fruit mixture on top, making a 2-inch wide band lengthwise in center of rectangle. Fold unfilled portion of dough over filling, first one side and then the other. Pinch dough together along seam and at ends to seal. Gently roll filled dough over on surface, forming a log. Repeat with remaining half of dough and remaining fruit mixture.

6. Grease a baking sheet. Lay logs side by side on work surface. Twist them together, holding one end firmly and twisting opposite end with your hand. Squeeze logs together at each end of twist and tuck ends under. Transfer to baking sheet. Cover with a clean kitchen towel or plastic wrap; let rise in warm place until doubled in volume, 45 minutes.

7. Heat oven to 350°.

8. Prepare topping: Mix together flour, granulated sugar and cinnamon in a small bowl. Add butter and blend in with back of a spoon until mixture is crumbly. Stir in chopped nuts.

9. When bread has risen, brush top with egg white and sprinkle with topping. Bake in heated 350° oven 25 minutes or until lightly browned. Transfer bread on baking sheet to a wire rack and cool 5 minutes. Serve bread warm or transfer to rack to cool completely.

Gingerbraid

This fragrant, gingery round can stand as a centerpiece—until you can no longer resist the temptation to cut it. Crystallized ginger adds glitter to the top.

MAKES *16 servings*
PREP *1 hour*
RISE *about 3 hours*
BAKE *at 350° for 35 minutes*

Dough

- 2 envelopes active dry yeast
- 1 cup warm water (105° to 115°)
- ½ cup (1 stick) butter, at room temperature
- 3 tablespoons sugar
- 2 eggs
- ⅓ cup dark molasses
- 3 tablespoons ground ginger
- 1 tablespoon finely chopped crystallized ginger
- ¾ teaspoon ground cinnamon
- 1 teaspoon salt
- ½ teaspoon black pepper
- 4 cups bread flour

Glaze

- ¼ cup sugar
- 2 tablespoons water
- 1 tablespoon finely chopped crystallized ginger for sprinkling

1. Prepare dough: Sprinkle yeast over warm water in a small bowl. Let stand until foamy, about 5 minutes.

2. With a mixer on medium speed, beat butter in a large bowl until creamy. Beat in sugar until fluffy. Beat in eggs. On low speed, beat in molasses, ground ginger, crystallized ginger, cinnamon, salt, pepper and 2 cups bread flour. Beat in yeast mixture and ⅓ cup flour until smooth.

3. Adding ⅓ cup at a time, stir in enough flour to make a dough that can be kneaded without sticking to sides of bowl. Turn out dough onto a lightly floured work surface. Knead until soft and elastic, about 5 minutes. Transfer to a large greased bowl, turning to coat. Cover with a clean kitchen towel. Let rise in a warm place until doubled in volume, about 2 hours.

4. Coat a 9½ x 4-inch tube pan with a removable center with nonstick cooking spray. Punch down dough; divide dough into 3 equal pieces. Using your hands, roll each piece into 22-inch-long rope. Place ropes side by side. At 1 end, gently press ropes together onto work surface to form top of braid. Braid ropes. Gently bring ends of braid together, forming a ring; press ends together and seal with a little water. Transfer braid to prepared pan. Cover with a clean kitchen towel. Let rise in a warm place until doubled in volume, 45 to 60 minutes.

5. Heat oven to 350°. Bake braid 35 minutes or until puffed and lightly browned. Run a knife around edges if bread is stuck to pan. Remove center section of tube pan, then remove bread from pan to a wire rack to cool.

6. Meanwhile, prepare glaze: Heat sugar and water in a small saucepan over medium heat until sugar is completely dissolved. Let syrup cool slightly. Brush over top of braid. Sprinkle with remaining crystallized ginger. Serve warm or at room temperature.

Gingerbraid

Chocolate Bread with Macadamia Crumb Topping

Serving lunch or brunch? This honey-flavored bread with a twist that shows off the creamy filling is guaranteed to be a hit.

MAKES *16 servings*

PREP *35 minutes*

RISE *2¼ hours to 3 hours*

BAKE *at 350° for 30 to 35 minutes*

Chocolate Bread

½ cup warm (105° to 115°) water
2 packages active dry yeast
⅓ cup honey
6 tablespoons (¾ stick) butter, at room temperature
1 egg
½ cup unsweetened cocoa powder
½ teaspoon salt
2½ to 3 cups bread flour

Cheese Filling

4 ounces cream cheese, at room temperature
¼ cup sugar
¼ cup all-purpose flour
1 egg, lightly beaten
1 teaspoon vanilla
¼ teaspoon ground nutmeg

Crumb Topping

¼ cup all-purpose flour
¼ cup sugar
½ teaspoon ground cinnamon
2 tablespoons unsalted butter, at room temperature
¼ cup chopped macadamia nuts

Garnishes (optional)

Fresh red currants
Strawberries
Grape-ivy leaves

1. Prepare bread: Combine water, yeast and 2 teaspoons honey in a large bowl. Let stand until foamy, about 10 minutes.

2. Add butter, egg, cocoa, salt, 1½ cups flour and remaining honey to yeast mixture. With a mixer on medium-low speed, beat 2 minutes, scraping down bowl frequently. Stir in enough of remaining flour, about 1¼ cups, to make a soft dough.

3. Turn out dough onto a floured surface. Knead 5 minutes or until smooth and elastic. Transfer to a greased bowl, turning to coat. Cover with plastic wrap or a clean kitchen towel. Let rise in a warm place until doubled in volume, 1½ to 2 hours.

4. Punch down dough; turn out onto a floured surface. Using a floured rolling pin, roll dough into a 16 x 11-inch rectangle.

5. Prepare filling: Beat together cream cheese, sugar, flour, egg, vanilla and nutmeg in a small bowl until blended. Spread filling over dough, leaving a 1-inch border all around. Starting with a long side, roll up jelly-roll fashion.

6. Grease a baking sheet. Using a serrated knife and beginning 3 inches from 1 end, cut dough roll in half lengthwise. Transfer to baking sheet; rotate each half so cut side faces up. Cross left half over right half. Repeat once. Pinch ends together to seal and tuck them under twisted roll. Cover with greased plastic wrap. Let rise in a warm place until doubled in volume, 45 to 60 minutes.

7. Meanwhile, prepare topping: Combine flour, sugar and cinnamon in a small bowl. Add butter; blend in with back of a spoon until crumbly. Stir in nuts.

8. Heat oven to 350°.

9. When bread has risen, sprinkle with topping. Bake in heated 350° oven 30 to 35 minutes. Transfer bread on baking sheet to a wire rack and cool 5 minutes. Serve bread warm or transfer to rack to cool completely. Garnish with currants, strawberries and grape-ivy leaves if desired.

Honey Nut Twist

An egg-rich dough encases a mix of walnuts, sugar and honey; after baking, a glaze of apricot preserves completes the package.

MAKES *20 servings*

PREP *40 minutes*

RISE *30 minutes* BAKE *1 hour*

Dough

1 cup sugar
1½ teaspoons salt
2 envelopes fast-acting yeast
7½ cups all-purpose flour
1½ cups milk
½ cup (1 stick) unsalted butter
3 eggs

Filling

2 cups chopped walnuts
½ cup sugar
½ cup honey
¼ cup (½ stick) unsalted butter, melted
1½ teaspoons ground cinnamon

Glaze

¼ cup apricot preserves

1. Prepare dough: Combine sugar, salt, yeast and 2 cups flour in a large bowl.

2. Heat milk and butter in a small saucepan until very warm (125° to 130°). With a mixer on medium speed, gradually beat milk mixture into flour mixture. Beat in eggs and 2 cups remaining flour to make a thick batter. With a wooden spoon, stir in 3 cups flour, ½ cup at a time.

3. Turn out dough onto a lightly floured surface. Knead until smooth and elastic, 5 minutes; work in remaining flour as needed to prevent sticking. Shape into a ball. Cover with a clean kitchen towel; let rest 10 minutes.

4. Prepare filling: Combine nuts, sugar, honey, butter and cinnamon in a small bowl.

5. Roll out dough on lightly floured surface with a lightly floured rolling pin to a 20 x 12-inch rectangle. Spread nut filling over dough. Starting from a long side, tightly roll up dough jelly-roll fashion; pinch seam to seal. Cut roll in half lengthwise, stopping cutting about 1 inch from 1 end. Rotate halves so cut sides face up. Cross left half over right half. Repeat until dough halves are twisted into a rope. Pinch ends to seal.

6. Grease a 10-inch tube pan with a removable bottom. Place twist in pan, cut side up, shaping into ring and pressing ends together to seal. Cover with plastic wrap. Let rise in a warm place until doubled in volume, about 30 minutes.

7. Heat oven to 350°. Place a sheet of aluminum foil on lower rack to catch any drips from pan.

8. Bake twist in heated 350° oven 1 hour or until golden brown. Tent pan with aluminum foil during last 30 minutes of baking to prevent overbrowning. Cool twist in pan on a wire rack 20 minutes. Run a knife around sides and center of pan to loosen twist. Remove sides of pan.

9. Prepare glaze: Melt apricot preserves in a small saucepan over medium heat, stirring occasionally. Brush over top and sides of twist. Cool twist on rack to room temperature before slicing.

Frozen Strawberry Zabaglione, *page 168*

Nutmeg Pots de Crème, *page 183*

Creamy Delights

Melon Granita, *page 177*

Golden Baked Alaska

It's a blast from the past, but our Baked Alaska is still fun after all these years.

MAKES *8 servings*

PREP *20 minutes*

FREEZE *several hours or overnight*

BAKE *crust at 350° for 12 to 15 minutes; meringue at 475° for 2 to 4 minutes*

Filling

1 pint strawberry ice cream or frozen yogurt, softened

1 pint chocolate ice cream or frozen yogurt, softened

Dough

9 ounces (half of 18-ounce tube) refrigerated chocolate-chip cookie dough (see note, right)

¼ cup finely chopped toasted walnuts

Meringue

⅓ cup pasteurized dried egg whites

⅔ cup warm water

½ cup sugar

1. Heat oven to 350°.

2. Prepare filling: Line a 1-quart round bowl with plastic wrap, leaving a generous overhang. Scoop strawberry ice cream into bowl; pack in and smooth top until level. Top with chocolate ice cream; pack and smooth. Fold overhanging plastic wrap over top of ice cream. Freeze several hours or overnight, until very firm.

3. Prepare dough: Line a baking sheet with aluminum foil; grease an area 8 inches in diameter in center.

4. Using a wooden spoon, work together dough and walnuts in a large bowl until well blended. Shape dough into disc. (If dough is too soft to work with, wrap it and return to refrigerator until firm, about 10 minutes.)

5. Place dough in center of greased foil. Pat with hands or roll with a floured rolling pin into 8-inch round. Bake in heated 350° oven 12 to 15 minutes or until cookie is lightly browned at edges. Transfer cookie, still on foil, to a wire rack to cool completely. Increase oven temperature to 475°.

6. Prepare meringue: Remove bowl with ice cream from freezer; let stand at room temperature while preparing meringue. Stir dried egg whites into warm water in a small bowl to dissolve completely. Beat with a mixer at high speed until fluffy. Gradually add sugar, beating until meringue forms stiff peaks.

7. Loosen cookie from foil, then return to same piece of foil; transfer to an insulated baking sheet.

8. Lift ice cream from bowl with its plastic wrapping. (It may be necessary to loosen sides by gently running a long, thin metal spatula between bowl and plastic wrap.) Fold back plastic wrap from top of ice cream; invert ice cream onto center of cookie. Peel off plastic wrap. Completely cover ice cream with meringue, swirling to seal within ¼ inch of cookie edge.

9. Bake in heated 475° oven 2 to 4 minutes or until meringue is lightly browned. Using a wide spatula, gently slide Alaska from foil onto a serving platter. Serve immediately.

NOTE: *For a homemade crust, prepare the dough for Chocolate Chip Sugar Cookies on page 57, adding ½ cup chopped toasted walnuts. Use half of the recipe, shaping into a disc and chilling 10 minutes. If making your own dough, skip step 4, left.*

Chocolate Almond Bars

Melted semisweet or bittersweet chocolate—or a medley of the two—blankets these ice cream bars for grown-ups. Who could possibly pass one up?

MAKES *12 bars*

PREP *1 hour*

FREEZE *5 hours or overnight*

½ gallon premium coffee- or vanilla ice cream (in a rectangular container)
12 flat wooden sticks
1 cup almonds, toasted (see page 231)
2 pounds semisweet or bittersweet chocolate or a combination of both, chopped
3 tablespoons solid vegetable shortening

1. Line a baking sheet with waxed paper.

2. Unwrap ice cream and place on a cutting board. Cut block crosswise into thirds; rewrap 2 pieces and return to freezer. Working quickly, cut ice cream on cutting board crosswise into 8 equal slices, each about ½ inch thick.

3. Using a spatula, transfer 4 ice-cream slices to prepared baking sheet. Gently press a wooden stick lengthwise onto half of each piece, extending end to make a handle. Top each piece with another ice cream piece to make a bar, lining up edges. Cover with waxed paper or plastic wrap. Place baking sheet in freezer. Repeat with each remaining third of ice cream and remaining 8 wooden sticks, transferring assembled bars to baking sheet in freezer. Freeze until firm but not solid, about 1 hour.

4. Finely chop almonds. Place in a pie plate. Using a spatula, remove bars, one at a time, from baking sheet and transfer to pie plate; press chopped nuts onto sides and edges. Return each bar to baking sheet, placing under wrapping. Freeze until solid, about 2 hours.

5. Place chocolate and shortening in a microwave-safe shallow dish. Microwave at 100% power 2 minutes. Stir until mixture is blended and chocolate is completely melted. If chocolate is not completely melted, microwave 30 to 60 seconds longer, then stir mixture again.

6. Remove wrapping from baking sheet in freezer. Remove bars from freezer, one at a time, and quickly dip into chocolate mixture; use a spoon or rubber spatula to coat any exposed nuts with chocolate. Return each bar to baking sheet. Chocolate should harden almost immediately. Freeze 2 hours. Serve or store in plastic food-storage bags in freezer.

ICE CREAM BAR BASICS

Lay a wooden stick, end extended, onto each ice cream slice. Top with second ice cream slice.

Berry–Ice Cream Torte

Don't be daunted when you see how long this layered beauty takes—most of the time the torte is resting in the freezer! Read the recipe from start to finish before you begin to make sure you'll have the ice cream at the right temperature for each step.

Berry–Ice Cream Torte

PREP *60 minutes*

BAKE *at 375° for 7 minutes*

REFRIGERATE *2 hours*

FREEZE *about 18 hours*

Chocolate Ganache

1½ cups heavy cream
1 package (12 ounces) semisweet chocolate chips (2 cups)
1½ teaspoons vanilla

Cake

⅓ cup sifted cake flour (not self-rising)
½ teaspoon baking powder
⅛ teaspoon salt
1 egg
¼ cup sugar
1½ tablespoons water
½ teaspoon vanilla

Ice Cream Layers

3 pints vanilla ice cream
⅓ cup shelled pistachios, coarsely chopped
2 tablespoons pistachio instant pudding-and-pie-filling mix
1 cup strawberries, hulled

Garnishes (optional)

Whipped cream
Strawberries

1. Prepare ganache: Bring cream to boiling in a small saucepan over medium-high heat. Remove from heat. Stir in chocolate chips until melted and smooth. Stir in vanilla. Pour into a pie plate or shallow bowl. Refrigerate until a good spreading consistency, 2 hours.

2. Prepare cake: Heat oven to 375°. Grease a 9 x 3-inch springform pan; dust bottom with flour. Line sides of pan (not bottom) with waxed paper.

3. Sift together cake flour, baking powder and salt onto a sheet of waxed paper.

4. With a mixer on medium-high speed, beat egg in a small bowl until fluffy. Increase speed to high, gradually add sugar, beating until a thick ribbon forms when beaters are raised, about 3 minutes. Gently stir in water and vanilla until well mixed. Fold in flour mixture. Pour batter into prepared pan.

5. Bake cake in heated 375° oven about 7 minutes or until top is golden and center springs back when lightly pressed with a fingertip. Cool cake in pan on a wire rack.

6. Meanwhile, prepare ice cream layers: Transfer 1 pint ice cream to refrigerator to soften about 30 minutes.

7. Spoon softened ice cream into a large bowl. Add pistachios and pudding-and-pie-filling mix; beat with a mixer on medium speed until combined. Spread over cooled cake in springform pan. Freeze until firm, 3 hours.

8. Remove pan from freezer. Evenly spread 1 cup plus 2 tablespoons ganache over top of hardened ice cream. Freeze until firm, about 4 hours.

9. Meanwhile, transfer 1 pint remaining ice cream to refrigerator to soften about 30 minutes.

10. Remove pan with layered dessert from freezer. Spoon softened ice cream on top of hardened ganache. Freeze until firm, about 3 hours.

11. Remove pan from freezer. Spoon in remaining ganache; spread on top of hardened ice cream. Freeze until firm, 3 to 4 hours.

12. Meanwhile, transfer remaining 1 pint ice cream to refrigerator to soften about 30 minutes. While ice cream softens, mash ¼ cup strawberries in a small bowl. Chop remaining ¾ cup berries; stir into mashed berries. Add softened ice cream and beat together on medium speed until blended.

13. Remove pan with layered dessert from freezer. Spoon strawberry ice cream on top of hardened ganache, spreading evenly. Freeze until firm, 3 to 4 hours, or preferably overnight.

14. When ready to serve, transfer torte to refrigerator to soften 15 to 20 minutes. Remove sides of pan; peel off waxed paper. If garnish is desired, pipe whipped cream around top edge of torte; embellish with whole or halved strawberries.

ICE CREAM TORTE TACTICS

Spread cooled chocolate ganache over frozen ice cream mixture in pan.

Frozen Strawberry Zabaglione

Here is a dessert with all the rich creamy flavor of the classic Italian custard specialty and none of the last-minute hassle. The zabaglione is folded into strawberry puree and whipped cream, then frozen. Come serving time, simply slice and serve with more berries. Shown on page 162.

MAKES *12 servings*

PREP *30 minutes*

COOK *about 15 minutes*

FREEZE *2 to 4 hours, then overnight*

3   cups chopped strawberries (about
     2 pints whole strawberries)
1   cup sugar
4   egg yolks
2   whole eggs
¾   cup dry white wine
     Red food coloring
1   cup heavy cream
     Sliced strawberries for garnish (optional)
     Fresh mint sprigs for garnish (optional)

1. Coat a 9 x 5 x 2½-inch loaf pan with nonstick cooking spray. Line pan with plastic wrap.

2. Whirl strawberries in a food processor until smooth. Pour into a small bowl. Stir in ¼ cup sugar; set aside.

3. In top of a double boiler over simmering, not boiling, water, whisk together egg yolks, whole eggs and remaining ¾ cup sugar. Whisk in wine; whisk constantly until custard registers 160° on an instant-read thermometer and forms mounding ribbons when whisk is lifted, about 15 minutes.

4. Remove top of double boiler and place in a larger bowl filled halfway with ice and water. Whisk custard until cool. Stir in reserved strawberry puree. Transfer 2⅔ cups custard to a medium-size bowl. Transfer remaining custard to a second bowl; stir in red food coloring to tint bright pink—the color will be softened with the addition of the uncolored custard and whipped cream.

5. Beat cream in a medium-size bowl until soft peaks form. Fold 1⅓ cups whipped cream into bright pink custard. Fold remaining whipped cream into uncolored custard. Refrigerate both mixtures until ready to use.

6. Spread half of bright pink custard in prepared pan. Place in freezer until set, 1 to 2 hours. Spoon uncolored custard on top of frozen layer. Chill in freezer until set, 1 to 2 hours. Spread remaining bright pink custard over frozen layer. Cover pan; place in freezer overnight.

7. To unmold and serve, briefly dip pan into warm water. Invert onto a serving plate; gently shake to release. Lift off pan and remove plastic wrap. Garnish with whole strawberries and mint sprigs if desired.

ZABAGLIONE TECHNIQUE

Place top of double boiler in an ice-water bath. Whisk custard until it is cool.

Chocolate Ice Cream Cake

Whipped cream, ice cream, chocolate cake—they're an irresistible combination.

MAKES *20 servings*

PREP *45 minutes*

BAKE *at 350° for 18 minutes*

FREEZE *several hours*

½ cup sifted cake flour (not self-rising)
½ cup sifted unsweetened cocoa powder
¼ teaspoon salt
5 eggs, separated
½ teaspoon cream of tartar
1 cup sugar
1 teaspoon vanilla
½ gallon any flavor ice cream (in a rectangular container)

Frosting

4 squares (1 ounce each) semisweet chocolate, chopped
2 cups heavy cream
2 tablespoons strong brewed coffee

1. Heat oven to 350°.

2. Grease a 15 x 10 x 1-inch baking pan, or coat with nonstick cooking spray. Line bottom of pan with waxed paper; grease paper, or coat with spray.

3. Sift flour, cocoa powder and ⅛ teaspoon salt into a shallow bowl.

4. With a mixer on high speed, beat egg whites, cream of tartar and remaining ⅛ teaspoon salt in a large bowl until frothy. Beat in sugar, 1 tablespoon at a time, until soft peaks form. On low speed, beat in egg yolks and vanilla just until blended. Gently fold flour mixture into egg mixture. Spread evenly in prepared pan.

5. Bake in heated 350° oven 18 minutes or until center springs back when lightly touched with a fingertip. Cool cake in pan on a wire rack 10 minutes. Invert pan onto rack; remove pan. Gently peel waxed paper from warm cake; allow cake to cool completely.

6. Carefully transfer cake to a cutting board. Cut cake lengthwise into thirds.

7. Cut a piece of cardboard the exact size of 1 cake rectangle; wrap in aluminum foil. Place 1 cake rectangle on top of cardboard.

8. Unwrap ice cream and place on a cutting board. Quickly cut block lengthwise into 4 equal slices (expect the ice cream to splinter). Place 2 ice cream slices on top of cake on cardboard, aligning ends of ice cream with ends of cake. Fill gap in center with ice cream splinters. Top with a second cake rectangle, then another layer of ice cream and a final layer of cake. Wrap in plastic wrap. Freeze several hours or until cake is firm.

9. When ready to serve, prepare frosting: Combine chocolate, ¼ cup cream and coffee in a small saucepan over low heat, and stir until mixture is smooth and chocolate is melted. Remove from heat and let cool.

10. Meanwhile, with a mixer on medium-high, beat remaining 1¾ cups cream in a small bowl until soft peaks form.

11. Remove cake from freezer; unwrap. Spread chocolate mixture over top of cake. Spread whipped cream evenly over sides of cake. Serve immediately.

EASY ICE CREAM CAKE

Arrange ice cream and cake in layers, aligning at ends and filling gap with ice cream splinters.

Strawberry-Banana Torta

Layers of gelatin, cream cheese, fruit and crushed cookies make our torta oh-so-tempting.

Strawberry-Banana Torta

MAKES *12 servings*

PREP *30 minutes*

REFRIGERATE *3 hours or overnight*

20   chocolate sandwich cookies, finely crushed
3   tablespoons unsalted butter, melted
1   package (8 ounces) cream cheese
1   container (8 ounces) sour cream
½   cup sugar
2   tablespoons boiling water
1   envelope unflavored gelatin
1   box (3 ounces) strawberry-flavored gelatin mix
1   firm medium-size banana, sliced into ¼-inch-thick rounds (about 1 cup)
1   cup sliced strawberries

1. Coat an 8 x 8 x 2-inch square glass serving dish with nonstick cooking spray.

2. Mix cookies and butter in a medium-size bowl. Press evenly onto bottom of prepared serving dish. Freeze until set, 10 minutes.

3. Beat cream cheese, sour cream and ¼ cup sugar in a small bowl until well blended.

4. Measure boiling water into a cup. Sprinkle 1½ teaspoons unflavored gelatin on top. Let stand until softened, about 5 minutes. Stir to dissolve gelatin. Beat gelatin mixture into cream cheese mixture until smooth and creamy.

5. Remove cookie crust from freezer. Spread half of cream cheese mixture (about 1⅓ cups) evenly over crust. Freeze 10 minutes, until set.

6. Meanwhile, whisk together remaining unflavored gelatin, remaining ¼ cup sugar and strawberry-flavored gelatin mix in a small bowl. Then prepare mixture according to strawberry gelatin package directions. Stir in sliced bananas and strawberries.

7. Remove crust with cream cheese from freezer. Pour 2 cups fruit-gelatin mixture over cream cheese, smoothing evenly. Freeze 20 minutes, until set.

8. Remove crust with fillings from freezer. Spread remaining cream cheese mixture evenly over fruit-gelatin layer. Freeze 10 minutes, until set.

9. Remove crust from freezer and pour remaining fruit-gelatin mixture over cheese; freeze 20 minutes, until set.

10. Cover dish with plastic wrap and refrigerate (don't return to freezer) 3 hours or overnight.

11. To serve, cut torta into squares; use a spatula to transfer squares to individual dessert plates.

Coconut Bonbons with Two Sauces

Butterscotch or chocolate sauce with your bonbons? No need to decide—we like to serve them both!

MAKES *8 servings*

PREP *1 hour*

COOK *1 minute*

FREEZE *2 hours*

1 pint vanilla ice cream
⅔ cup sweetened flake coconut, toasted (see page 231)
⅔ cup cornflake crumbs
¼ teaspoon ground cinnamon
Butterscotch and Chocolate Sauces (recipes follow)

1. Line 2 baking sheets with waxed paper. Scoop about 18 ice cream balls (about 1 heaping tablespoon each) onto 1 prepared baking sheet; cover with plastic wrap and place in freezer. Repeat with second baking sheet and remaining ice cream. Freeze 1 hour.

2. Mix coconut, cornflake crumbs and cinnamon in a plastic food-storage bag.

3. Remove 1 baking sheet from freezer. Transfer 9 balls to a shallow dish; place baking sheet with remaining balls in refrigerator. One at a time, add balls to bag with coconut mixture; shake to coat; press coating into sides, reshaping ball if necessary. As soon as each ball is coated, return it to baking sheet in refrigerator. Repeat with remaining 9 balls on baking sheet, then return baking sheet to freezer. Repeat with remaining 18 balls on second baking sheet. If balls begin to melt, return to freezer.

4. To serve, drizzle sauces on 8 dessert plates. Top each with 3 or 4 bonbons.

Butterscotch Sauce

Combine ½ cup packed light-brown sugar, ½ cup corn syrup, 2 tablespoons butter, ⅛ teaspoon cinnamon and ⅛ teaspoon ginger in a small saucepan (not nonstick). Cook over medium heat, stirring occasionally, until sugar is dissolved, 8 minutes. Increase heat to medium-high. Bring mixture just to boiling. Remove from heat. Stir in 2 tablespoons half-and-half. Serve warm or at room temperature.

MAKES 1¼ cups

Chocolate Sauce

Chop 8 ounces semisweet chocolate and melt in a small saucepan over medium heat with 2 tablespoons butter, stirring until smooth. Slowly add 1 cup heavy cream, stirring until smooth and glossy. Remove from heat. Stir in ¾ teaspoon almond extract or vanilla.

MAKES 1¾ cups

Cookies 'n' Cream

Not only is our soothing mocha mixture a mere 200 calories with 3 grams of fat, it is also amazingly easy to make.

MAKES *6 servings* PREP *5 minutes*
REFRIGERATE *several hours*

1   teaspoon instant coffee powder
1   tablespoon hot water
⅔   cup chocolate sweetened condensed milk
¼   teaspoon vanilla
1   container (8 ounces) nonfat frozen whipped topping, thawed
8   chocolate wafer cookies, crushed
6   rolled sugar wafer cookies

1. In a cup, stir coffee powder into hot water until dissolved. Pour condensed milk into a small bowl. Stir in coffee and vanilla. Pour into a medium-size bowl; fold in whipped topping. Gently stir in crushed cookies.

2. Divide mixture among 6 dessert glasses. Refrigerate several hours. Garnish with rolled sugar wafer cookies.

Tropical Sorbet

Scoop up a serving of these icy tropical tastes and pretend you're lounging at a beach under the palm trees. Fresh mint sprigs make a perfect garnish.

MAKES *8 servings* PREP *10 minutes*
FREEZE *6 to 7 hours*

2   cans (20 ounces each) crushed pineapple, packed in its own juice
½   cup evaporated skim milk
¼   cup light corn syrup
1   tablespoon coconut extract
1   tablespoon grated orange rind

1. Place pineapple with its juice, skim milk, corn syrup, coconut extract and orange rind in a food processor. Whirl to puree. Pour mixture into a 13 x 9 x 2-inch metal baking pan. Cover; freeze until partially frozen, about 3 hours.

2. Spoon mixture into a food processor. Whirl until almost smooth—do not overprocess. Return mixture to pan. Cover; freeze until firm, 3 to 4 hours. Remove sorbet from freezer 15 minutes before serving.

Peachy Ice Cream

Jazz up plain old vanilla ice cream with pecans, crushed wafer cookies and, of course, peaches. Serve it plain, or in waffle bowls, topped with a sliced peach garnish.

MAKES *8 servings* PREP *15 minutes*
FREEZE *6 hours or overnight*

1   quart vanilla ice cream
1¼ cups frozen peach pieces, thawed
⅓   cup peach nectar
    Pinch ground nutmeg
    Pinch ground cinnamon
¼   cup pecans, coarsely chopped and toasted (see page 231)
¾   cup coarsely broken vanilla wafers (about 15 cookies)

1. Let ice cream soften slightly at room temperature. Place half of peach pieces in a blender. Pour peach nectar into a glass measure; stir in nutmeg and cinnamon. Add to blender; whirl to puree. Add ice cream. Pulse 6 to 8 times or until blended. Pour ice cream mixture into an 8 x 8 x 2-inch square cake pan.

2. Finely dice remaining peach pieces. Stir diced peaches, pecans and cookie pieces into pan with ice cream mixture until well blended. Freeze until mixture is firm, about 6 hours or overnight.

Mastering Mixing Techniques

The method you use to combine ingredients is very different depending on the nature of the recipe. These are the key techniques to know in order to wind up with perfect mousses, soufflés and more.

CREAMING

The technique for blending a fat (butter, shortening or oil) with sugar or another dry ingredient is called creaming. Begin with room temperature butter or vegetable shortening, and soften it by beating with an electric mixer, wooden spoon or whisk. Then, continuing to beat, add the sugar or other ingredient gradually. When all the sugar has been incorporated, continue to beat the mixture for 2 to 3 minutes longer. To make sure all the ingredients are being incorporated, stop every few minutes and, using a wooden spoon or rubber spatula, scrape down the sides of the mixing bowl.

BEATING

By beating ingredients, you not only blend them thoroughly, you incorporate air, which makes the mixture lighter and increases its volume. You can beat with a fork, a wooden spoon, a wire whisk or an electric mixer; if the recipe indicates a specific tool, use it. To make sure all the ingredients make it into the blend, scrape down the sides of the mixing bowl frequently.

Recipes often indicate how much beating is required. Phrases such as "beat until smooth," "beat until thick" "or beat 2 minutes" are common.

WHIPPING CREAM

You can whip heavy cream with a wire whisk, rotary eggbeater or electric mixer. Whichever you use, be sure to chill the beaters and mixing bowl first—for 1 hour in the refrigerator or about 30 minutes in the freezer. If the weather is very warm, it's a good idea to chill the cream in the freezer also; let it get very cold—a few ice crystals won't affect the whipping.

To whip, begin beating on low speed and then, as the cream increases in volume, you should increase the beating speed. When the cream is lightly thickened, add any flavoring indicated by the recipe. (If no flavoring is called for, but you would like one, for each cup of heavy cream you can add 2 tablespoons confectioners' sugar or ½ teaspoon extract or 2 tablespoons liqueur.) Continue beating until the cream forms soft peaks. Don't overbeat—you'll have butter!

FOLDING

You must be gentle when you add a beaten mixture to other ingredients (or vice versa) or you run the risk of deflating it. To prevent collapse, you should fold the two together instead of stirring them. For instance, soufflé recipes usually instruct you to fold the beaten egg whites into the egg yolks.

Be sure whichever ingredients you will be adding to (the egg yolks in the case of a soufflé) are in a large bowl. Drop the ingredients to be incorporated (the beaten egg whites) on top in a single pile. To fold, use a spatula or wooden spoon, sliding it down the side of the bowl to the bottom and then lifting the mixture with a sweeping motion, turning it over. Rotate the bowl a quarter turn and repeat the process. Repeat only as many times as are needed to barely mix the ingredients—the mixture will not be completely blended or smooth.

TEMPERING

Custards and custard sauces will curdle if the eggs are added to the hot liquid. To prevent this, temper the eggs by slowly whisking a little of the hot liquid into them, and then, depending on your recipe, whisking in the remaining hot liquid or whisking the egg mixture into the hot liquid.

Chocolate-Cherry Sandwiches

Cherries in the cookies, cherries in the ice cream—it all adds up to a happy summertime treat.

Blackberry-Lime Sherbet, Mango Mandarin Sherbet and Raspberry-Strawberry Sherbet, *opposite*; Chocolate-Cherry Sandwiches

MAKES *12 sandwiches*
PREP *25 minutes*
BAKE *at 350° for 10 minutes*
FREEZE *4 hours or overnight*

½ gallon cherry ice cream (in a rectangular container)
1 box (about 18 ounces) chocolate cake mix
2 eggs
½ cup vegetable oil
1 jar (about 6 ounces) maraschino cherries, drained and chopped
½ teaspoon cherry extract

1. Line a baking sheet with waxed paper.

2. Unwrap ice cream and place on a cutting board. With ice cream block resting on one long side, using a sharp knife, cut 6 lengthwise slices, each ½ inch thick. Place each slice on prepared baking sheet. Rewrap remaining ice cream and return to freezer. Cover baking sheet with plastic wrap and freeze 45 minutes or until firm.

3. Meanwhile, heat oven to 350°.

4. Stir together cake mix, eggs, oil, cherries and cherry extract in a large bowl until a stiff dough comes together. Divide into 24 pieces, about 1½ tablespoons each. Roll into balls. Place 3 inches apart on ungreased baking sheets, about 8 balls per sheet. Using bottom of a glass, flatten each ball into a 3-inch round; if dough is sticky, grease bottom of glass.

5. Bake cookies in heated 350° oven 10 minutes or until firm. Cool on baking sheet 2 minutes, then transfer to a wire rack to cool completely.

6. Remove ice cream slices from freezer; remove covering. Using a 3-inch round or scalloped cookie cutter, quickly cut 2 rounds out of each slice, for a total of 12 rounds. Place 1 cookie on a piece of plastic wrap. Using a spatula, transfer 1 ice cream round onto the cookie; top with another cookie. Enclose sandwich in plastic wrap. Repeat, making a total of 12 sandwiches. (If ice cream begins to melt, return baking sheet to freezer.) Freeze 3 hours or overnight.

Blackberry-Lime Sherbet

No need to invest in an ice cream maker— you can make this creamy sherbet using a food processor and your refrigerator freezer.

MAKES *6 cups*

PREP *30 minutes*

FREEZE *4 to 6 hours*

1½ cups water
1½ cups sugar
1 bag (12 ounces) frozen blackberries, thawed, or 2½ cups fresh blackberries
1 bag (12 ounces) frozen blueberries, thawed, or 2½ cups fresh blueberries
¼ cup fresh lime juice
 Red and blue liquid food colors, to make purple (about 5 drops each)
2 cups heavy cream or half-and-half
 Pinch salt
 Ice cream cones for serving (optional)
½ pint fresh blackberries for garnish (optional)

1. Bring water and sugar to simmering in a small saucepan over medium heat, stirring until sugar dissolves, about 4 minutes. Pour sugar syrup into a large bowl to cool.

2. Puree blackberries and blueberries in a food processor (do not use a blender). Strain through a fine-mesh sieve into bowl with sugar syrup, forcing berry mixture through with a rubber spatula; discard solids. Stir in lime juice and food colors.

3. Add cream and salt to berry puree, stirring until blended. Pour into a 13 x 9 x 2-inch baking pan. Freeze 2 hours.

4. Spoon mixture into food processor. Pulse to break up—do not overprocess. Return mixture to pan. Freeze 2 hours.

5. Spoon mixture into food processor again and pulse as before. Return mixture to pan. Freeze until firm. If desired, spoon into ice cream cones to serve and garnish with fresh berries.

Mango-Mandarin Sherbet

Prepare step 1 of Blackberry-Lime Sherbet. In step 2, substitute 2 drained 11-ounce cans mandarin orange segments for berries. Puree orange segments in a food processor. Pour into a large measuring cup; add enough mango nectar to make 2½ cups. Stir in ¾ teaspoon grated fresh ginger; omit lime juice and food colors. Continue with step 3.

Raspberry-Strawberry Sherbet

Prepare Blackberry-Lime Sherbet, substituting raspberries and strawberries for blackberries and blueberries, omitting food colors and replacing lime juice with lemon juice.

Raspberry Mousse Mint Boxes

Once you get the hang of making our perfect little jewel boxes out of chocolate-covered mints, you can fill them with any favorite mousse or pudding.

MAKES *5 servings*

PREP *30 minutes*

STAND *1½ hours*

5   ounces white baking chocolate
20 (1½-inch) square chocolate-covered
    thin mints
5   squares (1 ounce each) semisweet
    chocolate
1   package (10 ounces) frozen raspberries
    in syrup, thawed
1½ teaspoons unflavored gelatin
3   tablespoons water
¾   cup heavy cream
¼   cup confectioners' sugar
    Fresh red currants (in clusters) for
    garnish (optional)

1. Melt white chocolate in top of a double boiler over barely simmering, not boiling, water, stirring until smooth. Spoon into a custard cup, filling about two-thirds full; allow chocolate to cool slightly.

2. Line a baking sheet with waxed paper. Hold 1 mint by a corner and dip diagonally into white chocolate, coating halfway; repeat with a second mint. With white edges down, position mints upright on waxed paper; press vertical white edges together at right angles to form box corner. Repeat with remaining 18 mints, two at a time. Allow chocolate to set.

3. Meanwhile, in a second double boiler (or a metal bowl) melt semisweet chocolate over barely simmering, not boiling, water, stirring until smooth. Spoon into a second custard cup, filling about two-thirds full; allow chocolate to cool slightly.

4. Using a small spatula or butter knife and working with mint box corners in pairs, spread a little semisweet chocolate onto unattached vertical edges and then press them together to complete box sides. With boxes still upright on waxed paper, spoon about 1 tablespoon semisweet chocolate into bottom of each box, spreading evenly with a small metal spatula or your fingertip. Let boxes stand until firm. Transfer boxes to a small tray or storage container, cover and keep cool or refrigerate until ready to serve (see note, opposite).

5. Place raspberries, with their syrup, in a food processor or blender; whirl to puree. Transfer to a medium-size bowl, pressing through a fine-mesh sieve with the back of a wooden spoon to remove seeds. Measure out ¼ cup puree; reserve for garnish.

6. Sprinkle gelatin over cold water in a small saucepan; let stand 1 minute to soften. Stir over low heat until gelatin is dissolved, about 1 minute. Stir into raspberry mixture. Let stand until consistency of raw egg whites.

7. Beat cream and confectioners' sugar in a medium-size bowl until stiff peaks form. Fold into raspberry mixture using a rubber spatula; when combined, mixture should be stiff enough to pipe. If mixture is too soft, refrigerate until sufficiently thickened.

8. Line a baking sheet with waxed paper. Remove mint boxes from refrigerator; position upright on waxed paper. Spoon raspberry mousse into a pastry bag fitted with a large star tip. Pipe mousse into boxes. Pipe any remaining mousse onto waxed paper, forming rosettes; refrigerate boxes and rosettes on baking sheet.

9. Prepare decorative hearts if desired: Scrape any leftover melted white chocolate (remelt, if necessary) into a small pastry bag fitted with small writing tip. Line a small tray with waxed paper. Pipe outline of hearts onto waxed paper, making each about 1 inch tall. Refrigerate until firm, about 10 minutes.

10. To serve, place a filled box in center of each dessert plate. Garnish with mousse rosettes, chocolate hearts and currant clusters if using.

NOTE: *Assembled, but unfilled, boxes will keep in refrigerator several days.*

SQUARE DEAL: MAKE A CHOCOLATE BOX

Using a small spatula, spread a little semisweet chocolate onto unattached vertical edges.

To complete box, press chocolate-coated edges together.

Melon Granita

On a hot summer's night, nothing refreshes like a cooling cup of granita—the Italian frozen mixture of water, sugar and flavorings. Shown on page 163.

MAKES 6 *servings*

PREP 10 *minutes*

FREEZE 3 *hours*

½   cup water
⅓   cup sugar
⅓   cup fresh lime juice (about 2 limes)
1   medium-size honeydew, cantaloupe or Crenshaw melon, peeled, seeded and cut into 1-inch pieces
2   teaspoons melon liqueur

1. Bring water and sugar to simmering in a medium-size saucepan over medium heat, stirring until sugar dissolves, about 4 minutes. Pour sugar syrup into a large bowl to cool. Stir in lime juice when cool.

2. Working in batches, place melon in a food processor and whirl to puree. Stir each batch into sugar syrup in bowl. Stir in liqueur. Pour melon mixture into a shallow metal pan and freeze 3 hours or until partially frozen, stirring with a fork every hour and mixing crystals from side of pan into middle of mixture.

3. Working in batches, spoon frozen melon mixture into a food processor; whirl 3 to 5 seconds to make a "snowlike" texture. Spoon granita into serving dishes and serve at once.

Nectarine Mousse Cake

Make ahead for a showy finale. Can't find nectarines? Peaches will fill in magnificently.

MAKES *12 servings*
PREP *20 minutes plus chilling*
COOK *5 minutes*
REFRIGERATE *5 hours*

1 pound cake loaf (12 ounces)
¼ cup cherry jam, strained
3 envelopes unflavored gelatin
½ cup cold water
2 nectarines, peeled, halved and pitted
3 tablespoons orange liqueur
1 teaspoon grated fresh ginger
¾ cup sugar
2 tablespoons powdered egg whites
6 tablespoons warm water
1 cup heavy cream
   Fresh cherries with stems for garnish
   (optional)

1. Trim crust from pound cake. Cut four ½-inch-thick slices from the bottom. Spread half of jam over slices, dividing equally. Stack slices, jam side up. Cut stack in half lengthwise, then cut crosswise into eighths.

2. Grease a 9-inch springform pan. Arrange cake stacks inside pan, standing them upright against pan sides and facing all jam-coated cake surfaces in the same direction to make a striped border. Crumble remaining cake into center. Cut a 9-inch round of waxed paper, lay on top of cake, and then firmly press to level cake surface. Remove waxed paper. Spread remaining jam over cake. Cover pan with plastic wrap and place in refrigerator (see note).

3. Sprinkle gelatin over cold water in a small saucepan; let stand 1 minute to soften. Stir over low heat until gelatin is dissolved, about 1 minute.

4. Place nectarines, orange liqueur, fresh ginger and ¼ cup sugar in a food processor; whirl to a smooth puree. Transfer to a large bowl; stir in gelatin mixture. Refrigerate, stirring often, until thickened to consistency of egg whites, about 45 minutes.

5. With a mixer on medium-high speed, beat egg whites and warm water in a medium-size bowl until soft peaks form. Gradually beat in remaining ½ cup sugar until stiff peaks form. With clean beaters, on medium-high speed, beat cream in a second medium-size bowl until firm, not stiff, peaks form.

6. Fold egg whites into nectarine mixture using a rubber spatula, then fold in whipped cream. Spread smoothly onto top of cake in pan. Cover pan with plastic wrap and refrigerate 5 hours or overnight. Before serving, garnish with cherries if using.

NOTE: *Recipe can be prepared through step 2 and refrigerated up to 2 days.*

Nectarine Mousse Cake

Amaretto Tiramisu

Loosely translated as "pick me up," this Italian classic found a new home on these shores as we fell for the combination of cream, cake, coffee and chocolate. The new twist here: almond-flavored liqueur.

MAKES *8 servings*

PREP *20 minutes*

REFRIGERATE *4 hours or overnight*

1   package (8 ounces) less-fat cream cheese, at room temperature
⅓   cup granulated sugar
5   tablespoons amaretto liqueur
½   teaspoon vanilla
1   container (8 ounces) reduced-fat nondairy whipped topping
1   package (7 ounces) ladyfingers (24 ladyfingers)
¾   cup strong brewed coffee
¼   cup unsweetened cocoa powder
2   tablespoons sliced blanched almonds for serving (optional)
1   tablespoon confectioners' sugar for serving (optional)
    Fresh mint sprigs for garnish (optional)

1. With a mixer on medium-high speed, beat together cream cheese and granulated sugar in a medium-size bowl until light and creamy, 3 to 4 minutes. Beat in amaretto and vanilla.

2. Using a rubber spatula, fold whipped topping into cream-cheese mixture.

3. Arrange 12 ladyfingers in a single layer in bottom of a 9 x 9-inch square casserole dish. Sprinkle with 6 tablespoons coffee. Spread half of cream-cheese mixture smoothly on top. Sprinkle with 2 tablespoons cocoa powder. Repeat layering with remaining 12 ladyfingers, 6 tablespoons coffee, cream-cheese mixture and 2 tablespoons cocoa powder.

4. Cover dish and refrigerate at least 4 hours, or preferably overnight. To serve, cut tiramisu into squares. If desired, sprinkle almonds with confectioners' sugar; use a fork to transfer to top of each square; garnish with a mint sprig.

Very Vanilla Baked Cream

This custard derives its characteristic flavor and aroma not only from vanilla extract—which is made by macerating chopped vanilla beans in alcohol and water—but from a piece of vanilla bean as well.

MAKES *6 servings*

COOK *about 5 minutes*

BAKE *at 300° for 1 hour*

REFRIGERATE *2 hours*

6   egg yolks
½   cup sugar
    Pinch salt
2   cups half-and-half
½   cup milk
1   piece (3 inches) vanilla bean, split
1   teaspoon vanilla

1. Heat oven to 300°.

2. In medium-size bowl, whisk together egg yolks, sugar and salt just until thickened.

3. Heat half-and-half and milk in a small saucepan over medium heat until small bubbles appear around edge. Scrape seeds from vanilla bean into milk mixture; add bean. Remove from heat and let stand 5 minutes.

4. Remove bean from saucepan. Slowly pour milk mixture into egg yolk mixture, whisking constantly but gently to avoid bubbles. Strain into a 4-cup glass measure. Stir in vanilla.

5. Pour mixture into six 5-ounce ramekins, dividing equally. Gently blot any foam from tops with paper toweling. Set ramekins in a large shallow baking pan on oven rack. Pour hot water into pan to depth of 1 inch.

6. Bake in heated 300° oven 1 hour, until custards are set. Remove ramekins from water and place on a wire rack. Let custards cool to room temperature, then refrigerate 2 hours, until chilled.

Mocha Flan

A brand new take on the classic Spanish dessert: Espresso and cocoa powders flavor the baked custard, while a white-chocolate sauce provides an addition to the standard caramel coating.

MAKES *10 servings*

PREP *20 minutes*

BAKE *at 325° for 65 minutes*

REFRIGERATE *2 hours or overnight*

Flan

⅓ cup unsweetened cocoa powder
1½ teaspoons instant espresso coffee powder
⅓ cup boiling water
1¼ cups sugar
3 whole eggs
3 egg yolks
1 can (12 ounces) evaporated milk
1 cup half-and-half
1 tablespoon vanilla

White-Chocolate Sauce

½ cup heavy cream
1 tablespoon sugar
3 ounces white baking chocolate, chopped (½ cup)
½ teaspoon vanilla

1. Heat oven to 325°.

2. Prepare flan: Stir together cocoa powder, espresso powder and boiling water in a small bowl until dissolved.

3. Place ¾ cup sugar in an 8-inch round metal cake pan. Place pan over medium-high heat. Very carefully, using pot holders, shake pan. When sugar begins to melt, stir until amber-colored; watch carefully since sugar will change color very quickly. With pot holders, remove pan from heat; carefully tilt and revolve pan until caramelized sugar thickens and coats sides and bottom of pan. Set aside to cool on a wire rack.

4. Whisk together whole eggs, egg yolks and remaining ½ cup sugar in a large bowl. Whisk in evaporated milk, half-and-half, cocoa mixture and vanilla. Pour into caramel-lined pan. Place in a larger baking pan on middle oven rack. Pour boiling water into large pan to depth of 1 inch.

5. Bake flan in heated 325° oven 65 minutes or until set and a knife inserted in center comes out clean. Carefully remove flan from water; let cool on wire rack 20 minutes. Run a knife between edge of flan and pan; refrigerate 2 hours or overnight.

6. Meanwhile, prepare sauce: Bring cream and sugar to boiling in a small saucepan over medium heat. Remove from heat. Add chocolate; let stand 3 minutes. Add vanilla and whisk until chocolate is melted and mixture is smooth. Transfer to a small bowl; cover and refrigerate until chilled, about 1 hour.

7. Twirl pan to make sure flan is loose. Invert a larger serving plate over pan; invert flan onto plate, lifting off pan and letting melted caramel pour over flan. Cut into wedges. Serve with sauce.

Double-Chocolate Soufflés

It's fun to give each person at the table his or her very own soufflé. If you like, an easy raspberry sauce makes a fine accompaniment, but a simple dusting of confectioners' sugar also does the trick.

Double-Chocolate Soufflés

MAKES *8 individual soufflés*

PREP *10 minutes*

COOK *12 to 13 minutes*

REFRIGERATE *20 minutes*

BAKE *at 350° for 25 minutes*

6 tablespoons plus 2 teaspoons superfine sugar
¼ cup unsweetened cocoa powder
1 envelope unflavored gelatin
3 tablespoons all-purpose flour
2 tablespoons instant espresso coffee powder
¼ teaspoon salt
1½ cups low-fat (1%) milk
1 egg yolk
2 tablespoons chocolate syrup
1 teaspoon vanilla
6 egg whites
½ teaspoon cream of tartar
1 package (10 ounces) frozen raspberries in syrup, thawed, for serving (optional)
Confectioners' sugar for dusting

1. Stir together 4 tablespoons superfine sugar, cocoa powder, gelatin, flour, espresso powder and salt in a medium-size saucepan.

2. Whisk together milk, egg yolk and chocolate syrup in a small bowl. Stir milk mixture into cocoa powder mixture in saucepan. Cook, stirring, over medium-low heat until mixture is thick enough to coat back of spoon, 12 to 13 minutes.

3. Remove saucepan from heat. Stir in vanilla. Scrape chocolate mixture into a medium-size bowl. Place in a larger bowl filled halfway with ice and water. Let chocolate mixture cool, stirring occasionally, until consistency of pudding, about 20 minutes.

4. Heat oven to 350°. Coat eight 1¼-cup ramekins with nonstick cooking spray (see note, below). Sprinkle inside of each ramekin with ¼ teaspoon superfine sugar, turning to coat evenly.

5. With a mixer on medium-high speed, beat together egg whites and cream of tartar in a clean large bowl until soft peaks form. Gradually add remaining 2 tablespoons superfine sugar, beating until stiff, glossy peaks form. Using a rubber spatula, fold one-fourth of egg white mixture into cooled chocolate mixture. Then fold in remaining egg white mixture until no white streaks remain.

6. Divide soufflé mixture among prepared ramekins. Immediately transfer to heated 350° oven; bake 25 minutes or until puffed and slightly browned.

7. While soufflés are baking, place raspberries with their syrup in a food processor or blender; whirl to puree. To remove seeds, press through a fine-mesh sieve with the back of a wooden spoon.

8. Lightly dust soufflé tops with confectioners' sugar. Serve immediately with raspberry sauce if desired.

NOTE: *Recipe can also be prepared in a 2½-quart soufflé dish. In step 4, coat dish with nonstick spray and sprinkle 2 teaspoons superfine sugar inside. In step 6, bake 45 minutes.*

Nutmeg Pots de Crème

Warm and spicy-sweet, nutmeg is even better when freshly ground, so buy the egg-shaped spice whole, along with a small fine grater. You'll use it happily to make custards like this one as well as in savory dishes like fettuccine Alfredo. Shown on page 163.

MAKES *6 servings*

PREP *10 minutes*

BAKE *at 350° for 30 to 33 minutes*

2   **cups heavy cream**
½   **cup packed light-brown sugar**
4   **egg yolks**
2   **teaspoons vanilla**
1   **teaspoon ground nutmeg**

1. Heat oven to 350°.

2. Combine cream and brown sugar in a small saucepan; bring just to boiling over medium heat, stirring to dissolve sugar.

3. Whisk egg yolks and vanilla in a small bowl. Gradually whisk in ½ cup hot cream mixture. Gradually whisk in remaining cream mixture, whisking gently to avoid bubbles.

4. Pour custard through a fine-mesh sieve into six 4- or 5-ounce custard cups. Sprinkle with nutmeg, dividing evenly. Place cups in a baking pan. Pour hot water into pan to come halfway up sides of custard cups.

5. Bake in heated 350° oven until custards are nearly set in center, 30 to 33 minutes. Transfer cups to a wire rack to cool 15 minutes. Serve warm and soft or refrigerate, covered, up to 8 hours.

Raisin Rice Pudding

Some like it hot, some like it cold. We invite you to try this both ways.

MAKES *6 servings*

PREP *5 minutes*

COOK *about 45 minutes*

REFRIGERATE *2 hours (optional)*

4   cups milk
1   cup long-grain white rice
    (not converted)
¾   cup sugar
½   teaspoon salt
1   cup heavy cream
1   cup dark seedless raisins
¾   cup boiling water
1   egg
1   teaspoon vanilla
¾   cup half-and-half

1. Bring milk, rice, sugar and salt to boiling in a medium-size saucepan over high heat. Adjust heat to medium-low; simmer, uncovered, until water is absorbed, rice is tender and mixture is thickened, 40 to 45 minutes. Near end of cooking, adjust heat to low to avoid scorching. Five minutes before end of cooking, stir in ½ cup cream.

2. Meanwhile, place raisins in a small bowl. Add boiling water; let stand 5 minutes to soften. Drain excess water. Stir raisins into cooked rice mixture in saucepan.

3. Whisk together remaining ½ cup cream and egg in a small bowl. Stir a small amount of hot rice mixture into egg mixture. Stir egg mixture into rice mixture in saucepan. Return to simmering; cook until thickened and internal temperature registers 160° on an instant-read thermometer, about 3 minutes.

4. Remove saucepan from heat. Stir in vanilla. Let pudding cool 15 minutes. Stir in half-and-half. If serving chilled, refrigerate at least 2 hours.

Black Forest Bread Pudding

Turn day-old Italian bread into a comforting dessert with the help of cherries and chocolate.

MAKES *8 servings*

PREP *15 minutes*

COOK *4 minutes*

STAND *30 minutes*

BAKE *at 325° for 30 minutes*

2½ cups low-fat milk
½   cup granulated sugar
8   squares (1 ounce each) semisweet
    chocolate, chopped
6   cups 1-inch cubes Italian bread (about
    one 8-ounce loaf)
¾   cup dried cherries
3   whole eggs
1   egg white
⅓   cup confectioners' sugar for dusting
    Whipped cream for serving (optional)

1. Bring milk and sugar to boiling in a small saucepan over medium heat. Add chocolate and stir until almost melted. Remove from heat; stir until smooth. Set aside to cool to room temperature.

2. Mix bread and cherries in a large bowl. Whisk whole eggs and egg white in a small bowl until blended. Whisk eggs into chocolate mixture. Pour over bread. Submerge bread in liquid by placing a second bowl on top. Cover; let stand at room temperature 30 minutes.

3. Heat oven to 325°. Butter an 11 x 7 x 2-inch baking pan. Butter a sheet of aluminum foil large enough to cover pan.

4. Pour bread mixture into prepared pan. Cover tightly with buttered foil. Bake in heated 325° oven 30 minutes. Transfer pan to a wire rack; remove foil. Let pudding cool slightly. Dust with confectioners' sugar and serve with whipped cream if desired.

Crescent Roll Bread Pudding

Scrumptious on its own, this pudding only gets better with a generous dollop of freshly whipped cream.

MAKES *12 servings*

PREP *20 minutes*

STAND *30 minutes*

BAKE *at 350° for 1½ hours*

8   egg yolks
4   whole eggs
4   cups milk
1   cup heavy cream
1   cup granulated sugar
2   teaspoons vanilla
½   teaspoon salt
2   packages (6.25 ounces each) prepared butter crescent rolls
1   package (6 ounces) milk chocolate chips (1 cup)
½   cup dark seedless raisins

Whipped Cream

1   cup heavy cream
2   tablespoons confectioners' sugar
1   teaspoon vanilla

1. Whisk together egg yolks, whole eggs, milk, cream, granulated sugar, vanilla and salt in a large bowl.

2. Coat a 2½-quart glass baking dish with nonstick cooking spray. Cut rolls in half horizontally; place bottom halves in prepared pan. Sprinkle chocolate chips and raisins over rolls. Place top half on each roll. Pour egg mixture over rolls. Submerge rolls in liquid by placing a second glass dish on top. Let stand 30 minutes.

3. Heat oven to 350°.

4. Remove top baking dish. Cover pudding in bottom dish loosely with aluminum foil; place in a large baking pan on oven rack. Pour hot water into large pan to depth of 1 inch.

5. Bake in heated 350° oven 1 hour. Remove foil. Bake 30 minutes or until center of pudding is set and registers 160° on an instant-read thermometer. Carefully remove pudding dish from water; transfer to a wire rack.

6. Prepare whipped cream: Beat cream in a medium-size bowl on medium speed until foamy. Add confectioners' sugar and vanilla; beat at medium-high speed until soft peaks form. Serve pudding warm, at room temperature or chilled, dolloped with whipped cream.

VANILLA FACTS

Vanilla extract is made by steeping long, thin, cured vanilla beans—seed pods from an orchid—in an alcohol-water solution. It can be stored in a tightly capped dark bottle at room temperature for about 6 months. For the best quality, choose pure, rather than imitation, vanilla extract.

Apple Christmas Tree Tart, page 208

Lollipops, *page 191*

Holiday Desserts

Halloween Muffins, *page 204*

Poached-Pear Tarts

Pale pink slices of pear adorn puff-pastry hearts. What a delectable way to whisper "I love you."

MAKES *4 tarts (2 servings each)*

PREP *30 minutes*

COOK *35 to 40 minutes*

BAKE *tarts at 400° for 12 minutes; cutouts for 6 minutes*

2 cups cranberry juice cocktail
⅓ cup packed light-brown sugar
1 teaspoon grenadine (optional)
½ teaspoon ground cinnamon
¼ teaspoon ground allspice
2 firm ripe pears, peeled, halved lengthwise and cored
2 teaspoons cornstarch dissolved in 2 tablespoons water
1 sheet frozen puff pastry, thawed
1 cup hazelnuts, toasted and skinned (see page 231)
½ cup confectioners' sugar
3 tablespoons unsalted butter
1 tablespoon hazelnut liqueur (optional)
Fresh mint sprigs for garnish

1. Bring cranberry juice, sugar, grenadine if using, cinnamon and allspice to simmering in a medium saucepan over medium-high heat, stirring to dissolve sugar. Add pears and arrange so they are submerged. Cover and simmer over medium-low heat 35 to 40 minutes or until tender. Remove with a slotted spoon to a small bowl.

2. Over high heat, boil liquid 10 minutes to reduce to 1 cup. Whisk in dissolved cornstarch; cook, whisking, until thickened. Cover and reserve sauce.

3. Heat oven to 400°. Coat a baking sheet with nonstick cooking spray.

4. Unfold pastry onto a floured work surface; roll to an 11-inch square. Using a 5-inch heart-shaped cutter, cut out four pastry hearts; transfer to prepared baking sheet. Using a sharp knife, cut pastry scraps into small Xs, Os and hearts; transfer to prepared baking sheet.

5. Bake pastry in heated 400° oven 6 minutes or until cutouts are golden; transfer cutouts to a wire rack. Continue to bake large hearts 12 minutes or until golden. Transfer hearts to rack with cutouts to cool.

6. Using a sharp knife and leaving ¾-inch sides, cut out center of large heart— be careful not to cut through bottom.

7. Place nuts and sugar in a food processor; whirl until nuts are ground. Add butter and liqueur if using. Whirl until mixture forms a paste. Spoon into center of heart, dividing equally; smooth tops.

8. Cut pear halves in half lengthwise. Cut each quarter lengthwise into thin slices, leaving attached at stem end. Arrange 2 quarters on each tart, placing stem ends at point of heart and fanning slices to cover hazelnut filling. Arrange tarts on a serving plate; surround with cutouts. Garnish with mint sprigs. Cut tarts in half to serve; pass reserved sauce separately.

EASY PUFF PASTRY CUTOUTS

Using a sharp knife, cut out center of each large heart, leaving bottom intact.

Cream Hearts

A puddle of pineapple sauce perfectly complements coconut-topped mousse hearts. You'll create some scraps while making these—happy snacking.

MAKES *6 hearts*

PREP *10 minutes*

REFRIGERATE *24 hours*

12 ounces cream cheese, at room temperature
1½ teaspoons coconut extract
1 cup heavy cream
½ cup confectioners' sugar
¼ cup light rum
1 tablespoon cornstarch
1 cup pineapple juice
2 tablespoons granulated sugar
⅓ cup unsweetened flake coconut, toasted

1. Line an 8 x 8 x 2-inch square baking dish with plastic wrap, leaving wrap extending over sides.

2. Beat together cream cheese and coconut extract in a medium-size bowl until light and fluffy, about 2 minutes.

3. Beat cream and confectioners' sugar in a second medium-size bowl until soft peaks form. Using a rubber spatula, gently fold one-quarter of whipped cream into cheese mixture. Fold in remaining whipped cream mixture. Spoon into prepared baking dish; smooth top with a spatula. Cover dish with plastic wrap. Refrigerate 24 hours.

4. To make pineapple sauce, whisk together rum and cornstarch in a small bowl until cornstarch is dissolved. Mix pineapple juice and granulated sugar in a small saucepan; bring to boiling. Whisk in cornstarch mixture; cook, whisking, until thickened, about 1 minute. Transfer to a small bowl; cover with plastic wrap. Refrigerate sauce until ready to use.

5. When ready to serve, remove cream-cheese mixture from baking dish by lifting out plastic wrap hanging over sides; place plastic with mixture on a work surface. Using a 2¾-inch heart-shaped cookie cutter, cut out 6 heart shapes.

6. Spoon pineapple sauce onto middle of 6 dessert plates, dividing equally. Using a spatula, place a cream heart on each pool of sauce. Garnish top of each with a sprinkling of toasted coconut.

CREAM HEART HINTS

Using a rubber spatula, gently fold whipped cream into beaten cream cheese.

Lift plastic with chilled mixture onto work surface; cut out heart shapes.

Chocolate Heart Cake

A chocolate extravaganza! Cake, glaze and berries all feature our favorite flavor. If you are pressed for time, you can prepare the strawberry topping while the cake is baking.

Chocolate Heart Cake

MAKES *14 servings*

PREP *30 minutes*

BAKE *at 350° for 25 to 30 minutes*

REFRIGERATE *cake 30 minutes;*
berries 30 minutes

Cake

- 2 squares (1 ounce each) unsweetened chocolate, chopped
- 1 cup all-purpose flour
- 1 teaspoon baking powder
- ½ teaspoon baking soda
- ¼ teaspoon salt
- 5 tablespoons unsalted butter, at room temperature
- ¾ cup granulated sugar
- 2 eggs
- 1 teaspoon vanilla
- ½ cup half-and-half or milk

Chocolate Glaze

- ½ cup unsweetened cocoa powder
- 2 cups confectioners' sugar
- 6 to 7 tablespoons water

Strawberry Topping

- 3 squares (1 ounce each) milk chocolate, chopped
- 1 teaspoon vegetable oil
- 3 ounces white baking chocolate, chopped
- 14 large strawberries, hulled
  Candy sprinkles for dipping
  Chopped nuts for dipping
  Candied violets for decoration

1. Prepare cake: Heat oven to 350°. Grease an 8-inch (6-cup) heart-shaped pan or a 9 x 2-inch round layer-cake pan; dust pan with flour.

2. Melt unsweetened chocolate in top of a double boiler set over barely simmering, not boiling water, stirring until smooth. Remove top of pan from above water.

3. Sift together flour, baking powder, baking soda and salt into a small bowl.

4. With a mixer on medium speed, beat butter and sugar in a medium-size bowl 1 minute. Beat in melted chocolate. Beat in eggs, one at a time, beating well after each addition, until fluffy. Beat in vanilla. Beat 1 minute. On low speed, beat flour mixture into butter mixture in 3 additions, alternating with half-and-half and ending with flour mixture; beat just until blended. Scrape batter into prepared pan.

5. Bake in heated 350° oven 25 to 30 minutes, until a wooden pick inserted in center comes out clean. Cool cake in pan on a wire rack 10 minutes. Turn out onto rack with flat (bottom) side up and cool completely. Brush off excess crumbs.

6. Prepare glaze: Whisk together cocoa powder, confectioners' sugar and water in a small bowl until a good coating consistency. Line a baking sheet with waxed paper; place cake on rack on top. Spoon glaze over top, spreading to cover top and sides. Refrigerate 30 minutes, until glaze is hardened; then let cake stand at room temperature until serving.

7. Prepare topping: Melt milk chocolate and oil in a small saucepan over low heat, stirring until smooth; remove from heat. Melt white chocolate in top of a double boiler set over barely simmering, not boiling water, stirring until smooth. Remove top of pan from above water.

8. Line a baking sheet with waxed paper. Arrange sprinkles and chopped nuts in separate small shallow bowls. One at a time, hold each of 7 strawberries horizontally and dip halfway into melted dark or white chocolate; immediately dip into sprinkles or nuts; stand, pointed end up, on waxed paper.

9. Dip remaining berries into chocolates; stand on waxed paper. Spoon remaining chocolates into separate small plastic food-storage bags; snip off a corner of each bag. Drizzle chocolates decoratively on top of berries. Press candied violets onto some of the berries.

10. Refrigerate berries on baking sheet until chocolate is hardened, about 30 minutes. Arrange berries on top of cake just before serving.

Heart Lollipops

Cinnamon extract and floating red cinnamon candies add zing to adorable homemade pops. Shown on page 187.

MAKES *24 lollipops*

PREP *10 minutes*

COOK *about 40 minutes*

Assorted candies for decorations (small red cinnamon candies, hearts and flowers)
2 cups sugar
1 cup water
¾ cup light corn syrup
½ teaspoon cinnamon extract
24 lollipop sticks

1. Lightly coat twenty-four 2-inch heart-shaped lollipop molds with nonstick cooking spray. Arrange red cinnamon candies, hearts and flowers in molds.

2. Combine sugar, water and corn syrup in a heavy saucepan and cook over medium heat about 5 to 7 minutes, stirring, until sugar dissolves.

3. Clip a candy thermometer to side of saucepan. Continue to cook over medium-high heat without stirring, about 30 to 35 minutes, until thermometer registers 300°. Remove pan from heat. Stir in extract.

4. Working quickly, ladle half of liquid into 12 molds, dividing equally. Press lollipop sticks into center. Repeat with remaining liquid, molds and sticks. Cool completely. Loosen lollipops from molds and remove.

Easter Treats

The tangy citrus filling in these candies is a delightful foil for layers of chocolate. Use mini cookie cutters of baby chicks, bunnies or eggs.

MAKES *about 100 candies*

PREP *45 minutes*

REFRIGERATE *about 50 minutes*

12 ounces semisweet chocolate chips or squares, chopped
¼ cup solid vegetable shortening
2 jars (7½ ounces each) marshmallow cream
5 cups confectioners' sugar
¼ cup grated orange rind
2 teaspoons orange extract
⅛ teaspoon salt
White baking chocolate for details (optional)

1. Line bottom of a 15½ x 10½ x 1-inch jelly-roll pan with aluminum foil.

2. Melt half of semisweet chocolate and 2 tablespoons shortening in top of a double boiler over barely simmering, not boiling, water, stirring until smooth. Pour into prepared pan; spread evenly with a long metal spatula. Refrigerate about 20 minutes or until firm.

3. Tape waxed paper to bottom of a second 15½ x 10½ x 1-inch jelly-roll pan. Invert chocolate onto paper. Peel off foil. Refrigerate.

4. Combine marshmallow cream, 4¼ cups confectioners' sugar, orange rind, orange extract and salt in a medium-size bowl. Stir with a wooden spoon until a thick mass forms; knead mixture with hands if necessary to incorporate ingredients.

5. Lightly dust a work surface with a little of remaining ¾ cup confectioners' sugar. Turn marshmallow mixture out onto prepared surface. Knead until smooth, 2 to 3 minutes.

6. Tape waxed paper to bottom of first jelly-roll pan. Lightly dust paper and a rolling pin with remaining confectioners' sugar. Roll filling out to ⅛- to ¼-inch thickness, covering bottom of prepared pan.

7. Remove pan of chocolate from refrigerator. Let stand to soften slightly, about 5 minutes. Carefully invert filling on top of chocolate; peel off waxed paper. Refrigerate 15 minutes.

8. Melt remaining semisweet chocolate and remaining 2 tablespoons shortening in top of a double boiler over barely simmering, not boiling, water, stirring until smooth. Remove pan with chocolate and marshmallow layers from refrigerator. Pour melted chocolate on top, spreading smoothly over entire surface with a spatula. Refrigerate 15 to 20 minutes or until firm.

9. Line a baking sheet with waxed paper. Using 1½- to 2-inch mini cookie cutters, cut chocolate-marshmallow layers into seasonal shapes. Or cut into 1-inch squares. Transfer cutouts to prepared baking sheets.

10. Add white chocolate details if desired: Melt white chocolate in top of a double boiler over barely simmering, not boiling, water, stirring until smooth. Remove from heat and cool slightly. Pour into a small plastic food-storage bag. Snip off a corner of bag to make a very small opening. Pipe chocolate over cutouts to add features or decorative patterns. Refrigerate until ready to serve.

Easter Eggs

Show you care with a batch of can't-say-no cream-filled Easter treats. Each of the three coatings given here will cover one batch of candy eggs. Take your choice.

MAKES *about 10 large or 20 small eggs*

PREP *45 minutes*

COOK *5 minutes*

REFRIGERATE *30 minutes*

Candy Eggs

⅓ cup butter or margarine
1 package (about 3 ounces) chocolate pudding-and-pie-filling mix (not instant)
¼ cup milk
⅛ teaspoon almond extract
1¾ cups confectioners' sugar
3½ ounces blanched almonds, finely ground (½ cup)

Chocolate Coatings *(see note)*

1 package (12 ounces) milk chocolate chips (2 cups) plus 6 tablespoons solid vegetable shortening
1 package (12 ounces) semisweet chocolate chips (2 cups) plus ¼ cup solid vegetable shortening
1 pound white baking chocolate plus ½ cup solid vegetable shortening

1. Melt butter in a small saucepan over medium-low heat. Stir in pudding-and-pie-filling mix until smooth. Gradually add milk, stirring constantly until mixture is thickened and creamy, about 5 minutes. Remove from heat. Stir in almond extract. Spoon into a large bowl. Place plastic wrap directly on surface of pudding. Set aside 20 minutes, until cooled to room temperature, stirring occasionally.

2. Beat confectioners' sugar into pudding mixture with a wooden spoon until smooth (mixture will be stiff). Stir in almonds. Cover; refrigerate 30 minutes or until mixture holds its shape.

3. Using 2 level measuring tablespoonfuls pudding mixture for each large egg or 1 level tablespoonful for each small egg, shape candies. Place on a small baking sheet. Cover loosely with plastic wrap. Refrigerate 1 hour or until eggs are firm.

4. Prepare your choice of chocolate coating: Melt together one kind of chocolate and shortening in top of a double boiler over barely simmering, not boiling, water, stirring until smooth. Pour into a small bowl. Let cool 5 minutes.

5. Line a baking sheet with waxed paper. Reshaping eggs if necessary, place them, one at a time, in chocolate coating; use a fork to roll each until completely coated. Lift egg with fork, let excess chocolate drip back into bowl and transfer egg to prepared baking sheet. Touch up coating with a small metal spatula if necessary.

6. Let eggs stand at room temperature until firm. If they became soft during dipping, place in refrigerator until firm.

7. Repeat dipping process to coat eggs in another layer of chocolate. Let firm completely on baking sheet. Loosen from waxed paper with a thin spatula.

NOTE: *If you wish, make a second coating and drizzle it in decorative swirls over finished eggs.*

Vanilla Egg Variation

Substitute 1 package (about 3 ounces) vanilla pudding-and-pie-filling mix (not instant) for chocolate, 1½ teaspoons vanilla for almond extract, and ¼ cup finely chopped red candied cherries for almonds.

Rosebud Cake

After a few practice runs, you'll be an old hand at making frosting roses. All you need is a pastry bag and flower nail (available at baking supply shops)—and patience! But rest assured, the pretty-as-a-picture results are worth it.

Rosebud Cake

MAKES *16 servings*

PREP *35 minutes plus decorating time*

BAKE *at 350° for 30 to 32 minutes*

Cake

- 3 cups all-purpose flour
- 4 teaspoons baking powder
- ½ teaspoon salt
- ¾ cup (1½ sticks) butter, at room temperature
- 2 cups granulated sugar
- 5 eggs
- 1 teaspoon vanilla
- ½ teaspoon lemon extract
- 1¼ cups water

Frosting and Filling

- ¾ cup (1½ sticks) butter, at room temperature
- 2 boxes (1 pound each) confectioners' sugar
- ¼ cup milk
- ¼ cup lemon juice
- 2 teaspoons vanilla
- ½ cup strawberry preserves

Royal Icing (recipe, page 201)
Leaf green soft gel paste food coloring
Fuchsia soft gel paste food coloring

1. Prepare cake: Heat oven to 350°. Coat three 9-inch round layer-cake pans with nonstick cooking spray. Line bottoms with waxed paper; coat with spray.

2. Whisk together flour, baking powder and salt in a large bowl.

3. Beat butter in a large bowl on medium speed about 1 minute or until creamy. Add sugar; beat 2 minutes or until fluffy. Add eggs, one at a time, beating well after each addition. Add vanilla and lemon extract; beat 1 minute.

4. On low speed, beat flour mixture into butter mixture in 3 additions, alternating with water and ending with flour. On medium-high, beat 3 minutes. Divide batter equally among pans.

5. Bake in heated 350° oven 30 to 32 minutes or until a wooden pick inserted in center of cake layers comes out clean. Cool cake layers in pans on wire racks 10 minutes. Turn out onto wire racks; remove waxed paper; let cool completely. Trim cake layers with a serrated knife to level if necessary.

6. Meanwhile, prepare frosting and filling: Beat butter in a large bowl on medium speed until fluffy, 1 minute. Add confectioners' sugar, milk, lemon juice and vanilla; beat on low until well blended. Beat 1 minute. Add additional milk if necessary for a good spreading consistency. For filling, mix 1 cup frosting and strawberry preserves in a small bowl; cover and set aside. Press plastic wrap onto surface of plain frosting; set aside.

Leaves, Roses and Rosebuds

1. Divide royal icing between 2 small bowls. Tint 1 bowl leaf green and 1 fuchsia. Press plastic wrap onto surface of icings and keep covered until ready to use.

2. Line 3 baking sheets with waxed paper.

3. Fit a medium-size pastry bag with a coupler and plain medium leaf tip; fill bag halfway with green icing. Pipe about 30 small leaves onto paper on 1 baking sheet. Cover end of tip with moist paper toweling and plastic wrap until ready to pipe vines.

4. Fit another medium-size pastry bag with a coupler and plain medium rose tip. Fill halfway with fuchsia icing. Using a flower nail with a small square of waxed paper attached (with a drop of icing) for each rose, pipe about 12 large roses (see Glorious Roses, page 197). To begin, pipe a small cone in center. Then pipe a vertical strip around cone. Continue,

piping about 4 concentric crescents around center. Transfer each rose on its paper square to paper on second baking sheet. Replenish bag with icing as needed.

5. Pipe about 20 rosebuds onto third baking sheet. Let leaves, roses and rosebuds dry completely.

Decorate

1. Place ½ cup white frosting in a pastry bag fitted with a large round tip. Measure out ½ cup frosting for piping around bottom of cake, cover and reserve. Keep remainder of frosting in bowl covered until ready to frost top and sides of cake.

2. Place 1 cake layer on a cake plate. Using white frosting in bag, pipe a border of white frosting around top edge of layer. Spread half of strawberry filling inside white border. Place second cake layer on top; pipe a border and fill in same way. Place remaining cake layer on top.

3. Frost top and sides of cake with remaining white frosting in mixing bowl.

4. Using a wooden pick, gently outline a trailing vine pattern on top and sides of cake. Place a small round tip on pastry bag with green icing. Pipe vines over pattern on cake.

5. Carefully remove leaves and rosebuds from waxed paper. Attach over vines, using a dab of green icing for glue. Remove roses from paper and glue onto cake with green icing. Spoon reserved ½ cup white frosting into bag fitted with large tip. Pipe a border around bottom of cake. Refrigerate at least 1 hour to set.

Cake Decorating Basics

The only thing standing between you and a gloriously decorated cake is practice. Everything you need to know is right here, from the proper tools to the best way to prep the layers. So practice away—besides it's a joy to eat the test samples!

FUSS-FREE FROSTING

- Be sure to let cake layers cool completely before you trim, cut, fill or frost them.

- If cooled cake layers have a rounded top, slice off domed portion with a long serrated knife. Or place bottom layer on cake plate rounded side down; when you add the top layer, place it rounded side up.

- It is easier to spread frosting on surfaces that have not been cut. If you slice cake layers horizontally—to trim rounded top or to divide into thinner layers—invert the layers when you stack them so you will spread frosting on bottom of each.

- Rub your hand over surface of cake layers before placing them on cake plate—this will loosen and brush off any crumbs.

- Before applying frosting to cake, tuck strips of waxed paper between bottom layer and cake plate, all the way around. Later, you'll be able to pull out the waxed paper, removing any stray frosting.

- A stainless-steel spatula with an 8-inch-long blade is great for spreading frosting.

- For best results, first apply a thin coating of frosting to surface, then place cake in the refrigerator for a few minutes. The chilled coating will seal the cake surface, making it easy to apply the rest of the frosting.

LEVEL THE FIELD

Use a long serrated knife to slice rounded top from cooled cake layer.

FROSTING PREP

- Make sure the frosting is the right consistency. If too thick and stiff, it will tear the cake. If too thin, it will slide off the surface.

- To thin a confectioners' sugar frosting, add more liquid. To stiffen, add more sugar.

- To soften a too-stiff butter-rich frosting, place bowl in a pan of warm water. To stiffen one that's too soft, place bowl in a pan of ice water. In either case, stir frosting until it assumes the desired consistency.

- If making frosting ahead, press plastic wrap onto surface of frosting before storing. In general, frostings can be refrigerated, tightly covered, 1 week or frozen up to 3 months.

COLOR-COATED

- Frosting can be tinted with liquid or soft gel paste food colors. The paste colors come in a greater variety of hues and give vibrant results. You can create custom colors by mixing liquid with liquid, or paste with paste.

PASTRY BAG LINGO

A pastry bag set-up may look tricky, but get your hands on one and you'll see how easy it makes your cake—or cookie—decorating.

- Be sure to pick up bags in a variety of sizes, plus extras. Some food colors stain the inside of the cloth bags, so it is a good idea to reserve some bags for white frosting only.

- Disposable clear plastic bags work just as well and may be more economical.

PASTRY BAG KNOW-HOW

Pastry bags and icing tips in assorted sizes make cake decorating a breeze.

Fit bag with a coupler and desired tip, then fold down top all around. Fill halfway with frosting.

Practice piping on waxed paper. Or if your recipe directs, pipe motifs on waxed paper and let them set before transferring to the cake.

GLORIOUS ROSES

Blossoms like the ones shown on the Rosebud Cake on page 194 are fun to make if you practice first to get the hang of the process.

Pipe a small icing cone in center of flower nail. Then for first petal, pipe a stand-up ring of icing around cone.

Continue, piping about 4 concentric stand-up petals around center.

- A basic icing tip set will be all you need for most projects. Buy a set that comes with an instruction sheet that shows the designs each tip will make and the steps to copy them.

- Alternatively, if you just want to test a few techniques, buy only the most frequently used tips: 1 small and 1 medium writing tip, a small star tip and a small leaf tip.

- Tips attach to the pastry bag with a coupler, which allows you to change tips without emptying the bag.

- For small piping jobs, use a plastic food-storage bag instead of a pastry bag. Just snip off a corner and drop a tip in, then fill with icing.

- Keep wooden skewers on hand for cleaning tips.

PIPING TRICKS

Any smooth stiff frosting can be piped with a pastry bag and icing tip. If you are using a whipped cream frosting, underbeat it slightly.

- Stir frosting briskly with a rubber spatula before transferring to bag. This will keep it smooth and air-bubble-free.

- Choose a bag that is larger than you think you will need. Fit it with coupler and tip.

- To fill the bag, fold down top all around, then fill halfway with frosting. Use a rubber spatula as a scoop. Twist the empty top portion of the bag to seal.

- To minimize mess, place bag, tip down, in a tall glass when not in use. Or wrap tip in plastic wrap.

- Hone your technique. Do a few practice runs on waxed paper to get the motions down and build confidence.

- Use a wooden pick to sketch words or freehand motifs on frosted cake. Make sure size and spacing are as you like before piping with decorative frosting.

- To pipe, apply a firm steady pressure to bag. Start to squeeze a split second before moving the bag and release the pressure just before coming to a stop. If your motif does not end crisply, it's because you are still squeezing as you finish the stroke.

Layered Berry Divine

Is it a cake or a mousse? Whatever we call it, these circles of cheesecake, berries and cookies will draw raves at your fanciest party—a wedding even. Be sure to have on hand nonstick 6½-inch, 8½-inch and 10-inch springform pans.

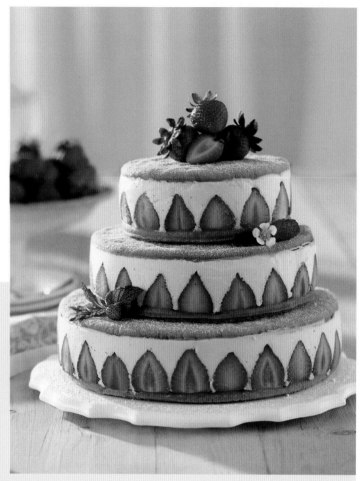

Layered Berry Divine

MAKES *34 servings* PREP *1 hour*

BAKE *cookie layers at 350°* *for a total of about 60 minutes*

COOK *15 minutes*

REFRIGERATE *overnight*

Cookies

1   cup all-purpose flour
2   packages (about 18 ounces each) refrigerated sugar-cookie dough

Cream-Cheese Filling

2¼ cups granulated sugar
¼   teaspoon salt
6   envelopes unflavored gelatin
2   teaspoons strawberry-flavored gelatin powder
9   egg yolks
3   cups milk
1   tablespoon vanilla
1½ tablespoons fresh lemon juice
6   packages (8 ounces each) cream cheese, at room temperature
3   cups heavy cream
2   cups lengthwise-sliced strawberries
¼   cup water

Decorations

Confectioners' sugar for dusting
Whole strawberries
Fresh mint sprigs
Strawberry blossoms

1. Heat oven to 350°. Disassemble 3 nonstick springform pans (one each 6½-inch, 8½-inch and 10-inch), setting each pan bottom at your work area.

2. Prepare cookies: On a lightly floured surface, knead ½ cup flour into 1 package cookie dough. Divide dough into 3 equal pieces; divide 1 piece in half. Shape all 4 pieces into discs; set aside 1 large disc and 1 small disc.

3. Place remaining smaller disc of dough in center of 6½-inch pan bottom; place larger disc in center of 8½-inch pan bottom. One pan at a time, and using a rolling pin, roll out dough almost to edges of pan bottom, then press dough to edge using your fingertips. Fit sides onto bottom of each pan. If necessary, press dough out to seam; do not press up sides of pan. Prick dough in both pans with a fork.

4. Bake cookies in heated 350° oven 11 to 13 minutes, until golden brown. Transfer pans to wire racks to cool slightly. Leave oven on. Remove sides of pans; let cookies cool on pan bottoms on racks. Remove cookies from pan bottoms.

5. Wash and dry pans. Repeat steps 3 and 4 with reserved discs of dough.

6. Knead remaining ½ cup flour into second package of cookie dough. Divide dough in half; shape each piece into a disc. Working with 1 disc of dough at a time and using 10-inch pan, repeat steps 3, 4 and 5 to prepare 2 more cookies; bake each 12 to 15 minutes. Wash, dry and reassemble all 3 springform pans.

7. Prepare filling: Whisk together granulated sugar, salt, unflavored gelatin, strawberry gelatin and egg yolks in a large saucepan. Whisk in milk until smooth. Cook over medium-low heat, stirring frequently, 15 to 18 minutes or until an instant-read thermometer inserted in mixture registers 170°— mixture should be slightly thickened and smooth. Strain through a fine-mesh sieve into a large bowl to remove any lumps. Stir in vanilla and lemon juice. Let mixture cool to room temperature, until slightly thickened. (To hasten cooling, place bowl of gelatin mixture in a larger bowl filled halfway with ice and water; be careful mixture doesn't cool too quickly and become lumpy.)

8. Meanwhile, beat cream cheese in a large bowl until smooth. Using clean beaters, beat cream in a medium-size bowl until soft peaks form. Gradually beat cream cheese into cooled gelatin mixture until no lumps remain. Fold in whipped cream using a rubber spatula.

9. Place a 10-inch cookie in bottom of 10-inch springform pan. Form a ring of strawberries against sides of pan, on top of cookie, standing slices upright and spacing them evenly. Spoon cream cheese mixture into pan, filling almost to top and smoothing surface. Place remaining 10-inch cookie on top; brush with 2 tablespoons water. In the same way, assemble remaining cookies and filling in remaining pans; brush water over 8½-inch pan only. Wrap each pan tightly with plastic wrap; refrigerate overnight.

10. When ready to serve, unwrap all pans and remove sides. Using 2 large wide metal spatulas, lift 10-inch cookie-and-cream sandwich from pan bottom and transfer to a serving plate. Dust top with confectioners' sugar. Center 8½-inch sandwich on top; dust with confectioners' sugar. Top with 6½-inch sandwich; dust with sugar. Arrange whole strawberries on top; garnish with mint sprigs and strawberry blossoms. Serve immediately.

NOTE: *For a smaller cake, divide recipe in half and make only the top 2 layers.*

BERRY DIVINE HOW-TO

Form a ring of evenly spaced strawberries against sides of pan, on top of cookie.

Ribbons and Bows Cake

To create a showy swag for this celebration cake, use a plain rose icing tip. The soft peach-colored icing gives a hint of the chopped peaches in the cake itself.

MAKES *16 servings*

PREP *30 minutes plus decorating time*

BAKE *at 350° for 25 to 30 minutes*

REFRIGERATE *1 hour*

Cake

3½ cups cake flour (not self-rising)
1¼ teaspoons baking soda
½   teaspoon salt
1   cup solid vegetable shortening
2   cups granulated sugar
3   tablespoons peach schnapps
1   teaspoon vanilla
1   cup buttermilk
½   cup diced canned peaches (4 peach halves in heavy syrup, drained)
6   egg whites
1   teaspoon cream of tartar

Frosting

½   cup (1 stick) unsalted butter, at room temperature
½   cup solid vegetable shortening, at room temperature
2   boxes (1 pound each) confectioners' sugar
6   tablespoons milk, more if needed
1   tablespoon plus 1 teaspoon peach schnapps
    Green, yellow and red soft gel paste food coloring

1. Prepare cake: Heat oven to 350°. Coat three 8-inch round cake pans with nonstick cooking spray. Line bottoms with waxed paper; coat paper with spray.

2. Whisk together flour, baking soda and salt in a large bowl.

3. Beat shortening in a large bowl on medium speed, gradually adding 1½ cups granulated sugar, schnapps and vanilla; beat mixture 1 minute.

4. On low speed, beat flour mixture into shortening mixture in 3 additions, alternating with buttermilk and ending with flour mixture. Beat 2 minutes on medium-high speed. With a rubber spatula, gently fold in peaches.

5. Beat egg whites in a medium-size bowl on medium speed until foamy. Add cream of tartar; beat on high speed until soft peaks form. Gradually beat in remaining ½ cup granulated sugar until stiff, glossy peaks form.

6. Stir about one-fourth of beaten egg whites into cake batter to lighten. Carefully fold in remaining whites. Divide batter equally among 3 prepared pans.

7. Bake in heated 350° oven 25 to 30 minutes or until a wooden pick inserted into center of cake layers comes out clean. Cool cake layers in pans on wire racks 10 minutes. Turn cake layers out onto racks; remove waxed paper; let cool completely.

8. Meanwhile, prepare frosting: Beat together butter and vegetable shortening in a large bowl on medium speed 1 minute, until blended. Add confectioners' sugar, milk and schnapps; beat on low speed until mixture is well blended. Scrape down sides of bowl with a rubber spatula. Beat on high speed 1 minute or until frosting is very smooth and spreadable. Add additional milk if necessary for good spreading consistency.

9. Spoon ½ cup frosting (white) into a pastry bag fitted with a small star tip. Cover tip with plastic wrap until ready to use. Tint 1 cup frosting medium green. Place in another pastry bag fitted with a plain medium-size rose tip. Cover tip until ready to use. Tint remainder of frosting peach, using 3 parts yellow to 1 part red food coloring.

Decorate

1. Place 1 cake layer on a cake plate. Spread ½ cup peach frosting over top. Place another cake layer on top of first. Spread ½ cup peach frosting over top. Top with third cake layer. Frost top and sides of cake with remaining peach frosting.

2. For ribbon garland, use a wooden pick to make 6 equidistant marks around top edge of cake. Using pastry bag filled with green frosting, pipe a shallow swag on side of cake between 2 marks; below it, pipe a second swag between same marks. Repeat to pipe double swags between remaining marks.

3. Continuing with bag of green frosting, pipe a bow at each mark (where double swags meet); use a figure-8 motion for the bow loops, then use a downward motion to give each bow 2 tails.

4. Using pastry bag filled with white frosting, pipe a ring of stars along top edge of cake. Pipe a second ring of stars around base at cake plate. Refrigerate 1 hour to set.

FESTIVE RIBBONS AND BOWS

Use a downward motion to pipe 2 tails hanging from each bow, between the swags.

Basic Frostings

Here are two frostings that every baker should have in her repertoire: Buttercream for sweet gooey curls all over and Royal Icing for decorating cookies and cakes.

BUTTERCREAM FROSTING

MAKES *5 cups*   PREP *15 minutes*

½ cup (1 stick) unsalted butter, at room temperature
½ cup solid vegetable shortening, at room temperature
2 boxes (1 pound each) confectioners' sugar
6 tablespoons milk
1 teaspoon vanilla

Beat together butter and vegetable shortening in a large bowl on medium until blended, about 1 minute. Add confectioners' sugar, milk and vanilla; beat on low speed until mixture is well blended. Scrape down side of bowl with a rubber spatula. Beat on high speed 1 minute or until frosting is very smooth and spreadable.

ROYAL ICING

MAKES *about 3 cups*   PREP *15 minutes*

1 box (1 pound) confectioners' sugar
3 tablespoons meringue powder or egg white powder
6 tablespoons warm water

Whisk together confectioners' sugar and meringue powder in a medium-size bowl until well combined. On medium speed, gradually beat in water. Continue beating until peaks form and icing is thick enough to pipe, about 10 minutes. Press plastic wrap onto surface of icing and keep covered until ready to use.

NOTE: *Divide the ingredients by thirds to make 1 or 2 cups icing.*

Basketweave Cake

Once you master the technique of creating a basketweave out of frosting, you can turn any old cake into a triumph. The whimsical bumblebees topping this cake are Jordan almonds in disguise.

Basketweave Cake

MAKES *16 servings*

PREP *30 minutes plus decorating time*

BAKE *at 350° for 25 minutes*

REFRIGERATE *1 hour*

Cake

2¼ cups all-purpose flour
1 tablespoon baking powder
½ teaspoon salt
¼ cup (½ stick) butter, at room temperature
1½ cups granulated sugar
4 eggs
2 teaspoons vanilla
1¼ cups milk

Vanilla and Chocolate Frostings

½ cup (1 stick) butter, at room temperature
½ cup solid vegetable shortening
2 boxes (1 pound each) confectioners' sugar
10 tablespoons milk
2 teaspoons vanilla
6 squares (1 ounce each) unsweetened chocolate, melted and slightly cooled

Decorations

Assorted prepared candy flowers and leaves (see note, opposite)
Yellow Jordan almonds

1. Prepare cake: Heat oven to 350°. Coat two 8 x 8 x 2-inch square cake pans with nonstick cooking spray. Line bottoms with waxed paper; coat paper with spray.

2. Whisk together flour, baking powder and salt in a large bowl.

3. Beat butter in a large bowl on medium speed 1 minute or until creamy. Add sugar; beat 2 minutes or until fluffy. Add eggs, one at a time, beating well after each addition. Beat in vanilla. Beat 1 minute.

4. On low speed, beat flour mixture into butter mixture in 3 additions, alternating with milk and ending with flour mixture. Beat 2 minutes on medium speed. Divide batter equally between prepared cake pans.

5. Bake in heated 350° oven 25 minutes or until a wooden pick inserted in center of cakes comes out clean. Cool cake layers in pans on wire racks 10 minutes. Turn cake layers out onto racks. Remove waxed paper; let cool completely.

6. Meanwhile, prepare frostings: Beat butter and shortening in a large bowl on medium speed until blended, about 1 minute. Add confectioners' sugar, milk and vanilla; beat on low speed until blended. Beat on medium-high 1 minute. Transfer ¾ cup frosting to a small bowl; cover with plastic wrap.

7. On low speed, beat melted chocolate into larger amount of frosting until smooth. Add additional milk if needed for good spreading consistency. Cover with plastic wrap.

Decorate

1. Place 1 cake layer on a cake plate. Spread ½ cup chocolate frosting over top. Place second layer on top of first. Spread reserved white vanilla frosting over top. Using ¾ cup chocolate frosting, spread thin layer over sides of cake.

2. Fit a pastry bag with a coupler and basketweave tip. Fill bag halfway with chocolate frosting. To make a basketweave pattern, begin by piping a vertical band up one side of cake. At top, pipe a short horizontal band across and to the right of this vertical band. Leave a space the width of band, and pipe another horizontal band beneath it. Repeat until you reach bottom of cake. Pipe another vertical band adjacent to first vertical band and over horizontal bands. To fill in the open spaces, bury tip under first vertical band and pipe short horizontal bands across second vertical band. Continue in this manner to cover sides of cake. Refill bag as needed.

3. With same pastry bag, make a zigzag pattern around top edge of cake where chocolate frosting meets white frosting.

4. Decorate top with flowers and leaves. Use frosting as glue.

5. For bumblebees, press almonds onto top of cake. Fit a small writing tip onto pastry bag with chocolate frosting. Draw bumblebee stripes, wings, antennae and stinger over each almond. Refrigerate cake 1 hour to set.

NOTE: *To make your own decorative flowers and leaves, prepare Royal Icing, page 201. Use soft gel paste food colors to tint small amounts in various colors. Refer to Rosebud Cake, page 199, for a method of flower- and leaf-making.*

FOOLPROOF BASKETWEAVE

Fill in intervals with short horizontal bands; begin at first vertical band and pipe across the second.

Halloween Cupcakes

The "cobwebs" cloaking the cupcake tops are easier to make than they look—just pipe a thin spiral of melted chocolate and then drag the tip of a sharp knife lightly from center to edge. Shown on page 187.

MAKES *24 cupcakes*

PREP *20 minutes plus decorating*

BAKE *at 350° for 30 to 35 minutes*

Cupcakes

- 4 cups all-purpose flour
- 2 teaspoons baking soda
- 2 teaspoons ground cinnamon
- 1 teaspoon ground ginger
- ½ teaspoon ground nutmeg
- ½ teaspoon salt
- 2 cups packed light-brown sugar
- 1 cup butter (2 sticks), at room temperature
- 4 eggs
- 1 can (15 ounces) pumpkin puree (not pie filling)
- 1½ cups chopped pecans (6 ounces)

Frosting

- 1 package (8 ounces) cream cheese, at room temperature
- 6 tablespoons (¾ stick) butter, at room temperature
- 2 tablespoons frozen orange juice concentrate, thawed
- ½ teaspoon orange extract
- 1 box (1 pound) confectioners' sugar

Decorations

Candy sprinkles in seasonal colors

⅓ cup semisweet chocolate chips for cobwebs

1. Prepare cupcakes: Heat oven to 350°. Line cups in 2 standard 12-muffin pans with paper liners.

2. Sift together flour, baking soda, cinnamon, ginger, nutmeg and salt into a medium-size bowl.

3. With a mixer on medium speed, beat together sugar and butter in a large bowl until smooth. Beat in eggs, one at a time, beating well after each addition. Beat in pumpkin—mixture may look a little curdled.

4. On low speed, beat flour mixture into pumpkin mixture just until blended. Stir in pecans by hand. Divide batter equally among prepared muffin cups.

5. Bake in heated 350° oven 30 to 35 minutes or until a wooden pick inserted in centers comes out clean. Remove cupcakes from pans to wire racks to cool completely.

6. Prepare frosting: On medium speed, beat together cream cheese and butter in a large bowl until smooth. Beat in orange juice concentrate and orange extract. On low speed, gradually beat in confectioners' sugar until smooth and well blended.

7. Spread top of each cupcake with about 2 tablespoons frosting. Scatter sprinkles on tops of 12 cupcakes, mixing colors as desired. Reserve remaining 12 cupcakes for "cobweb" decoration.

8. Prepare cobwebs: Melt chocolate chips in top of a double boiler over barely simmering, not boiling, water, stirring until smooth. Spoon into a small plastic food-storage bag. Snip off a very small corner. Starting in center and ending at edge, pipe chocolate in a spiral on top of each cupcake. To create a cobweb pattern, lightly drag tip of a paring knife or wooden pick through spiral from center to edge; repeat 7 or 8 times, wheel-spoke fashion.

Holiday Surprise Cake

Candies brighten a "tunnel" of cream cheese that spirals through this rich chocolate cake.

MAKES *12 servings*

PREP *20 minutes*

BAKE *at 350° for 1 hour.*

Filling

1　package (8 ounces) cream cheese, at room temperature
1　egg
⅓　cup granulated sugar
2　tablespoons all-purpose flour
1　teaspoon vanilla
½　cup red and green mini candy-coated chocolates

Cake

3　cups all-purpose flour
1　cup granulated sugar
½　cup unsweetened cocoa powder
½　teaspoon salt
2　teaspoons baking soda, sifted
⅔　cup vegetable oil
2　tablespoons distilled white vinegar
1　tablespoon vanilla
2　cups water

Glaze and Garnish

1　cup confectioners' sugar, sifted
3　to 3½ tablespoons milk
1　square (1 ounce) semisweet chocolate
½　tablespoon vegetable oil
　 Red and green mini candy-coated chocolates

1.　Heat oven to 350°. Coat a 10-cup Bundt pan with nonstick cooking spray.

2.　Prepare filling: Beat together cream cheese, egg, granulated sugar, flour and vanilla in a small bowl. Stir in candies.

3.　Prepare cake: Whisk together flour, granulated sugar, cocoa powder, salt and baking soda in a large bowl. Add oil, vinegar, vanilla and water; beat until blended.

4.　Pour almost half of the batter into prepared pan. Spoon filling on top, forming a ring centered between sides of pan and tube. Pour remaining batter evenly over top.

5.　Bake in heated 350° oven 1 hour or until cake cracks on top and shrinks from sides of pan. Cool in pan on a wire rack 30 minutes. Invert cake onto rack; allow to cool completely.

6.　Prepare glaze and garnish: Stir together confectioners' sugar and 3 tablespoons milk in a small bowl until combined. If too thick, add remaining milk. Spoon glaze over cake, letting it drizzle down sides. Let dry slightly. Heat semisweet chocolate and oil in a glass measuring cup in a microwave on 100% power 30 seconds; stir until chocolate is melted and mixture is smooth. Drizzle over cake on top of glaze. Sprinkle with colored candies.

Pepparkaka

Christmastime in Sweden conjures up visions of saffron buns to celebrate St. Lucia's feast day (December 13), ginger-cookie cutouts and this dark, pudding-moist spice cake.

MAKES *8 servings*
PREP *20 minutes*
BAKE *at 350° for 40 minutes*
COOK *about 5 minutes*

Cake

- 2 tablespoons very fine dry unseasoned bread crumbs, for dusting pan
- 1½ cups sifted all-purpose flour
- 2 teaspoons ground cinnamon
- 1½ teaspoons ground ginger
- 1 teaspoon baking powder
- ½ teaspoon baking soda
- ½ teaspoon ground cardamom
- ½ teaspoon ground cloves
- ½ teaspoon ground nutmeg
- ½ teaspoon salt
- ¼ teaspoon black pepper
- ½ cup (1 stick) unsalted butter, at room temperature
- ¾ cup granulated sugar
- ¼ cup molasses
- 2 eggs
- 1 cup sour cream, at room temperature

Topping

- ⅓ cup warm water
- 2 tablespoons honey
  1-inch piece cinnamon stick
- 2 tablespoons confectioners' sugar

  Gooseberries for garnish (optional)

1. Prepare cake: Heat oven to 350°. Generously butter a 9-inch (8-cup) bundt pan; coat with crumbs.

2. Sift together flour, cinnamon, ginger, baking powder, baking soda, cardamom, cloves, nutmeg, salt and pepper into a medium-size bowl.

3. With a mixer on low speed, beat butter and granulated sugar in a large bowl 2 minutes. Scrape down sides of bowl. Adjust speed to medium-low, beat until fluffy, 2 minutes. Beat in molasses, then eggs, one at a time.

4. On low speed, beat flour mixture into butter mixture in 3 additions, alternating with sour cream and ending with flour mixture; beat just until combined. Spoon batter into prepared pan, spreading evenly to edge.

5. Bake in heated 350° oven until cake pulls away from sides of pan and a cake tester inserted in center of cake comes out clean, about 40 minutes. Cool cake in pan on a wire rack 10 minutes. Loosen cake around edge and center tube with a thin knife. Invert cake onto rack and remove pan; place rack over a sheet of waxed paper.

6. Prepare topping: Heat water, honey and cinnamon stick in a small saucepan over medium heat, stirring to melt honey; simmer 3 to 5 minutes, until mixture is a thin syrup. Remove cinnamon stick. Spoon syrup over warm cake. Let cake cool completely. Sift sugar over top. Fill center with gooseberries if desired.

Pepparkaka

Apple Christmas Tree Tart

With "ornaments" made from cherries and blueberries, your apple-y tree is complete. We use a piecrust mix, but you could also prepare your favorite sweetened two-crust pie pastry (double the recipe on page 84). Shown on page 186.

MAKES *8 servings*

PREP *25 minutes*

BAKE *at 400° for 20 to 25 minutes*

⅓ cup apricot preserves
2 Golden Delicious apples, peeled, cored and thinly sliced (3 cups)
1 teaspoon fresh lemon juice
1 package (11 ounces) piecrust mix
⅓ cup plus 1 tablespoon sugar
   Sugared fresh cranberries, blueberries and/or cherries (recipe page 231) for garnish (optional)

1. Press preserves through a fine-mesh sieve into a small saucepan; cover and set aside. Toss apples with lemon juice in a medium-size bowl and set aside.

2. Heat oven to 400°. Lightly flour a baking sheet.

3. Prepare piecrust mix for a 2-crust pie according to package directions but adding ⅓ cup sugar. On a lightly floured surface, shape piecrust dough into a block. Roll dough into a 12 x 11-inch rectangle. Roll up dough onto rolling pin; unroll onto prepared baking sheet.

4. Using tip of a small paring knife, lightly outline a Christmas tree shape lengthwise on dough; make 3 branch indentations, about 1-inch deep, on each side and a short trunk at base. Use a cookie cutter to cut out a small star from a corner of the dough border; set star aside and cover with dampened paper toweling. Cut out tree; reserve trimmings.

5. Working on floured surface, gather about one-fourth of reserved trimmings into a ball, then roll it with your hands into a rope long enough to go halfway around tree. Repeat once. Build up perimeter of tree by outlining each side from tip to center of base with a rope; pinch edges together to adhere and then flute as for a piecrust.

6. Arrange apples over tree, overlapping slightly to fill in. Heat strained preserves just until hot and bubbly. Uncover star; brush star and apple slices with half the preserves. Place star on baking sheet. Sprinkle apples with 1 tablespoon sugar.

7. Bake tart and star in heated 400° oven 20 to 25 minutes, until crust is golden and apples are tender; remove star from oven when golden. If parts of tart crust brown too quickly, cover with pieces of aluminum foil.

8. Remove tart from oven when done. Brush underside of star with apricot preserves for "glue." Place star on top of tree. Brush apples with remaining preserves. Cool tart on baking sheet on a wire rack about 20 minutes. Remove to a serving plate and garnish with frosted berries if using.

Peppermint Ice Cream Roll

Our chocolate-glazed marvel, topped with crushed peppermints, has a high "Wow!" factor but is easy to put together. Be sure to let it stand at room temperature 10 minutes before slicing.

MAKES *12 servings*
PREP *30 minutes*
BAKE *at 375° for 12 to 15 minutes*
FREEZE *4½ hours or overnight*

Cake

- ¾ cup all-purpose flour
- ¼ cup unsweetened cocoa powder
- 1 teaspoon baking powder
- ¼ teaspoon salt
- 4 eggs
- ¾ cup granulated sugar
- ¼ cup milk
- 1 teaspoon vanilla
- 1 tablespoon confectioners' sugar mixed with 1 tablespoon unsweetened cocoa powder

Filling

- 3 cups vanilla ice cream
- ¼ teaspoon peppermint extract
- ¼ cup crushed candy canes

Chocolate Glaze

- 6 squares (1 ounce each) semisweet chocolate, chopped
- ⅔ cup heavy cream
- ⅛ teaspoon peppermint extract (optional)
- 6 to 7 hard peppermint candies, crushed

1. Prepare cake: Heat oven to 375°. Grease a 15 x 10 x 2-inch jelly-roll pan; line with waxed paper; grease paper.

2. Sift together flour, cocoa powder, baking powder and salt into a medium-size bowl.

3. With a mixer on medium-high speed, beat eggs in a second medium-size bowl until lemon-colored, about 5 minutes. Gradually beat in granulated sugar until well blended. Beat in milk and vanilla. Fold in flour mixture. Scrape batter into prepared pan.

4. Bake cake in heated 375° oven 12 to 15 minutes or until center springs back when lightly pressed with a fingertip.

5. Loosen cake around edges with a thin knife. Sift confectioners' sugar–cocoa powder mix over top. Cover with a clean kitchen towel. Top with a slightly larger baking sheet; invert. Remove pan, then waxed paper. Starting from a short end, roll up cake and towel together. Place seam side down on a wire rack to cool completely.

6. Meanwhile, prepare filling: Soften ice cream in a medium-size bowl. Line a 13 x 9 x 2-inch pan with plastic wrap. Beat peppermint extract and crushed candy canes into ice cream. Scrape into prepared pan, spreading evenly. Freeze until firm, 15 to 20 minutes.

7. Place a wire rack in a baking pan. When ice cream is firm, unroll cake on a work surface. Invert ice cream onto cake, leaving a 1½-inch border on 1 short end. Leaving the border, spread ice cream with a rubber spatula to edges of cake. Starting at end with border, reroll cake without towel. Place seam side down on rack in pan; place pan in freezer.

8. Prepare glaze: Place chocolate in a medium-size bowl. Bring cream just to simmering in a small saucepan. Pour over chocolate in bowl; stir until mixture is smooth, adding peppermint extract if using. Let cool slightly, 3 to 5 minutes or until mixture registers 85° on an instant-read thermometer.

9. Remove pan with cake roll from freezer. Pour glaze over cake, spreading evenly with a spatula. Sprinkle crushed candies in a band along center of cake top. Return cake in pan to freezer until frozen, 4 hours or overnight.

Gingerbread Layer Cake

Molasses, cinnamon and ground cloves meld wonderfully with orange in the creamy frosting. Make the layers ahead and store well-wrapped in plastic for a few days until you're ready to frost and serve to great acclaim.

Gingerbread Layer Cake

MAKES *14 servings* PREP *15 minutes*
BAKE *at 350° for 25 minutes*

Cake

- ¾ cup boiling water
- ½ cup molasses
- 1 teaspoon baking soda
- 2¼ cups all-purpose flour
- 2 teaspoons ground cinnamon
- 1 teaspoon baking powder
- ½ teaspoon ground cloves
- 1 teaspoon ground ginger
- 2 tablespoons grated fresh ginger
- ½ teaspoon salt
- 10 tablespoons (1¼ sticks) butter or margarine, at room temperature
- 1¼ cups granulated sugar
- 2 eggs

Orange Buttercream Frosting

- ¾ cup (1½ sticks) unsalted butter or margarine, at room temperature
- 1 tablespoon grated orange rind
  Pinch salt
- 1 box (1 pound) plus 1 cup confectioners' sugar
- ¼ cup milk

Garnishes (optional)

Orange rind, cut into thin strips
Fresh raspberries

1. Prepare cake: Heat oven to 350°. Grease two 8-inch round layer-cake pans; dust pans with flour.

2. Combine boiling water, molasses and baking soda in a 2-cup glass measure; mixture will bubble up. Whisk together flour, cinnamon, baking powder, cloves, ground and fresh ginger and salt in a small bowl.

3. With a mixer on medium speed, beat butter and granulated sugar in a medium-size bowl until light and fluffy. Beat in eggs, one at a time, beating well

after each addition. Stir flour mixture into butter mixture in 3 additions, alternating with molasses mixture and ending with flour mixture. Divide batter between prepared pans.

4. Bake in heated 350° oven 25 minutes. Cool cake layers in pans on wire racks 10 minutes. Turn out onto racks to cool.

5. Prepare frosting: With mixer on medium-high speed, beat together butter, orange rind and salt in a medium-size bowl until light and fluffy. Stir in confectioners' sugar and milk until frosting is a good spreading consistency.

6. Using a long serrated knife, slice each cake layer in half horizontally for a total of 4 layers. Place 1 layer on a serving platter, cut side up. Spread about ⅔ cup frosting on top. Repeat 3 times with remaining cake layers and remaining frosting. Refrigerate until serving time. Garnish with strips of orange rind and raspberries if desired.

White Fruitcake

Here's a fruitcake you're going to love; honest, we're not kidding. It avoids the traditional glacé fruit in favor of dried pineapple and dried cranberries, resulting in a lighter version of the much-maligned Christmas classic.

MAKES *2 loaves (12 servings each)*

PREP *35 minutes*

BAKE *at 350° for 55 to 60 minutes*

Cake
¾ cup (1½ sticks) butter, at room temperature
1½ cups packed brown sugar
5 eggs
¼ cup brandy
2½ cups all-purpose flour
2 teaspoons baking powder
1 cup dried cranberries
1 cup diced dried pineapple
1 cup golden seedless raisins
1 cup chopped pecans

Brandy Glaze
½ cup light corn syrup
2 tablespoons brandy

1. Prepare cake: Heat oven to 350°.

2. Butter and flour two 8½ x 4½ x 2⅝-inch loaf pans. Line pans with waxed paper. Butter paper; dust with flour.

3. Beat together butter and sugar in a medium-size bowl until light and fluffy, about 3 minutes. Beat in eggs, one at a time. Beat in brandy.

4. Whisk together flour and baking powder in a small bowl. Stir into butter mixture. Stir in cranberries, pineapple, raisins and pecans. Divide batter between prepared pans; smooth tops.

5. Bake in heated 350° oven until loaves are brown on top and a wooden pick inserted in center comes out clean, 55 to 60 minutes. If loaves brown too quickly, cover pans with aluminum foil. Cool loaves in pans on wire racks 15 minutes. Remove loaves from pans; peel off waxed paper. Cool loaves completely on racks.

6. Prepare glaze: Combine corn syrup and brandy in a small heavy saucepan. Bring to a rolling boil over medium heat; boil 1 minute.

7. Generously pierce top of cakes with a fork. Pour half of glaze over each.

Pumpkin Cheesecake

To make this dessert extra-special, embellish each serving with crystallized ginger, half a gingersnap cookie and a cinnamon stick.

MAKES *12 servings*

PREP *20 minutes*

BAKE *at 350° for 1 hour;*
at 450° for 10 minutes

REFRIGERATE *8 hours or overnight*

Crust

¼ cup (½ stick) butter or margarine,
at room temperature
2 cups gingersnap crumbs (about
30 gingersnap cookies)
2 tablespoons packed light-brown sugar

Filling

3 packages (8 ounces each) cream cheese,
at room temperature
1¼ cups packed light-brown sugar
6 eggs
1 can (1 pound) pumpkin puree
(not pie filling)
1 teaspoon vanilla
1 teaspoon ground cinnamon
½ teaspoon ground ginger
¼ teaspoon ground nutmeg

Topping

1½ cups reduced-fat sour cream
⅓ cup packed light-brown sugar
½ teaspoon vanilla

1. Heat oven to 350°.

2. Prepare crust: Generously coat sides of a 10-inch springform pan with 1 tablespoon of the butter. Sprinkle with 3 tablespoons crumbs. Thoroughly blend remaining crumbs, remaining 3 tablespoons butter and brown sugar in a medium-size bowl. Press mixture evenly onto bottom of prepared pan. Place on a baking sheet.

3. Prepare filling: Beat cream cheese and brown sugar in a medium-size bowl until smooth. Beat in eggs, pumpkin, vanilla, cinnamon, ginger and nutmeg until blended. Scrape filling over crust in pan, spreading evenly.

4. Bake in heated 350° oven 1 hour or until center is set. Transfer pan to a wire rack. Increase oven temperature to 450°. Let cake cool in pan on rack 20 minutes.

5. Meanwhile, prepare topping: Stir together sour cream, brown sugar and vanilla in a small bowl until well blended. Spread evenly over top of cooled cheesecake.

6. Return cheesecake to heated 450° oven; bake 10 minutes. Let cool in pan on rack. Refrigerate, covered, at least 8 hours. Remove sides of pan to serve cake.

Spiced Eggnog Cheesecake

One whiff will give you lots of heady scents of the season: cinnamon, nutmeg, ginger, cloves and more. Use eggnog made with liquor if you like.

MAKES *12 servings*

PREP *30 minutes*

BAKE *at 350° for 1¼ hours*

Crust

- 1 cup graham cracker crumbs (about 8 whole graham crackers)
- 1 teaspoon sugar
- ¼ teaspoon ground ginger
- ¼ teaspoon ground nutmeg
- ¼ teaspoon ground cinnamon
- ¼ cup (½ stick) butter, melted

Filling

- 4 packages (8 ounces each) cream cheese, at room temperature
- ¾ cup sugar
- ¼ cup all-purpose flour
- ¼ teaspoon ground nutmeg
- ¼ teaspoon ground cinnamon
  Pinch ground cloves
- 1 egg
- 1¾ cups eggnog
- 1 teaspoon vanilla
- 1 container (8 ounces) sour cream

Garnish (optional)

- 6 ounces white baking chocolate
  Pinch ground nutmeg

1. Prepare crust: Heat oven to 350°.

2. Combine crumbs, sugar, ginger, nutmeg, cinnamon and butter in a small bowl until well blended. Press over bottom of a 9-inch springform pan.

3. Bake crust in heated 350° oven 10 minutes. Transfer pan to a wire rack to cool. Leave oven on.

4. Meanwhile, prepare filling: Beat cream cheese in a medium-size bowl until smooth. Mix sugar, flour, nutmeg, cinnamon and cloves in a small bowl. Add to cream cheese; beat until smooth. Beat in egg. Add eggnog in a slow stream, beating continuously. Beat in vanilla. Pour filling onto crust in pan; tap pan lightly to release air bubbles.

5. Bake in heated 350° oven 1 hour. Remove from oven; spread sour cream over top of cake. Bake 5 minutes longer. Cool in pan on rack until cake is cool to touch, then refrigerate until serving.

6. Prepare garnish if desired: Line an 8 x 4 x 3-inch loaf pan with aluminum foil, leaving an overhang on both ends. Melt chocolate in top of a double boiler over barely simmering, not boiling, water, stirring until smooth. Stir in nutmeg. Pour chocolate into prepared pan, spreading evenly; refrigerate until firm. Lift foil out of pan to remove chocolate bar. Using a vegetable peeler, scrape chocolate to make loose curls. Arrange curls on top of cake. Reserve any remaining chocolate bar for another use.

Neapolitan Christmas Cake

Come dessert time, you'll score big with a tricolor cake inspired by its pink-white-and-green ice cream–block namesake.

MAKES *10 servings*

PREP *30 minutes*

BAKE *at 350° for 12 minutes*

REFRIGERATE *45 minutes*

Cake

1 cup cake flour (not self-rising)
½ cup ground almonds
1 teaspoon baking powder
¼ teaspoon salt
8 egg whites (about 1 cup)
¼ teaspoon cream of tartar
¾ cup granulated sugar
¼ teaspoon almond extract
  Green and red food coloring

Filling and Topping

1 teaspoon unflavored gelatin
1¾ cups heavy cream
3 tablespoons confectioners' sugar
¼ cup strawberry jam

Garnishes

¾ cup sweetened flake coconut
  Fresh red currants, cut into clusters
  (optional)

1. Prepare cake: Heat oven to 350°. Coat three 9¼ x 5¼ x 2¾-inch loaf pans with nonstick cooking spray. Line pans with waxed paper.

2. Whisk together flour, almonds, baking powder and salt in a small bowl.

3. With a mixer on medium speed, beat egg whites and cream of tartar in a large bowl until foamy. Gradually add granulated sugar, beating on medium-high until stiff peaks form. Sprinkle half of flour mixture over beaten egg whites; fold in gently. Repeat with remaining flour. Fold in almond extract.

4. Measure 1¼ cups batter into each of 2 separate bowls. Tint batter in 1 bowl light green; pour into a prepared pan. Tint batter in second bowl pink; pour into another prepared pan. Pour remaining white batter into third pan.

5. Bake in heated 350° oven 12 minutes, until center of cake layers springs back when lightly pressed with a fingertip. Invert cake layers onto wire racks; peel off paper. Let cool.

6. Prepare filling and topping: Sprinkle gelatin over ¼ cup cream in a small saucepan; let stand 1 minute to soften. Stir over low heat until gelatin is dissolved. Remove from heat.

7. With mixer on medium-high speed, beat remaining 1½ cups cream and confectioners' sugar in a small bowl until slightly thickened and frothy. Add gelatin mixture. Beat until stiff peaks form.

8. Place green cake on a platter. Spread 2 tablespoons jam over cake, then spread ½ cup whipped cream on top. Sprinkle with ¼ cup coconut. Repeat layering with white cake, remaining 2 tablespoons jam, ½ cup whipped cream and ¼ cup coconut. Place pink cake on top. Frost top and sides of cake with remaining whipped cream. Place remaining ¼ cup coconut in a small plastic food-storage bag. Add 1 drop green food coloring; knead to tint coconut. Sprinkle coconut over cake.

9. Refrigerate cake 45 minutes or until whipped cream is firm. Serve garnished with currants if desired.

Neapolitan Christmas Cake

Santa Claus Cake

The secret of our chubby-faced St. Nick? A heart-shaped baking pan.

MAKES *20 servings*
PREP *35 minutes*
BAKE *at 350° for 35 to 40 minutes*
DECORATE *1 hour*

Cake

- 2 cups all-purpose flour
- 1 tablespoon baking powder
- ½ teaspoon salt
- ½ cup solid vegetable shortening
- 1¼ cups granulated sugar
- 4 egg whites
- 2 tablespoons vanilla
- 1 cup milk
- ½ cup maraschino cherries, drained and chopped

Frosting

- ½ cup (1 stick) butter, at room temperature
- ½ cup solid vegetable shortening
- 2 boxes (1 pound each) confectioners' sugar
- 2 teaspoons peppermint extract
- 2 teaspoons vanilla
- 6 to 7 tablespoons heavy cream

Decorations

- Pink and red soft gel paste food colors
- 2 medium blue gumdrops
- 1 red jelly bean
- 1 large red gumdrop

1. Prepare cake: Heat oven to 350°. Coat a large heart-shaped cake pan (9½ x 8½ x 2½ inches) with cooking spray. Line bottom with waxed paper; coat paper with spray.

2. Whisk together flour, baking powder and salt in a large bowl.

3. In another large bowl, beat together shortening and sugar on medium-high speed until well combined, about 2 minutes. Beat in egg whites until combined. Add vanilla; beat 1 minute.

4. On low speed, beat flour mixture into shortening mixture in 3 additions, alternating with milk and ending with flour mixture. Fold in cherries. Pour batter into prepared cake pan.

5. Bake in heated 350° oven 35 to 40 minutes or until cake springs back when lightly pressed with a fingertip. Let cake cool in pan on a wire rack 15 minutes. Turn out onto rack and cool completely.

6. Prepare frosting: On low speed, beat butter, shortening, confectioners' sugar, peppermint extract, vanilla and 6 tablespoons cream in a medium-size bowl until smooth. Add 1 tablespoon cream if needed to make a good consistency for spreading and piping.

Decorate

1. Tint ¾ cup frosting light pink. Place cooled cake on a cake plate. Spread pink frosting in a thin coat over top of cake.

2. Spread about ¾ cup white frosting in a thin coat on sides of cake.

3. Position cake with pointed end away from you. Using a wooden pick, mark a placement line across cake top for Santa's hat, about 3½ to 4 inches from point. Also outline an area about 2½ inches in diameter in middle of cake, where face will be framed by hair and beard.

4. Tint ¾ cup frosting red. Place in a small pastry bag fitted with a coupler and small star tip. Pipe onto pointed end of cake for hat.

5. Place remaining white frosting in a large pastry bag fitted with a coupler and shell tip. Pipe in a tight zigzag across base of hat, making a ruffle.

6. Using a "C" motion, pipe swirls of white frosting to make hair and beard around face area and on sides of cake. Pipe a white pom-pom on hat point.

7. Place blue gumdrops on face for eyes. Place red jelly bean for nose. Slice large red gumdrop in half crosswise; place, cut sides up, on face for cheeks. Pipe on a white moustache. Pipe on a red mouth.

Christmas Stollen

Bake three at a time, then serve one and give away the rest to your grateful friends.

MAKES *3 stollen (8 servings each)*
PREP *30 minutes*
RISE *2½ to 3 hours*
BAKE *at 350° for 35 minutes*

Dough

¾ cup milk
½ cup water
½ cup (1 stick) butter, cut into pats
4¼ cups bread flour (not self-rising)
½ cup granulated sugar
2 teaspoons salt
2 envelopes (¼ ounce each) active dry yeast
1 egg
¾ cup candied fruit
¾ cup nuts, such as almonds, pecans and/or walnuts, chopped
½ cup raisins
1 teaspoon grated lemon rind
1 teaspoon grated orange rind
¾ teaspoon ground mace

Topping

2 tablespoons butter, melted
¼ cup granulated sugar
3 tablespoons confectioners' sugar

1. Prepare dough: Heat milk, water and butter in a small saucepan over medium heat until temperature of mixture registers 120° on an instant-read thermometer.

2. Whisk together 1¼ cups flour, granulated sugar, salt and yeast in a large bowl. Add warm milk mixture; beat with a mixer on medium speed 2 minutes. Add egg and 1 cup flour; beat on high speed 2 minutes. Stir in remaining 2 cups flour until batter is stiff. Transfer to a greased large bowl; turn to coat. Cover with plastic wrap. Let rise in a warm place until doubled in volume, 1½ hours.

3. Combine candied fruit, nuts, raisins, lemon rind, orange rind and mace in a small bowl. Turn out dough onto a lightly floured surface. Knead fruit mixture into dough.

4. Divide dough into thirds. Shape each third into a loaf, first rolling it into a 10 x 8-inch oval, then folding oval in half lengthwise and curving each end slightly. Transfer each to a greased baking sheet. Cover with plastic wrap; let rise in a warm place until doubled, 1 to 1½ hours.

5. Heat oven to 350°.

6. Bake stollen 35 minutes or until bottom of loaves sounds hollow when tapped. Transfer loaves from baking sheet to wire racks to cool 1 hour.

7. Add topping: Brush loaves with melted butter. Sprinkle with granulated sugar. Dust tops with confectioners' sugar.

Kourabiedes

In the Greek Orthodox faith, the Christmas meal features special breads and sweets, including almond cookies buttery and tender as shortbread. According to tradition, they are shaped into little crescents or logs, then, while still warm, thickly coated with confectioners' sugar.

Kourabiedes

MAKES *about 4 dozen cookies*

PREP *30 minutes*

REFRIGERATE *1 hour*

BAKE *at 350° for 18 to 20 minutes*

1½ cups (3 sticks) unsalted butter, at room temperature
⅔ cup sifted confectioners' sugar
1 tablespoon brandy, orange juice or lemon juice
1 tablespoon vanilla
1 teaspoon almond extract
¼ teaspoon salt
1 egg yolk
3½ ounces blanched almonds, toasted (see page 231) and finely ground (½ cup)
3½ cups sifted all-purpose flour, or more as needed
1½ cups confectioners' sugar (not sifted)

1. With a mixer on low speed, beat butter, ⅔ cup sifted confectioners' sugar, brandy, vanilla, almond extract and salt in a large bowl until smooth and fluffy, 2 minutes. Scrape down sides of bowl. On medium-low speed, beat mixture until light and fluffy, about 2 minutes. Beat in egg yolk, then ground almonds.

2. On lowest speed, beat in flour just until blended. Dough should be stiff, but still soft; add flour if needed.

3. Turn out dough onto a floured surface. Shape into a block about 1 inch thick. Wrap in aluminum foil. Refrigerate 1 hour.

4. Heat oven to 350°.

5. Pinch off chunks of dough the size of walnuts; shape into small crescents or logs on ungreased baking sheets, spacing about 1½ inches apart—do not try to get more than 12 cookies on each sheet.

6. Bake cookies in heated 350° oven 18 to 20 minutes or until uniformly tan.

7. Meanwhile, sift ¾ cup confectioners' sugar evenly onto a 15½ x 10½ x 1-inch jelly-roll pan. When cookies are done, cool 1 minute on baking sheet. Then, using a spatula, lift cookies and arrange in neat rows on confectioners' sugar in pan. Sift remaining ¾ cup confectioners' sugar evenly on top. Let cookies cool to room temperature.

8. To store, layer cookies between sheets of waxed paper in airtight containers.

Raspberry-Pistachio Swirl Cookies

Ground pistachios and raspberry jam add flavor as well as color. The key to success for these? A very sharp knife to cut through the rolled-up dough.

MAKES *3 dozen cookies*
PREP *20 minutes*
REFRIGERATE *2 hours*
BAKE *at 375° for 10 to 12 minutes*

½ cup (1 stick) **unsalted butter, at room temperature**
½ cup sugar
1 egg
1 teaspoon vanilla
1¾ cups all-purpose flour
½ teaspoon baking powder
¼ teaspoon salt
⅓ cup finely ground pistachios (1½ ounces)
10 drops green food coloring
2 tablespoons raspberry jam
10 drops red food coloring

1. With a mixer on low speed, beat butter and sugar in a large bowl until smooth and creamy. Whisk egg and vanilla in a small bowl until frothy.

2. Sift together flour, baking powder and salt into a medium-size bowl. Stir into butter mixture until a dough forms.

3. Transfer half of dough to a medium-size bowl; stir in pistachios and green food coloring until blended. Stir together jam and red food coloring in a small bowl; stir into other half of dough.

4. Place green dough on a sheet of plastic wrap; pat into an 11 x 8-inch rectangle. Place red dough on another sheet of plastic wrap; with well-floured hands, pat dough into an 11 x 8-inch rectangle. Invert red dough onto green dough; peel off plastic wrap from red dough. Starting from a long side, roll up dough, jelly-roll fashion; wrap with plastic wrap. Refrigerate at least 2 hours or until firm.

5. Heat oven 375°. Lightly coat a large baking sheet with nonstick cooking spray.

6. Unwrap dough. Using a thin sharp knife, cut dough cylinder into ¼-inch-thick slices. Place on prepared baking sheet, spacing 1 inch apart.

7. Bake in heated 375° oven 10 to 12 minutes or until edges just begin to color—be careful not to overbake. Cool cookies on baking sheet on a wire rack 5 minutes. Transfer cookies to wire rack to cool completely.

Snowball Cakes

The candied cherry jauntily topping each tiny coconutty tea cake immediately says Season's Greetings!

MAKES *about 2½ dozen tea cakes*

PREP *15 minutes*

BAKE *at 350° for 20 to 25 minutes*

¾ cup all-purpose flour
½ teaspoon baking powder
¼ teaspoon salt
½ cup (1 stick) unsalted butter, melted
½ cup granulated sugar
½ cup packed light-brown sugar
2 eggs
¼ teaspoon coconut extract
3 cups unsweetened flake coconut
30 glacé cherries, optional

1. Heat oven to 350°. Arrange thirty-six 1¼-inch aluminum-foil baking cups on a baking sheet.

2. Whisk together flour, baking powder and salt in a small bowl.

3. Beat butter, sugars, eggs and coconut extract in a medium-size bowl until fluffy and smooth. Stir in flour mixture until blended. Stir in 1 cup flake coconut.

4. Spoon batter into baking cups, dividing equally. Sprinkle remaining 2 cups coconut evenly over tops. Place a glacé cherry in each cup.

5. Bake cups on baking sheet in heated 350° oven 20 minutes or until coconut is lightly golden. Tent with foil. Bake 5 minutes longer. Transfer to a wire rack to cool completely. Store in an airtight container.

Black Forest Squares

Sour cherries are the defining ingredient in these bars, which are reminiscent of the famous chocolate torte from Germany's Black Forest region.

MAKES *16 squares*

PREP *15 minutes*

BAKE *at 350° for 20 to 25 minutes*

Cake

1 cup all-purpose flour
½ teaspoon baking powder
¼ teaspoon salt
½ cup (1 stick) unsalted butter, melted
½ cup granulated sugar
½ cup packed light-brown sugar
½ cup unsweetened cocoa powder
2 eggs
1 teaspoon vanilla
½ cup milk chocolate chips
½ cup white chocolate chips
½ cup plus 2 tablespoons dried sour cherries

Topping

¼ cup milk chocolate chips
¼ cup white chocolate chips
2 tablespoons dried sour cherries
1 tablespoon solid vegetable shortening

1. Prepare cake: Heat oven to 350°. Lightly grease a 9 x 9 x 2-inch square cake pan.

2. Whisk together flour, baking powder and salt in a small bowl.

3. Beat butter, sugars, cocoa powder, eggs and vanilla in a medium-size bowl until fluffy and smooth. Stir in flour mixture until blended. Fold in milk chocolate chips, white chocolate chips and cherries. Spoon batter evenly into prepared pan.

4. Bake cake in heated 350° oven 20 to 25 minutes or until center is firm.

5. Meanwhile, prepare topping: Melt milk chocolate chips in top of a double boiler over barely simmering, not boiling, water, stirring until smooth. Melt white chocolate chips and shortening in a small saucepan over low heat, stirring until melted and smooth. Coarsely chop cherries.

6. When cake is done, remove it from oven and immediately cut into 16 squares; leave in pan. Drizzle melted milk chocolate diagonally over warm cake. Sprinkle cherries over top. Drizzle melted white chocolate diagonally over cake at a right angle to milk chocolate. Cool cake in pan on a wire rack. Remove squares from pan; store in an airtight container.

Christmas Stars

In addition to stars, try bells or trees, even Santa cookie cutters to shape these melt-in-your-mouth confections. If you have 4 large baking sheets and lots of counter space, you can make stars in both colors at once. If not, start several days ahead to allow time for each color to dry.

MAKES *about 8 dozen stars*

PREP *30 minutes*

REFRIGERATE *each color 45 to 60 minutes*

STAND *24 to 36 hours (per color)*

1 package (8 ounces) cream cheese, at room temperature
2 tablespoons milk
10 cups confectioners' sugar, sifted
½ teaspoon peppermint extract or 3 to 4 drops peppermint oil
 Green food coloring
½ teaspoon cherry extract or 3 to 4 drops cherry flavoring
 Red food coloring

1. With a mixer on low speed, beat half of cream cheese and 1 tablespoon milk in a large bowl until smooth and well blended. Gradually beat in 5 cups confectioners' sugar, peppermint extract and desired amount of green food coloring. If dough becomes difficult to beat with mixer, beat by hand using a wooden spoon.

2. Turn out dough onto a work surface lightly dusted with confectioners' sugar. If necessary, knead dough by hand until color is well blended.

3. Line a large baking sheet with waxed paper; place dough in center. Flatten dough; cover with a second sheet of waxed paper. Roll dough to ⅜-inch thickness. Refrigerate on baking sheet 45 to 60 minutes or until dough is firm enough to cut.

4. Line another large baking sheet with waxed paper. Remove baking sheet with dough from refrigerator, peel off top sheet of waxed paper. Using a 2-inch star cookie cutter, cut out stars and transfer to prepared baking sheet. Let stars stand at room temperature 24 to 36 hours or until dry; using a thin metal spatula, turn stars over every 12 hours.

5. Gather dough scraps. Reroll between fresh sheets of waxed paper and refrigerate as before.

6. Repeat steps 1 through 5, making another dough using remaining cream cheese, remaining milk, remaining sugar, cherry extract and red food coloring.

Ginger Checkerboards

Perky rectangles of brown and white checks, these cookies will add professional polish to a holiday cookie tray or gift package.

Chocolate-Pecan Thumbprints, *page 224;* Holiday Truffles, *opposite;* Cranberry Roll-Ups, *page 225;* Maple-Walnut Cakes, *page 226;* Mint Meltaways, *page 224;* Ginger Checkerboards

MAKES *4 dozen cookies*

PREP *30 minutes*

REFRIGERATE *2 hours*

BAKE *at 375° for 10 minutes*

¾ cup (1½ sticks) unsalted butter, at room temperature
¾ cup sugar
1 egg
1½ teaspoons vanilla
1 tablespoon ground ginger
½ teaspoon ground white pepper
¼ teaspoon salt
¼ cup mild molasses
3 cups all-purpose flour
¼ cup light corn syrup

1. With a mixer on medium speed, beat butter and sugar in a large bowl until creamy, about 3 minutes. Add egg and vanilla; beat well. Beat in ginger, white pepper and salt.

2. Transfer half of mixture to a medium-size bowl and set aside. Beat molasses into remaining butter mixture in large bowl. On low speed, beat in 1½ cups flour until a dough forms.

3. Transfer dough to a sheet of plastic wrap. Cover with a second piece of plastic wrap. Using a rolling pin, roll dough into a 10 x 8-inch rectangle, about ⅓ inch thick. Transfer plastic wrap with dough to a baking sheet. Refrigerate.

4. Meanwhile, with mixer on medium speed and using clean beaters, beat corn syrup into reserved half of butter mixture. On low speed, beat in remaining 1½ cups flour until a dough forms.

5. Roll light-colored dough between plastic wrap as in step 3. Transfer to a second baking sheet. Refrigerate both doughs 1 hour or until firm.

6. Remove 1 chilled dough rectangle from refrigerator. Peel plastic wrap from 1 side; invert onto a cutting board and peel off remaining plastic. Slice rectangle lengthwise into ⅓-inch-wide strips. Repeat with second chilled dough rectangle.

7. Alternating colors, arrange 2 light strips of dough and 1 dark strip side by side on a work surface; press lightly together. Top with 2 dark and 1 light strip, alternating as before. Repeat with 2 light and 1 dark. If strips of dough tear, press them lightly back together. Transfer checkerboard log to a baking sheet; refrigerate.

8. Repeat to assemble a second log, but begin with 2 dark strips of dough and 1 light strip; continue with alternating colors. Repeat with remaining strips of dough, assembling an equal number of logs in each color sequence. Cover logs on baking sheets and refrigerate until firm, about 1 hour.

9. Heat oven to 375°.

10. One at a time, remove logs from refrigerator and place on a cutting board. Cut crosswise into ¼-inch-thick slices. Transfer to an ungreased baking sheet, reshaping cookies if necessary.

11. Bake cookies in heated 375° oven 10 minutes or until light-colored portions just begin to brown. Cool cookies slightly on baking sheets on wire racks; transfer cookies to racks to cool completely.

CHECKERBOARDING TECHNIQUE

Alternating colors, arrange 3 strips of dough side by side on a work surface.

Holiday Truffles

A cloak of white chocolate encases dark chocolate mixed with cherries and nuts; gather four in a small box as a gift for the candy lover. Shown opposite.

MAKES 3½ dozen

PREP 20 minutes

REFRIGERATE 1½ hours

12 squares (1 ounce each) semisweet chocolate, chopped
3 squares (1 ounce each) unsweetened chocolate, chopped
1 can (14 ounces) sweetened condensed milk
¼ teaspoon salt
2 tablespoons cherry-flavored liqueur (optional)
½ cup maraschino cherries, drained and chopped
¼ cup chopped nuts
12 ounces white baking chocolate, chopped
2 teaspoons vegetable oil
Assorted colored sprinkles

1. Heat semisweet chocolate, unsweetened chocolate, condensed milk and salt in a medium-size saucepan over medium heat, stirring, until chocolates are melted, about 7 minutes. Remove from heat. Add liqueur if using, and cherries and nuts. Cover surface directly with waxed paper; refrigerate until cold, 1½ hours.

2. Line a baking sheet with waxed paper. Using your hands, roll chocolate mixture by slightly heaping tablespoonfuls into balls. Place on prepared baking sheet.

3. Heat white chocolate and oil in a small saucepan over low heat, stirring until melted and smooth. Remove from heat; let stand until cool to touch, 1 minute. Using 2 forks, dip balls into white chocolate. Return to waxed paper. Decorate with sprinkles while coating is fluid. Set aside to dry.

Mint Meltaways

There's a brownie tucked away under the smooth layer of peppermint-flavored frosting. Shown on page 222.

MAKES *4 dozen bars or 8 dozen mini-squares*

PREP *25 minutes*

BAKE *at 350° for 30 minutes*

Brownie

1½ cups (3 sticks) butter
6 squares (1 ounce each) unsweetened chocolate, chopped
6 eggs
2½ cups granulated sugar
2 teaspoons vanilla
1½ cups all-purpose flour
1¼ teaspoons peppermint extract

Peppermint Frosting

1 box (1 pound) confectioners' sugar
6 tablespoons heavy cream
¼ cup (½ stick) butter, at room temperature
¼ teaspoon peppermint extract
¼ cup crushed peppermint candies for sprinkling

1. Prepare brownie: Heat oven to 350°. Line a 10 x 15 x 1½-inch jelly-roll pan with waxed paper; leave overhang on 2 short ends; coat paper with cooking spray.

2. Melt butter and chocolate in a small saucepan over low heat, stirring until smooth. Transfer to a medium-size bowl. Beat in eggs, sugar and vanilla. Stir in flour and extract. Spread batter in prepared pan.

3. Bake brownie in heated 350° oven 30 minutes or until edges begin to firm. Cool brownie in pan on a wire rack.

4. Prepare frosting: Beat sugar, cream, butter and peppermint extract in a medium-size bowl until smooth. Lift waxed paper out of pan to remove brownie. Spread frosting over brownie top. Sprinkle with crushed candies. Cut into 48 bars or 96 mini-squares.

Chocolate-Pecan Thumbprints

Work quickly to fill the indentations with melted chocolate and a perfect pecan half. Then for a fast set-up, pop in the fridge. Or let stand at room temp until they're ready to take their rightful place on your holiday cookie tray. Shown on page 222.

MAKES *about 4½ dozen cookies*

PREP *20 minutes*

REFRIGERATE *1 hour*

BAKE *at 350° for 10 to 11 minutes*

2 cups all-purpose flour
1 cup finely ground pecans
¼ teaspoon salt
¾ cup (1½ sticks) unsalted butter, at room temperature
½ cup granulated sugar
½ cup confectioners' sugar
2 eggs
2 teaspoons vanilla
⅓ cup heavy cream
4 squares (1 ounce each) semisweet chocolate, finely chopped
4½ dozen pecan halves

1. Heat oven to 350°.

2. Whisk together flour, ground pecans and salt in a medium-size bowl.

3. With a mixer on medium speed, beat together butter, granulated sugar and confectioners' sugar in a second medium-size bowl until light and fluffy, about 3 minutes. Beat in eggs, one at a time, until well blended. Beat in vanilla. On low speed, beat in flour mixture just until a dough forms. Cover and refrigerate at least 1 hour, until dough is firm.

4. With your hands and using 2 teaspoons dough for each, roll dough into balls. Transfer balls to an ungreased baking sheet, spacing 1½ inches apart. With a wooden spoon handle or your fingertip, make a slight indentation in top of each ball.

5. Bake cookies in heated 350° oven 10 to 11 minutes or until lightly browned. Let cookies cool slightly on baking sheets on wire racks; transfer cookies to racks to cool completely.

6. Meanwhile, heat cream to simmering in a small saucepan over medium heat. Pour over chocolate in a small bowl, stirring to melt chocolate completely. Let cool slightly.

7. Spoon chocolate into indentation in each cookie. Press a pecan half on top. Let stand at room temperature until chocolate is firm. Or refrigerate to firm quickly.

Cranberry Roll-Ups

Baking these treats in mini-muffin cups helps them hold their shape. Shown on page 222.

MAKES *32 roll-ups*

PREP *20 minutes*

COOK *10 minutes*

BAKE *at 425° for 15 to 18 minutes*

1 cup fresh or frozen cranberries
⅓ cup packed light-brown sugar
⅛ teaspoon ground cinnamon
 Pinch ground nutmeg
½ cup dried apricots
2 tablespoons apple juice or cranberry juice
1 box (17.3 ounces) frozen puff pastry sheets, thawed
½ cup walnuts, coarsely chopped

1. Combine cranberries, brown sugar, cinnamon, nutmeg, apricots and apple juice in a small saucepan. Bring to boiling over medium-high heat. Cover; lower heat to medium-low. Cook 8 minutes or until thickened.

2. Transfer cranberry mixture to a food processor or blender. Whirl until nearly smooth but with some small pieces remaining—you should have about 1 cup filling. Set aside to cool.

3. Heat oven to 425°.

4. Unroll 1 pastry sheet on a work surface. Spread half of cranberry filling over pastry. Cut sheet in half lengthwise; cut each half crosswise into 8 equal strips. Starting at a short end, roll up each strip, enclosing filling. Repeat with remaining sheet of pastry and remaining filling, for a total of 32 roll-ups.

5. Place three 12-mini-muffin pans on work surface (see note, below). Spoon about ½ teaspoon chopped nuts into each of 32 cups. Place a roll-up, cut side up, on top of nuts in cups.

6. Transfer 2 pans to refrigerator. Bake remaining pan in heated 425° oven 15 to 18 minutes or until roll-ups are puffed and golden. Transfer pan of roll-ups to wire rack; cool roll-ups in pans 5 minutes. Remove to rack to cool completely. Bake remaining roll-ups, one pan at a time.

NOTE: *If you do not have 3 mini-muffin pans, work in batches; keep unbaked roll-ups refrigerated and let pan cool after baking each batch, then wash and dry pan before refilling.*

Maple-Walnut Cake

Invest in pure maple syrup to flavor this three-tiered majesty, which can also be made as a sheet cake and cut small to grace a dessert platter.

MAKES *12 servings*

PREP *20 minutes*

BAKE *at 350° for 25 to 30 minutes*

Cake

2	cups all-purpose flour
1	tablespoon baking powder
1	teaspoon baking soda
1	teaspoon ground cinnamon
½	cup (1 stick) unsalted butter, at room temperature
¾	cup granulated sugar
½	cup maple syrup
2	eggs
1	can (about 16 ounces) sweet potatoes in syrup, drained and mashed
½	teaspoon maple extract
¾	cup walnuts, chopped

Frosting

12	ounces cream cheese, softened
6	tablespoons (¾ stick) unsalted butter, at room temperature
¼	cup heavy cream
¼	teaspoon maple extract
1	box (1 pound) confectioners' sugar

Red and green glacé cherries for garnish (optional)

1. Prepare cake: Heat oven to 350°. Grease three 8 x 2-inch round layer-cake pans; dust pans with flour (see note, right).

2. Sift together flour, baking powder, baking soda and cinnamon into a medium-size bowl.

3. With a mixer on medium speed, beat butter in a large bowl until smooth and creamy. Beat in granulated sugar and maple syrup. Add eggs, one at a time, beating after each addition. Add sweet potatoes and maple extract to butter mixture; beat until smooth. On low speed, beat in flour mixture just until incorporated. Fold in walnuts. Spoon batter into prepared pans, dividing equally.

4. Bake in heated 350° oven 25 to 30 minutes, until cake layers are golden brown on top. Cool cake layers in pans on wire racks 10 minutes. Turn out onto racks to cool completely.

5. Prepare frosting: Beat cream cheese, butter, cream and maple extract in a medium-size bowl until smooth. Add confectioners' sugar; beat until a good spreading consistency. If frosting is too soft, refrigerate until thickened.

6. Place 1 cake layer on a platter. Spread with ¾ cup frosting. Place second layer on top; spread with ¾ cup frosting. Place third cake layer on top. Spread remaining frosting over top and sides of cake. Garnish with glacé cherries if desired.

NOTE: *For small snacking cakes, shown on page 222, prepare a 10 x 15 x 2-inch baking pan. Bake cake in 350° oven 20 to 25 minutes. Cool as for cake layers. Frost and cut into small squares or diamonds. For garnish, cut cherries into small pieces and dot onto cakes.*

Anise-Pine Nut Drops

The hint of licorice from the anise flavoring melds well with the buttery pine nuts.

MAKES *about 2 dozen cookies*

PREP *20 minutes*

REFRIGERATE *several hours*

BAKE *at 350° for 10 to 12 minutes*

1¼ cups all-purpose flour
½ teaspoon baking powder
¼ teaspoon salt
3 tablespoons butter
3 tablespoons margarine
½ cup sugar
1 egg
¾ teaspoon anise extract
½ cup pine nuts (pignoli)

1. Whisk together flour, baking powder and salt in a small bowl.

2. Beat butter, margarine and sugar in a medium-size bowl until creamy. Beat in egg and anise extract until well blended. Stir in flour mixture. Shape dough into a disc; wrap in plastic wrap. Refrigerate several hours or overnight.

3. Heat oven to 350°. Lightly coat 2 baking sheets with nonstick cooking spray.

4. Place pine nuts in a small shallow bowl. Using your hands, roll dough by rounded teaspoonfuls into balls; roll each ball in pine nuts. Place on prepared baking sheets.

5. Bake in heated 350° oven 10 to 12 minutes. Remove cookies from baking sheet to a wire rack to cool.

Anise-Pine Nut Drops; Nut Crescents, *page 229*; Apricot Wraps, *page 228*; Double-Mint Drops, *page 228*

Double-Mint Drops

Little bits of red peek through the white dough, giving just a hint of what's in store; a dip of melted mint chocolate reiterates the theme. Shown on page 227.

MAKES *about 4½ dozen cookies*

PREP *20 minutes*

REFRIGERATE *several hours*

BAKE *at 350° for 10 to 12 minutes*

1¼ cups all-purpose flour
½ teaspoon baking powder
¼ teaspoon salt
3 tablespoons butter
3 tablespoons margarine
½ cup sugar
1 egg
½ teaspoon vanilla
3 tablespoons crushed red and white peppermint candies (about 1½ ounces)
¼ cup mint chocolate chips

1. Whisk together flour, baking powder and salt in a small bowl.

2. Beat butter, margarine and sugar in a medium-size bowl until creamy. Beat in egg and vanilla until well blended. Stir in crushed peppermints and flour mixture. Shape dough into a disc; wrap in plastic wrap. Refrigerate several hours or overnight.

3. Heat oven to 350°.

4. Drop dough by rounded teaspoonfuls onto ungreased baking sheets. Bake in heated 350° oven 10 to 12 minutes. Transfer cookies to wire racks to cool.

5. Line a work surface with waxed paper. Melt chocolate chips in top of a double boiler over barely simmering, not boiling, water, stirring until smooth. Dip half of each cookie into melted chips. Place cookies on sheet of waxed paper and let stand until chocolate hardens.

Apricot Wraps

Simmering the apricots in orange juice adds extra flavor to the filling of these gorgeous goodies. But the best part is the elegance they add to any cookie platter. Shown on page 227.

MAKES *about 2 dozen cookies*

PREP *20 minutes*

REFRIGERATE *3 hours or overnight*

BAKE *at 350° for 10 to 12 minutes*

Dough

1¼ cups all-purpose flour
½ teaspoon baking powder
¼ teaspoon salt
3 tablespoons unsalted butter
3 tablespoons margarine
½ cup granulated sugar
1 egg
2 teaspoons grated orange rind
½ teaspoon vanilla

Filling

½ cup chopped dried apricots (4 ounces)
⅓ cup orange juice, plus more if needed
2 tablespoons light-brown sugar
Confectioners' sugar for sprinkling

1. Prepare dough: Whisk together flour, baking powder and salt in a small bowl.

2. With a mixer on medium speed, beat butter, margarine and granulated sugar in a medium-size bowl until creamy. Beat in egg, orange rind and vanilla. Stir in flour mixture. Shape into a disc; wrap in plastic wrap. Refrigerate until well chilled, 3 hours or overnight.

3. When ready to bake cookies, prepare filling: Combine apricots, orange juice and brown sugar in a small saucepan. Cover; bring to simmering over medium heat; simmer until apricots are very soft, 10 minutes. Transfer mixture to a food processor; whirl to puree. If apricot pieces do not break down evenly, add more orange juice; whirl again.

4. Heat oven to 350°. Coat 2 baking sheets with nonstick cooking spray.

5. Divide dough into thirds. On a lightly floured work surface, roll one piece to a 6-inch square; cut into 9 squares. Spread 1 scant teaspoon filling diagonally, from corner to opposite corner, on each square. Fold remaining opposite corners over filling; press to seal. Arrange cookies on prepared baking sheets. Repeat with remaining dough and filling.

6. Bake in heated 350° oven 10 to 12 minutes, until golden. Transfer cookies from baking sheets to wire racks to cool. Sprinkle confectioners' sugar over cookies.

Nut Crescents

Half-moons of nutty dough are a Christmas classic; this one goes a step further with a lacy garnish of melted dark and white chocolates. Shown on page 227.

MAKES *about 1½ dozen cookies*

PREP *20 minutes*

REFRIGERATE *several hours*

BAKE *at 350° for 10 to 12 minutes*

Dough

1   cup all-purpose flour
½   teaspoon baking powder
¼   teaspoon salt
6   tablespoons butter
½   cup sugar
1   egg
½   teaspoon almond extract
1   cup ground blanched almonds
     Sugar for rolling

Glaze

¼   cup semisweet chocolate chips
¼   cup white chocolate chips

1. Prepare dough: Whisk together flour, baking powder and salt in a small bowl.

2. Beat butter and sugar in a medium-size bowl until creamy. Beat in egg and almond extract until well blended. Stir in ground almonds and flour mixture. Shape dough into a disc; wrap in plastic wrap. Refrigerate several hours or overnight.

3. Heat oven to 350°. Lightly coat a baking sheet with nonstick cooking spray.

4. Roll dough by rounded tablespoonfuls into 3-inch-long ropes. Place on prepared baking sheets, shaping each cookie into a crescent.

5. Bake in heated 350° oven 10 to 12 minutes. Fill a small shallow bowl with granulated sugar. Remove cookies from oven; while still warm, roll in sugar; place on a wire rack to cool.

6. Meanwhile, prepare glaze: Melt semisweet chocolate chips in top of a double boiler over barely simmering, not boiling, water, stirring until smooth. Melt white chocolate chips in a small bowl over a small saucepan of barely simmering, not boiling, water over low heat, stirring until melted and smooth.

7. Place rack with cookies over a sheet of waxed paper. Place each melted chocolate in a separate small plastic food storage bag. Snip off a corner of each bag. Drizzle melted chocolates back and forth over cookies. Let harden.

About Chocolate

Chocolate starts as a bean from the tropical cacao tree. When roasted and ground, the beans become chocolate liquor (a paste); when cooled, this becomes baking chocolate. Chocolate liquor is also processed into cocoa butter and cocoa powder.

UNSWEETENED (BAKING) CHOCOLATE

Bitter, dark and brittle. You wouldn't want to eat it on its own, but used in baked goods, it delivers lots of rich flavor.

COCOA POWDER

Unsweetened chocolate with about 75% of the fat removed. In Dutch-process cocoa, the chocolate is treated with a mild alkali, which causes the cocoa to become less intense, darker and more easily mixed into liquid. (3 tablespoons cocoa powder + 1 tablespoon vegetable shortening = 1 square baking chocolate.)

BITTERSWEET AND SEMISWEET CHOCOLATE

Partially sweetened blends of chocolate liquor, cocoa butter and sugar; tend to vary in flavor and sweetness (and name), depending upon the manufacturer. Excellent for eating or cooking.

SWEET CHOCOLATE

Dark, fully sweetened blend of chocolate liquor, cocoa butter and sugar. Excellent for eating or cooking.

MILK CHOCOLATE

Fully sweetened blend of chocolate liquor, cocoa butter and sugar plus milk or cream and vanilla. Excellent for eating or cooking.

WHITE CHOCOLATE

Blend of cocoa butter, milk, sugar and flavoring, without any chocolate liquor. White chocolate is very mild and sweet-flavored, but difficult to melt—watch carefully and be sure not to overheat.

MELTING CHOCOLATE

Chocolate should be melted carefully to keep it from curdling, separating or scorching; take particular care to avoid getting any water in chocolate or it will seize. Here are failsafe techniques.

To melt on the stovetop: Place chocolate squares in a heavy saucepan over the lowest heat or in the top of a double boiler over (not in) simmering water. With a wooden spoon or spatula, stir constantly until chocolate is just melted.

To melt in the microwave: Place chocolate squares in a microwave-safe bowl; do not cover. Microwave on 100% power for 30 seconds. Remove and stir; if only partially melted, repeat microwaving.

- When preparing a recipe, use the melting technique specified in the recipe; otherwise, use either technique described above.

- When you want to melt chocolate completely, begin with squares. Chop them first for speedier melting. When heated, chocolate chips become gooey inside but retain their shape, so save them for cookies and cakes.

Beyond Basics

Here are some tips you will find helpful when making recipes from this book.

BEATING WHOLE EGGS AND EGG YOLKS

You won't increase the volume of whole eggs and egg yolks as dramatically as you do when beating egg whites, but plenty of air will be incorporated. Beaten whole eggs and egg yolks play an important role in leavening many cakes, quick breads and muffins, so be sure not to underbeat them; beat for the time indicated in your recipe.

MAKING SUGARED FRUIT

Sugar-coated fruit makes a pretty garnish or table decoration. You can use any fruit with a smooth, or nearly smooth, skin. Peaches, pears, grapes and berries are all attractive. Fill a shallow dish with granulated sugar. Brush fruit with honey, corn syrup or maple syrup and then roll in sugar. Place on a wire rack or waxed paper to dry. (You can use reconstituted egg white powder instead of a sweet syrup.)

SIFTING FLOUR

If a recipe calls for sifted flour and doesn't give specific directions for the sifting method, sift over and onto a piece of waxed paper. Then spoon the sifted flour into a dry measure of the appropriate size; pass the straight edge of a knife or spatula over the top to level off the excess. But if your recipe gives specific directions, follow them.

SIFTING SUGAR

Granulated sugar needs sifting only if it is lumpy. Confectioners' sugar should be sifted before measuring because it tends to cake, especially if the package has been open for a while.

SOFTENING BUTTER OR CREAM CHEESE

When a recipe ingredients list calls for butter or cream cheese at room temperature, take it out of the refrigerator about 20 minutes before beginning. It should be soft enough to have a slight give all over. Or refer to your microwave oven manual to see how to soften in the microwave.

TOASTING NUTS

Toast a small quantity of nuts in a small dry skillet over medium-high heat, stirring, until lightly browned and fragrant, about 3 minutes. Transfer to a plate to cool.

TOASTING COCONUT

Toast a small quantity of coconut in a small dry skillet over medium heat, stirring occasionally and shaking skillet from time to time, until lightly browned, about 1 minute.

USING EGG WHITE POWDER

Egg white powder and meringue powder are available in select supermarkets, gourmet shops and health-food stores. Because of health concerns about eating raw eggs, be sure to use either meringue powder or egg white powder for uncooked icings or other no-cook recipes calling for egg whites.

Index

Acknowledgments

The editors of *Family Circle* want to thank the entire food department for its energy and enthusiasm in creating desserts that are at once stylish and delicious: Diane Mogelever, Julie Miltenberger, Keri Linas, Althea Needham, JoAnn Brett, Donna Meadow, Patty Santelli, Michael Tyrrell and Robert Yamarone. Thanks as well to our contributors: Jean Anderson, Marie Bianco, Sylvia Carter, Bea Cihak, Jim Fobel, Libby Hillman, Michael Krondl and Andrew Schloss. To the writers, editors and designers who bring to life our recipes, our thanks: David Ricketts, Jonna M. Gallo and Diane Lamphron. Kudos to the books and licensing team of Tammy Palazzo and Carla Clark. And, finally, thanks to Roundtable Press for all its expertise: Marsha Melnick, Susan E. Meyer, Julie Merberg, Carol Spier, Sara Newberry and Bill Rose.

PHOTOGRAPHY CREDITS

Antonis Achilleos: page 227

Steve Cohen: pages 2, 29, 66, 89 (all), 102, 110, 119, 131, 139 (top), 156 (all), 163 (bottom), 170

Brian Hagiwara: pages 3 (all), 7 (top), 14, 15, 19, 39, 42, 46, 55 (top), 58, 67, 77, 82, 83 (bottom), 87, 94, 99, 115 (bottom), 122, 127, 135, 138, 143, 146, 159, 165, 166, 167, 174, 187 (top), 194, 196, 197 (all), 202, 207, 215, 218, 222

Robert Jacobs: page 115 (top)

Michael Luppino: page 198

Rita Maas: pages 11 (top), 50, 142

Steven Mark Needham: pages 7 (bottom) and 169

Dean Powell: pages 7 (middle), 36 (all), 45 (all), 51, 80 (all), 85, 113 (all), 116 (all), 145 (all), 151 (all), 155 (all), 168, 177 (all), 188, 189 (all), 199, 201, 203, 223

Alan Richardson: pages 35, 74, 111, 114, 134, 179, 186, 190, 210

Mark Thomas: pages 6, 10, 11 (bottom), 23, 26, 31, 54, 55 (bottom), 63, 70, 78, 83 (top), 86, 90, 103, 106, 107, 118 (all), 126, 139 (bottom), 150, 162, 163 (top), 182, 187 (bottom)